Praise for
Transforming Trauma with Jiu-Jitsu

"My grandfather, Helio Gracie, created Brazilian Jiu-Jitsu to assist the smaller, less athletic person in staying safe under attack. Using jiu-jitsu in the service of healing trauma survivors honors his legacy. I applaud Anna's and Jamie's efforts to spread the word and take healing to the next level. I highly recommend this book to instructors and practitioners everywhere."

—RENER GRACIE, fourth-degree Black Belt,
cofounder and co-owner of Gracie University

"I've closely followed Dr. Jamie's collection of movement work because of her unique ability to simplify critical concepts while providing clear and practical tools to reconnect with your body and heal. Jamie and collaborator Anna help trauma survivors like myself see new possibilities and options for managing daily life, which builds a sense of resilience and a feeling of empowerment in our decisions. Together they give ideas for how people can sensitively and effectively access movement and the martial arts, which provide immediate short-term benefits as well as long-term shifts in our nervous system, overall posture, and self-expression. This book is a gateway to a full, expansive, and authentic life and I'm so thankful they've made this kind of deep transformation available for everyone."

—ALYSON STONER, founder of Movement
Genius and mental health advocate

"*Transforming Trauma with Jiu-Jitsu* pushes psychotherapy beyond the siloed role that it normally holds in a person's healing process and extends those benefits into a real-world, practical, and empowering place for people overcoming trauma. Marich and Pirkl demonstrate the healing effects of jiu-jitsu explained through the lens of how someone who has undergone trauma would experience the process and give practical direction for clinicians, gyms, and people who may wish to incorporate martial arts in their trauma recovery. This book helps to break down the barriers of the overlapping but often partitioned worlds that can serve in the roles of providing healing. This kind of extension is a necessary step forward for the mental health field to better support recovery!"

—CURT WIDHALM, MA, MS, LMFT,
cofounder of the Therapy Reimagined Conference

"Marich and Pirkl's new book is a treasure trove of insight and empirically based information. This book clearly explains how healing from trauma, utilizing somatic-oriented methods (in particular jiu-jitsu), is possible and very attainable. . . . Over the years I have recommended martial arts in general to trauma survivors, instinctively knowing that learning to move their bodies in new and skilled defensive ways could help their overall trauma healing, very much complementing our EMDR therapy together. However, I only knew of a couple local dojos I felt comfortable sending survivors (women in particular). With the information in this book on the basic techniques and interesting history of jiu-jitsu, I now can confidently place this martial art recommendation at the top of the list (and better help trauma survivors discern if a potential dojo is healthy, positive, and welcoming), with research to back this up."

—STEPHANIE BAIRD, LMHC, EMDRIA
approved consultant and former karate practitioner
and author of *EMDR and Sexual Health*

"There are many pathways to successful healing. In their excellent discussion of jiu-jitsu's role in healing trauma survivors, Jamie Marich and Anna Pirkl provide the theory and practical knowledge helpful to both the healer and trauma survivor in need of healing. I didn't know much about jiu-jitsu before reading this book. I found it to be useful and informative."

—S. GEORGE KIPA, MD, MS
Detroit, MI

TRANSFORMING
TRAUMA
WITH
JIU-JITSU

TRANSFORMING TRAUMA
WITH
JIU-JITSU

A Guide for Survivors, Therapists, and
Jiu-Jitsu Practitioners to
Facilitate Embodied Recovery

JAMIE MARICH, PhD
AND ANNA PIRKL, LMFT

North Atlantic Books
Huichin, unceded Ohlone land
aka Berkeley, California

Published by
North Atlantic Books
Huichin, unceded Ohlone land
aka Berkeley, California

Cover photo © gettyimages.com/lindsay_imagery
Cover design by Jasmine Hromjak
Photography by John Kovalsky
Interior design by Happenstance Type-O-Rama

Printed in the United States of America

Transforming Trauma with Jiu-Jitsu: A Guide for Survivors, Therapists, and Jiu-Jitsu Practitioners to Facilitate Embodied Recovery is sponsored and published by North Atlantic Books, an educational nonprofit based in the unceded Ohlone land Huichin (*aka* Berkeley, CA) that collaborates with partners to develop cross-cultural perspectives, nurture holistic views of art, science, the humanities, and healing, and seed personal and global transformation by publishing work on the relationship of body, spirit, and nature.

North Atlantic Books' publications are distributed to the US trade and internationally by Penguin Random House Publishers Services. For further information, visit our website at www.northatlanticbooks.com.

CONTENT DISCLAIMER: This book contains material that may be triggering, including references to self-harm, sexual abuse, or trauma.

PLEASE NOTE: The creators and publishers of this book are not and will not be responsible, in any way whatsoever, for any improper use made by anyone of the information contained in this book. All use of the aforementioned information must be made in accordance with what is permitted by law, and any damage liable to be caused as a result thereof will be the exclusive responsibility of the user. In addition, they must adhere strictly to the safety rules contained in the book, both in training and in actual implementation of the information presented herein. This book is intended for use in conjunction with ongoing lessons and personal training with an authorized expert. It is not a substitute for formal training. It is the sole responsibility of every person planning to train in the techniques described in this book to consult a licensed physician in order to obtain complete medical information on their personal ability and limitations. The instructions and advice printed in this book are not in any way intended as a substitute for medical, mental, or emotional counseling with a licensed physician or health-care provider.

Library of Congress Cataloging-in-Publication Data

Names: Marich, Jamie, author. | Pirkl, Anna, author.
Title: Transforming trauma with Jiu-jitsu : a guide for survivors,
    therapists, and Jiu-jitsu practitioners to facilitate embodied recovery
    / Jamie Marich, PhD, and Anna Pirkl, LMFT.
Description: Berkeley, CA : North Atlantic Books, [2022] | Includes
    bibliographical references and index. | Summary: "An introduction to
    jiu-jitsu as an embodied modality for healing from trauma"— Provided by
    publisher.
Identifiers: LCCN 2021038497 (print) | LCCN 2021038498 (ebook) | ISBN
    9781623176150 (Trade Paperback) | ISBN 9781623176167 (eBook)
Subjects: LCSH: Exercise therapy.
Classification: LCC RM725 .M368 2022 (print) | LCC RM725 (ebook) | DDC
    615.8/2—dc23
LC record available at https://lccn.loc.gov/2021038497
LC ebook record available at https://lccn.loc.gov/2021038498

2 3 4 5 6 7 8 9 KPC 27 26 25 24 23

North Atlantic Books is committed to the protection of our environment. We print on recycled paper whenever possible and partner with printers who strive to use environmentally responsible practices.

To Brendan and Ethan Reiter, my "bonus boys"
and sons in every sense of the word . . .
Thank you for getting me onto the mat.
—Jamie

To Alice D. Peebles, AKA my adoptive "Mom" . . .
Thank you for teaching me that life was
worth fighting for.

To my awesome daughter and daily sunshine . . .
Whenever things are difficult, all I need is a
monkey hug and I know I'll be okay.
—Anna

Contents

Acknowledgments

We first met formally over the phone in December of 2017 after Anna heard Jamie talk about jiu-jitsu and mental health on a men's mental health podcast called *The Man Rules*. Thus, the first acknowledgments we owe in this book coming to fruition are to the host of that show, Dan Griffin, and to Anna's client who suggested she give the show a listen. This experience proves to us the power in planting seeds. When you have something to say, speak out, and the people who are meant to find you will find you!

We also owe a debt of gratitude to our teachers and influencers along the way. Jamie wishes to thank Staci May, Micah Bender, Brian Needham, Tada Hozumi, and members of the Gracie family—Eve, Rener, Sage, Ryron, and Victoria, whom she first met through the *Women Empowered* remote study videos. Anna extends gratitude to Alex Ueda, Alex Stuart, Guido Jenniges, Jimmy Deluca, Evandro Nunes, Chris Saunders, Jordan Collins, Sam Fernandez, Zac Cunningham, Mike Everett, Bobbie Timario, and members of the Gracie Family—Eve, Rener, Ryron, and Victoria. Anna would also like to thank the awesome support staff team and countless fellow students who have encouraged her every step of the way.

During the writing of this book, Anna identified more than forty people she would have liked to personally interview! However, given the limitations of scope and length of this book, we needed to stop further interviews in 2020. Anna had plans to connect with and train in a wide variety of jiu-jitsu schools. This was cut short by the COVID-19 pandemic. Anna will continue working to elevate the voices of those she did not get to and wants to express her gratitude for all that they do to elevate the humanity and practice of jiu-jitsu.

In making sure that we were as accurate as possible in sharing our understanding of a few jiu-jitsu techniques, we asked Alex Ueda, first-degree black belt instructor at Gracie University and founder of Grounded Grit, to review and edit our descriptions. Being the kind and generous soul that he is, he reviewed everything and enhanced much more than just the techniques. Thank you, Alex, for making this book more accessible to laypeople and non-laypeople alike. This book would not be as useful as it is without your insights.

A heartfelt thanks to Shayna Keyles and the team at North Atlantic Books for their faith in this project from before its inception and for working with us to bring it to life. In doing so, we hope to serve as many people as possible who can benefit from the healing power of jiu-jitsu.

Special gratitude goes out to the individuals who shared their stories and expertise with us as we researched and wrote this book. Your lived experience adds an essential dimension to describing the art of jiu-jitsu as a healing practice. Deep bow to Eve Torres Gracie, Guilherme (Gui) Valente, Dr. Gino Collura, Micah Bender, Alex Ueda, Brian Needham, Tony White, Nick "Chewy" Albin, Marty Josey, Ayesha Kamal, Guido Jenniges, Matthew Lee, Mark Barentine, Gwendolyn Samuels, Jami Jeffcoat, Katie Gollan, Katie Maloney, Brendan Reiter, Ramona Skriiko, and Destiny Aspen Mowadeng. And last but not least, thank you to Sven Pirkl for his assistance with the photographs and to John Kovalsky for doing such a wonderful job in receiving these images.

Basic Jiu-Jitsu Glossary

The language of jiu-jitsu can feel intimidating at first if you are new to training. In an effort to help survivors feel more confident, we are outlining a variety of basic terms and expressions that you may wish to consult as a quick reference as you read the book. If you are new to jiu-jitsu and decide to begin training, learning this vocabulary will empower you with the skills to communicate on the mat with your partner. Our goal is to help you feel more knowledgeable, to strengthen your voice, and to help you communicate effectively with your partners and instructors. More specifics on these terms are given in Chapters 5 and 6. For additional jiu-jitsu terminology, we recommend "The (Almost) Complete Jiu Jitsu Dictionary," which can be found at https://jiujitsux.com/the-jiu-jitsu-dictionary/.

Armlock or armbar Submissions (defined later on) in which you position an opponent's arm in relation to your body in such a way that you have the possibility of hyperextending their elbow and/or over-rotating their shoulder. Sometimes pressure on the joint is all you need to bring the person to yield (or submit) to your authority and stop what they were doing. Unfortunately, in cases in which a person has a high pain tolerance or is not registering pain due to drugs and/or alcohol, injury of the limb might be the only option to neutralize their attack.

Back mount/hooks in A position in which you attach yourself to the back of the opponent. Your torso is connected to their back, with your legs and arms wrapped around them for control. You put your "hooks in" by placing your legs inside your opponent's thighs and using your arms to attach to and control their upper body. If you are practicing this with a male partner, be careful to be mindful in placing your hooks in so you do not unintentionally heel them in their genitals.

Base The stability of your connection to the ground. If you have good base, it means it is difficult to push, pull, or move you. Base is a way of positioning your body to maximize your ability to apply and absorb force. Base is covered more extensively in Chapter 1.

Belt rank Many schools of jiu-jitsu have a belt ranking system from least experienced to most as follows (stripes indicate gradient levels of progress within a particular belt category):

1. White (1–4 stripes)

2. Blue (1–4 stripes)

3. Purple (1–4 stripes)

4. Brown (1–4 stripes)

5. Black (1–6 degrees)

6. Seventh-degree black belt = coral belt is awarded (also known as Master).

7. Ninth-degree black belt = red belt is awarded (Grandmaster, of which there are very few in the world).

Some programs have additional differentiated belts:

- For children under 18 (yellow stripe, solid yellow, orange stripe, solid orange, green stripe, solid green)

- Women (pink)

- Self-defense street fighting "combative belt" (white with blue stripe)

Break falling Specifically in jiu-jitsu, this typically refers to a "controlled" fall from standing to being on the ground. The goal is to learn how to take the energy of the fall and disperse it away from your trunk, head, and neck and instead distribute it through the arms and legs. The technique often looks like a rolling slap to the ground. In this way, the person works to protect their body and especially their head and neck from injury.

Clinch A technique outlined in more depth in Chapter 5 intended to help protect from powerful punches. Using it, you get in so close that your opponent's punching becomes low impact and ineffective in knocking you out. It is essentially a position similar to a really tight hug.

Closed guard A position in which the practitioner traps an opponent in between their legs by wrapping their legs around the opponent and crossing their ankles behind their opponent's back. This can help to prevent them from standing up. At the same time, arms are often working to control the opponent's head and to keep them close to avoid severe punches. The goal is for the practitioner to practice their ability to use their legs and arms to control an opponent while the practitioner is on their back with the opponent between their legs.

Foot locks A submission (defined later) in which you position an opponent's foot, in relation to your body, in such a way that you have the possibility of injuring it or their ankle. Sometimes pressure on the joint is what you need to bring the person to yield (or submit) to your authority and stop what they were doing. Unfortunately, in cases in which a person has a high pain tolerance or is not registering pain due to drugs and/or alcohol, injury of the limb might be the only option to neutralize their attack. Foot locks are often only taught to more advanced students or in early competitive sport gyms. If you are sparring in a new gym or with a new partner, be sure to highlight what you do and don't know and that you want to go slow until you are more experienced. If you are both moving slowly, you can spot if your foot is trapped and tap early.

Gi vs. No Gi A gi is a uniform for jiu-jitsu training, sometimes referred to as a kimono. A gi is typically a heavy cotton jacket, drawstring trousers, and a belt indicating your color rank. The term gi also refers to practice in which the participants are wearing gi. For example, "Today is gi day," or "Today is no-gi day." Some say that gi is more realistic because in a real fight on the street, people often grab your clothing. Gi helps you learn how to escape and defend against submissions in which clothing is used to submit. Gi also allows you to practice using an attacker's clothing against them. No gi is typically leggings, shorts, and a rash guard top. No gi or rash guards help you learn to control your opponent and submit them without using clothing. No gi also prepares you for an attack in warmer weather where jackets and thicker clothing will not necessarily be available, eliminating some submissions. Preparing for defense against a person without a shirt, for example, is also useful and can feel similar to the rash guard top worn in no gi trainings.

Good guy/bad guy Jiu-Jitsu slang often used during instruction to indicate which partner is taking which role in training. The bad guy can often be referred to as the aggressor or the opponent, yet, in talking to many instructors, we have not found a highly applicable and usable counterpoint for good guy. Many instructors emphasize that because good guy/bad guy is very quick and easy to articulate, the terms are easy to apply when instructing. Be prepared to hear these terms in a school, even as inclusive and gender-neutral language is becoming more widespread and we personally support this movement. If the terminology bothers you, bring it up with your instructor, especially if you have any viable alternatives to propose. Attacker/defender is the best alternative that we have found, and we use it often throughout the book. Although less common, in some jiu-jitsu settings, the Japanese terms torite 取り手 (partner, specifically the executor or connector of technique), and aite 相手 (partner, receiver) are used. Many variations of these terms exist across other Japanese martial arts.

Grips (C-grip and monkey grip) C-grip and monkey grip are two different ways to use your hands to grip onto something. Depending on the scenario and whether you are needing to push or pull, one has more strength than the other. In order to conceptualize these grips, take your hand and hold all your fingers together and straight up, as if you were going to high-five someone. Keeping them all glued together, bend your fingers forward, together. This is the monkey grip. The difference between monkey grip and C-grip is the direction of the thumb. In C-grip, your fingers keep this same position but rather than being lined up with your other fingers, your thumb comes around from the opposite direction to grab something. This is the more common everyday grip we use to pick something up, for example. You would use a particular grip for many different reasons. Good instructors explain why one is better than the other for a particular technique. C-grip is also referred to as C-clamp.

Guard or in-guard The practitioner is in the supine position with their legs wrapped around their partner. In the event that you are practicing a move with your partner and they are the aggressor, they might say, "For this move, I am in your guard." This means that you are on your back on the ground, and they kneel to get in between your legs. The move is then executed from "in-guard."

Indicator A signal that something is coming, or a sign that you will need to prepare for or engage in a certain technique. For example, if your instructor or partner wants you to practice the wrist release, the indicator would be them grabbing your wrist.

Leverage Or Alavanca (in Portuguese), is one of the core concepts of jiu-jitsu. In jiu-jitsu, we use our limbs and torso like mechanical levers, pushing and pulling, to put an opponent in a compromising position. Leverage is a key factor in what allows a smaller person to defeat a bigger opponent. If you position yourself in the right way, it is your bones that are holding back an opponent versus your muscle strength. Consider two same-weight children sitting on a seesaw; the further out one child sits, the more force and control they exert over the other. Jiu-Jitsu teaches us to use our body position to create a mechanical advantage that often works over considerably larger opponents.

Mount A position in which the good guy is sitting astride, with a leg on each side of the opponent's stomach. When students are just beginning to learn these techniques, it is important to have the bad guy on the bottom, expressing how much weight is okay and how much is not. It is not necessary to put all your weight, as the person on top, on the person lying on the ground. You can use your quads and knees to support part or all of your weight. If you have health issues that prevent you from getting into this position, make sure to communicate this to your instructor and partner. In some cases, and in some training environments, you may be paired with a different partner who has no problem with you sitting with your entire weight on their stomach.

Partnering In group jiu-jitsu instruction, it is often up to the participants to pair up with each other or for the advanced students to ask newer students to partner.

Posting Positioning a part of your body (often times an arm) so it is on your opponent or on the mat to support base (defined earlier), to neutralize an opponent's attack, or to set up for movement.

Prep drill An exercise that prepares you for a technique by repetitive practice of a specific and key movement that is part of the technique. In the guard get up referred to as giant killer triangle technique and others, shrimping (defined later) is the key movement and is often practiced as a warm-up to learning the full technique. For example, shuffling forward, without crossing your feet (that is, moving forward by leading with the foot that is closer to your bad guy), is a prep drill that can be used to prepare for the Clinch (defined earlier). Repetitions of simply lifting your hips off the floor make up a prep drill for getting up in base.

Punch block series A technique that involves staying safe from knockout punches when the practitioner is on their back on the ground. It is referred to as a series because it provides five techniques to respond to the aggressor depending on whether they are (1) standing and circling around you, (2) standing right above you, (3) close in your guard, (4) close in your guard trying to punch your ribs, and (5) pushing away from your guard. This is described in more depth in Chapter 5.

Reflex development After you have worked to learn the specifics of a par-ticular technique, the next challenge is to build muscle memory (reflexes). Muscle memory allows your body to respond quickly and not to have to wait on the brain to figure out the correct response. This has a significant impact on the efficacy of a technique. On the streets, real attacks don't allow you great amounts of time to consider what the right reaction is to a punch or to someone grabbing you. As a result, many jiu-jitsu gyms work with students on building muscle memory. This is done first via numerous repetitions of a specific technique. Once this is mastered, drills are performed in which your partner may use a variety of attacks without explanation or warning. It is your body's job to recognize the type of attack and respond as quickly and accurately as possible.

Shrimping A technique in which you use your legs to propel your hips to one side and away from the opponent. Shrimping is a key component in escapes. From above, it can look similar to the movement a shrimp makes as it swims through the water.

Side control A technique where the practitioner positions their body on top of and across the opponent's chest using the weight of their own chest to put pressure on and control the person below. Arms and legs are positioned in cer-tain ways to optimize this control. When students are just beginning to learn these techniques, it is important to have the bad guy on the bottom, expressing how much pressure is okay and how much is not. If a person has any injuries to their ribs or chest area, or if they are smaller than their partner, communication is key to keeping everyone as comfortable as possible in the beginning.

Sparring/Rolling Terms used interchangeably; you and your partner are using whatever jiu-jitsu knowledge you have to free fight. Sometimes instructors will limit sparring to the techniques taught that day or to standing or ground techniques. Sometimes they will explicitly ask you to go at 50 percent capacity or less, to go slow, and to be mindful so you do not to hurt your partner. In addition, sometimes instructors will suggest that there be no submissions (defined later) in the first round.

Stacking A technique where you use your weight to press down on an opponent's legs and knees while they are on their upper back with legs and hips off the floor (similar to an inverted lotus yoga pose). This is, for example, part of a technique called "passing the guard." Often this move can put pressure on their neck. People with neck injuries or issues should be careful to tap (defined later) early if they are getting stacked and/or let their partner know that they prefer not to be stacked.

Street vs. sport Street refers to defense against typical street violence without rules or regulations. Sport refers to techniques that apply in competition, where rules against striking and time limits are enforced, making defense against strikes not as important. Many techniques in sport jiu-jitsu can leave you open to severe injury in a street fight, often due to the potential for strikes. Principles such as managing the distance and efficiency are critical to staying safe in a street fight. Points and time limits in sport jiu-jitsu are the primary reasons behind people's rush to escape. In rushing, they can leave themselves open to strikes and other defense vulnerabilities. The initial goal in trauma recovery is to have a corrective experience through jiu-jitsu. If you are in a school environment that is primarily sport, some of these issues could make the experience contraindicated. It can be argued that quality schools will teach street first.

Striking The act of hitting. This is typically done with arms and fists and/or held objects. In a jiu-jitsu setting, it is more often referring to punches or palm strikes.

Submission Applying locking pressure to a joint or cutting off blood flow to a part of the brain. Emphasis by instructors should be made on safety in practicing submissions. In the beginning, partners should apply pressure very slowly and gently until their partner taps. If submissions are not applied slowly, there is potential for injury.

Sweep A movement that reverses the position of a grappler from bottom to top.

Takedown Any technique in which you take an opponent from standing to the ground. This is also referred to as a throw or a trip.

Tap When you and your partner are practicing a specific technique that ends in a submission (such as an armlock), it is critical that you are prepared to let your partner know when to let go. If you feel the tension (not pain) on your arm in an armlock, you use your hand to tap on your partner's body. This tap should not be hard to inflict pain on them, but firm enough that they will feel it and let you go. The reverse is also true. If you are practicing making an armlock submission, you should be moving slowly enough to allow your partner to recognize their arm is at risk and paying attention to the moment they tap to tell you to let go. This is one of the key reasons why sparring when you don't know many of the most basic techniques is very risky. You may recognize this word from the popular fashion brand Tap Out connection to the Mixed Martial Arts (MMA) and Ultimate Fight Championship (UFC) culture.

Trap and Roll (Upa) The trap part of this technique involves trapping the parts of your opponent's body that would normally allow them to block your ability to flip them off of you while you Upa. Upa is also known as bridging, which involves raising your hips while your opponent is mounted on you. If you have successfully trapped their posting options, then you will roll them off of you when you raise your hips.

One

The Transformative Power of Jiu-Jitsu

Jiu-Jitsu is for the protection of the individual, the older man, the weak, the child, the lady and the young woman—anyone who doesn't have the physical attributes to defend themselves.

—HELIO GRACIE, GRACIE JIU-JITSU

In trauma-informed discourse, the word *transformation*, which literally means "to change in shape," gets used a great deal; it's almost become trite. Yet the very essence of the word teaches us what we need to know about what is required to heal from the wounds of traumatic experience.

If we want to bring about change in ourselves and how we are with the world at all levels, we must experiment with taking on different shapes. Traumas of all kinds can leave survivors feeling rigid or inflexible about how they feel or how they see the world. Taking on different shapes can happen by trying out new behaviors as we interact with others and continue to navigate our inner world in as effective a manner as possible. The change process can be difficult if unhealed trauma—which is stored in our brain in a primarily nonverbal capacity—remains unaddressed. While people often explain that *unhealed trauma is stored in the body*, anything related to memory is stored in the brain; in the case of unhealed trauma and unaddressed stress, the effects play out in what medical doctor and trauma scholar Robert Scaer calls *the theater of the body*.[1] Part of the solution for healing the impact of trauma in a meaningful way is to begin exploring what it feels like to make new shapes in the body. The practice of jiu-jitsu contains a world of possibilities that allow survivors of trauma to engage in this exploration.

Embodied, holistic treatment is imperative to deeply heal the impact of traumatic stress and its various manifestations on the total person. Approaches like yoga, dance, the expressive arts, somatics, and various forms of body work have dominated the conversation in clinical circles over the last decade. The martial arts are gaining traction in these conversations as a possible option for helping survivors of trauma to heal. An aim of this book is to highlight the necessity. We specifically draw awareness to the power of jiu-jitsu for survivors of trauma because the qualities of this practice, especially when instructed in a trauma-sensitive manner, make it uniquely suited as a healing art.

Jiu-Jitsu and Martial Arts as Healing Practices

The martial arts are generally described as "various sports which originated chiefly in Japan, Korea, and China as forms of self-defense or attack, such as judo, karate, and kendo."[2] Although eventually anglicized around 1875 as *jiu-jitsu*, the practice of *jūjutsu* originated in Japan, heavily influenced by other Asian philosophies, particularly Daoism and Zen Buddhism. *Jūjutsu* is formed from two Japanese characters: *jū* (柔), meaning yielding flexibility or softness, and *jutsu* (術), which means the art of, as practiced within a particular system. Both characters *(kanji)* can be especially relevant for trauma survivors in their healing journey: learning to embrace the art of flexibility in an embodied way can be powerful medicine. Unhealed trauma can leave us in a place of both physical and mental rigidity that can make adapting to the challenges of life nearly impossible.[3] Any practice that can healthfully teach a trauma survivor to become more flexible in both body and mind has potential to assist in their overall goals for trauma recovery. Although more on the history and philosophy of jiu-jitsu, which includes its parallels to judo, is covered in Chapter 3, please consider for the moment what jiu-jitsu literally means as we begin our exploration together. The practice teaches the art of flexibility and adaptation. Such practices may indeed feel like a huge step out of the comfort zone for bodies socialized in Western or European traditions where focus on the *head* and the *heart* tend to dominate and tend to be internalized.

The popularity of jiu-jitsu in the United States and in other countries in the West is largely credited to Brazilian brothers Helio and Carlos Gracie. Helio was small of stature and struggled with the impact of chronic illness, with many describing him as *sickly*. He studied these Japanese arts and then modified them so that he could defend himself against larger opponents or aggressors. One of the reasons that jiu-jitsu can be particularly effective for survivors of trauma is that brute strength or size has less to do with a practitioner being effective. Alex Ueda, black belt and instructor at Gracie University and founder of Grounded Grit, explains that "size and strength is always an advantage, but it can be out-worked and out-foxed."

The late Pedro Valente Sr., a medical doctor and grandmaster who studied under Helio Gracie, taught that the jiu-jitsu techniques that emerged were the result of humans' instinct toward survival. In jiu-jitsu, the principle of body leverage, or how you learn to use your body, is the imperative. Making different shapes in the body, in the context of a rich environment to work out mental blocks that may arise, is a major reason why training in jiu-jitsu can be particularly transformative for survivors. If this idea does not resonate with you now, we hope it will after you explore what we offer in this book. Or better yet, we hope it's something you may be learning for yourself through your own training in jiu-jitsu or another embodied practice.

Helio Gracie's son Rorion went on to create the Ultimate Fight Championship (UFC), which propelled the sporting aspects of jiu-jitsu into the more popular realms of modern Western culture. While the impact of the UFC and sporting jiu-jitsu has undoubtedly created interest in the martial art, we've also found that the association people make with UFC as combat sport can be a barrier, especially for survivors of trauma. In this book we endeavor to introduce you to the larger art of jiu-jitsu as a healing practice that has deep and rich philosophical roots in Eastern practice. The healing potential exists in this depth and richness. Similar to yoga, what the practice of jiu-jitsu becomes in the West varies widely; some criticize the various permutations as overly commercialized and even harmful due to some schools and traditions overly emphasizing the sporting aspects. As with yoga, we maintain that if the sporting appeal can get people in the door and allow them to discover something deeper about themselves and the process, that's a beautiful thing! However, for survivors of trauma who are interested in learning a martial art like jiu-jitsu, especially for self-defense, schools that emphasize this sporting approach may not always be the best fit.

We wrote this book for anyone who might have an interest in jiu-jitsu and healing, regardless of your role: jiu-jitsu practitioners (or "players"), coaches, instructors, school owners, therapists, educators, or other helping professionals interested in incorporating the martial arts into the treatment process with clients. Trauma survivors who are seeking solutions are also more than welcome—we primarily wrote this book to serve you. While research on jiu-jitsu and other martial arts is not as extensive as a healing modality in trauma recovery as other embodied practices (e.g., yoga), ample evidence in this area merits a wider conversation. Both of us (Jamie and Anna) gladly submit our lived experience with jiu-jitsu as part of this evidence.

What Makes Jiu-Jitsu Special?

Both of us found the practice of jiu-jitsu through the *Women Empowered* program developed by the family of Helio Gracie at Gracie University in Torrance, California. Anna lives near the academy and is able to train in person. Jamie, who is based in Ohio, found the *Women Empowered* video study program online and worked with a jiu-jitsu coach at a local gym where she was taking lessons to guide her through the program. At the time jiu-jitsu entered our lives, we'd already received years of trauma-focused therapy. As complex trauma survivors, we both recognized the need for embodied and expressive practices fairly early into our healing journeys, with each of us receiving healthy doses of cognitive therapy, eye movement desensitization and reprocessing (EMDR) therapy, yoga, and creative arts therapies. Moreover, both of us were established clinical trauma specialists when jiu-jitsu found us, working with a wide range of survivors in our practices. Jamie is a specialist in EMDR therapy and travels the world training clinicians in this modality, and Anna is a registered art therapist with the American Art Therapy Association. Yet for so many reasons, jiu-jitsu proved to be the missing link that took our healing to the next level.

For both of us, jiu-jitsu provided an element of direct exposure to the triggers that we most feared, an opportunity that became more real when training with male instructors. Both of us were privileged to primarily work with instructors who understood trauma and its impact on human experience. They recognized how encountering certain challenges was difficult for us and allowed us to go slowly and make modifications in training so that we could eventually meet the challenge. Jamie directly credits her jiu-jitsu training as the practice that helped her work through blocks around being ladylike and people-pleasing, eventually allowing her to leave a toxic marriage. Anna's experience of directly working with Rener Gracie (Helio's grandson), who bore a striking physical resemblance to someone who assaulted her, allowed her to diffuse the primary triggers around that traumatic injury. Throughout this book, we share elements of our personal relationships with jiu-jitsu. Coupled with the stories of other practitioners, we hope to put a human face to the research and practice guidelines that we present.

Dr. Gino Collura is one such practitioner whom we were delighted to meet in this process. Gino is gaining a great deal of attention as a practitioner and a researcher of Brazilian Jiu-Jitsu as a tool for veteran reentry into civilian life. Collura observed training in Tampa, Florida, and used a neuroanthropological perspective to examine how participation in sport, specifically jiu-jitsu, positively impacts reassimilation into a nonmilitary context. Results indicated that jiu-jitsu promoted reassimilation through socialization, healthy outlets for prior combat identity, exercise, and familiar experience of cultural hierarchy within the jiu-jitsu instructors and students.[4] In 2019, Alison Willing and her team at the University of South Florida concluded that Brazilian Jiu-Jitsu shows value as a complementary practice to standard treatment for PTSD after investigating veterans who went through a five-month training regimen.[5] Study participants showed marked improvement in their PTSD symptoms, although effect sizes varied. Chinkov and Holt studied the transfer of life skills in both adults and youth through participation in Brazilian Jiu-Jitsu. Through qualitative inquiry, they found that learning respect for others, perseverance, self-confidence, and improved health habits were all related to training in jiu-jitsu.[6]

Jamie and Anna led a team that conducted a major research study specific to Brazilian Jiu-Jitsu in the tradition of Helio Gracie following our initial explanation of Anna's case study that now appears in the peer-reviewed literature. Our research surveyed the experience of sixty-three female practitioners of Gracie Jiu-Jitsu in a program called *Women Empowered*, developed by Rorion Gracie of Ultimate Fight Championship fame, the son of Helio Gracie. The program has since been refined by Helio's grandsons Rener and Ryron and their wives Eve and Victoria. Our research team used a grounded theory framework to read the data; the power of jiu-jitsu to facilitate transformation emerged as the major summary theme of the study, inspiring the title and direction of this book. The specific experiences within the framework that facilitated this transformation include (a) having a corrective emotional experience through jiu-jitsu (e.g., an opportunity to heal by relearning something about themselves or the world, correcting previously faculty information), (b) declaring self-worth, building positive coping strategies, (c) developing self-efficacy, (d) expanding awareness and possibilities, (e) collaborating toward a shared goal, (f) having an embodied practice, and (g) developing purpose. Many of the experiences described in this study parallel experiences described by women and survivors of sexual assault and other trauma in research examining other forms of martial arts–based self-defense. The most common experience reported in these studies was an increased feeling of self-efficacy and reduction in fear around sexual assaults.[7]

There is also a body of literature stemming from a psychodynamic framework. Twemlow, Sacco, and Fonagy examined the use of martial arts training as a container for unhealthy aggressions. They used clinical vignettes to exemplify work with people who had committed violence, using a combined approach of psychotherapy and physically oriented adjunctive treatments like yoga and martial arts. Results from this study indicated this approach contributed to the healing of psychological traumas, with the authors emphasizing the importance of the social context of the therapeutic relationship, but they reported more study is needed on these contextual factors in the embodied treatment of trauma.[8] Irish researchers Bird, McCarthy, and O'Sullivan published a study in 2019 examining the impact of a ten-week mixed martial arts (MMA) program combined with individual psychotherapy for at-risk young men. Among other benefits noted, participants reflected that engaging in sport felt less stigmatizing than engaging in traditional psychotherapy alone.[9] Having access to positive male role models in MMA training was also a key factor for participants in seeing improvements in self-esteem, improved relationships, and improved work life. The participants also noted that the structured activity of the sport was especially useful in impacting wellness outcomes.

These researchers echo the contention of an earlier psychodynamic study from Weiser, Kutz, Kutz, and Weiser, supporting the combination of adjunctive martial arts training with traditional psychotherapy approaches.[10] In her landmark work on the concept of *bodyfulness*, Christine Caldwell posits that martial arts training is ideal for allowing survivors of trauma to engage in movements of completion tendency (e.g., allowing the body to move in a way it may have needed to for protection at the time of a traumatic incident). The container of martial arts allows survivors to engage in this completion tendency without turning them into a bully or aggressor.[11]

Evidence also showcases the benefit of martial arts for youth populations. Zivin, Hassan, DePaula, et al. studied the impact of a traditional martial arts program for violence prevention with at-risk boys in middle school.[12] After taking the program, they found statistically significant improvements on teacher ratings regarding resistance to rules, inappropriate social behaviors, and impulsive behaviors, but no reduction in violence. Croom examined mental health factors that are strengthened through martial arts practice.[13] Psychological well-being (e.g., positive emotion, engagement, relationships, meaning, and accomplishment) can be improved through the practice of martial arts.

Both of us firmly believe that we were able to stick around and experience the healing power of jiu-jitsu because we had tremendously attuned instructors. Our own research and talking to other practitioners have taught us that this is not always the case. Hence, a main aim of this book is to describe a pathway for how a martial art like jiu-jitsu, which can still conjure up images of rough and tumble MMA fighters, is actually ideal for survivors of trauma. However, instructors, practitioners, and clinicians who refer their clients to jiu-jitsu training in order for the experience to be optimally beneficial must understand the realities of trauma and its impact on the human brain. Jiu-Jitsu, especially with its emphasis on body positioning (leverage) over strength or force, allows survivors to develop a healthier relationship with their bodies and can assist to transform the triggers that are keeping them stuck. We will highlight many other features of jiu-jitsu throughout this book that make the practice ideally suited to complement trauma healing. To commence with this flow, we'd like to present a few of them in this opening chapter for your consideration.

Base

Imagine for a moment that you are about to walk out the door into a heavy wind coming from the left. You probably instinctively prepare your body to lean into the wind (to the left). You might also take a wider stance (feet further apart) and even bend your left knee a little, with your right knee and leg more straight depending on the strength of the wind. Unless it's hurricane strength, most of us are probably not afraid of wind and can easily lean into it. Achieving a solid base can be intuitive for many of us. The practice does, however, become much more difficult if we introduce an attacker into the equation.

Imagine now an actual person with bad intent is waiting to the left outside the door. They want to push you to the right, perhaps into a vehicle where another person is waiting to help you in. All of a sudden, your natural instinct changes and you probably even lean in the direction they want you to go (away from them). Maybe you try to punch, kick, or run. Without training in other options, many of us are inclined to attempt a strike. Punching or kicking is likely ineffective and is not the best decision, because it puts you moving in the direction they want you to go. If a striking doesn't work (a hard-to-dismiss possibility), it actively ruins your better options. A punch pulls focus from doing the right thing with your legs, and a kick eradicates the possibility of forming a two-legged base.

In actuality, the best thing to do is the same you did when you walked into the wind. You need to lean the opposite direction from the way they want you to go. So, if they are coming at you from the left and trying to push you to the right, then you lean into them, pushing back to the left. The trouble is that it is counterintuitive to get closer to the attacker.

The brilliance of jiu-jitsu is that it doesn't matter how big or small you are compared to the "bad guy." Anna's preteen child, whom she outweighs by fifty pounds, can now use this technique to successfully prevent Anna or her husband from moving her if she doesn't want to be moved. It depends mainly on the angle of her upper body. She needs to form a straight line from her shoulder to her rear foot. Think in terms of a buttress you see on buildings or churches; stone or brick is built to project support against a wall. Against a stronger lateral force, Anna's daughter only needs to get a little lower to the ground to increase resistance.

In other words, she needs to angle into the bad guy. The harder the bad guy pushes, the lower her angle. Her bone structure holds Anna away, not her strength or size. And now that you know this, it may still be difficult to execute. It can take practice to build the reflex, when in fact your brain still wants you to run, punch, or kick. Practice is required to get your positioning and angle correct when the concept, and perhaps direct body contact, is so unfamiliar. Having people of different sizes and shapes to practice techniques like these with can really help prepare you for every scenario.

If you'd like to try out this foundational technique of jiu-jitsu here as our journey through the book begins, follow the instructions in the text box. Although working with a qualified instructor is ideal, we've prepared these exercises in a way that any reader can try them out either by themselves (certain elements) or with a trusted partner who is also committed to learning safely. *Please use discretion and caution, as the point of these exercises is never to push an edge or cause physical pain. If you feel better opting out of trying these on your own until you can work with an instructor, at least consider reading them and visualize yourself putting the technique into action.*

TRY THIS   Getting Up in Base and
Defense against Pushing

The key concept of base is being able to stop an aggressor from controlling your location. Think about the amazing metaphors to trauma recovery that this practice can teach. The aggressor wants to prevent you from getting up from the ground. Jiu-Jitsu teaches you how to get up despite their efforts. This is the essence of getting up in base. Jiu-Jitsu teaches us to position our bodies in such a way as to make it extremely difficult for a bad guy to stop us from standing up.

Imagine a baby moving from crawling to standing. The baby keeps its hands on the ground until it is steady enough to attempt to come to standing. The baby creates at least three if not four points of contact with the ground (two hands and two feet). In this position with both your legs spread wide (base) and your hands on the ground, you have become very difficult to push back down. In order to gain muscle memory, it can be best to make it a habit to get up this way from sitting on the floor. This may seem like a very simple concept. The challenge is in doing it in a way that an aggressor cannot prevent you from getting up, and the solution is in the fine details. Now let's examine the types of details you would expect to see in a jiu-jitsu lesson on "Base get up."

1. Begin by sitting on the floor in any position. While you can start with legs crossed, you also want to make this realistic. How might you sit on the ground in the park, for instance? For simplicity's sake, let's assume that the aggressor is to your left. Position your left leg (leg closest to the aggressor) bent with knee up, and your foot flat on the floor. Your right leg is bent, resting on the floor, with your right foot under your left knee (see Figure 1.1). The specific positioning of your body in jiu-jitsu is half the battle in executing any technique.

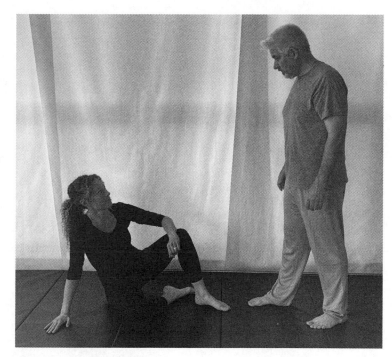

Figure 1.1: Position your legs.

2. Post your arms out straight with your hands on the ground to your right.

3. Lean forward so that your head dips down toward the ground. This will allow you to use your left leg and your arms to lift your hips off the ground and pull your flat, tucked leg out and swing it out backward to the right (see Figures 1.2 and 1.3). The rear foot must land outside your posted hand(s). You now have a wide stance with four points of contact on the floor. Again (see Figure 1.3), it's all in the details: if your feet are too close together, you can potentially be pushed back to the ground. What constitutes "too

close together" varies by body type, yet you tend to know it when you feel it because you can't establish a strong base. High-quality instruction will assist people with modifications to meet differing physical needs. If it is a struggle to go directly to your feet, you can also put your right knee on the ground first and then move to having your foot on the ground.

Figure 1.2: Lift hips.

Figure 1.3: Four points of contact on the floor.

Instructors will typically provide more details concerning where the aggressor is located and what they are doing. They will explain how to lean your body in order to counteract any pushing and how to protect yourself from any punches. They will also explain how to shuffle away to maintain good base, creating distance and keeping an eye on the aggressor (see Figure 1.4).

Figure 1.4: Shuffle backward while keeping an eye on them.

4. As you now let go of the four points of contact with the ground and move to standing (see Figure 1.4), the aggressor may try to push you. Lean your body in the opposite direction of where an aggressor would want you to go (see Figure 1.5). This can feel counterintuitive because it puts your upper body closer to the aggressor. Trauma survivors may find getting used to this close contact a challenge. In Chapter 5, we will discuss different ways of easing into the practice if you need to and how to communicate with partners and instructors about your specific training needs. Repetition helps us get used to the idea of close proximity.

Figure 1.5: Defending against pushing.

5. Instructors will provide more specific details to help you prevent pushing, but the most important thing is to keep a straight line from your head down to your back leg. This is vital. If you are leaning your legs but your upper body is vertical, then you are pushable. Your instructor will often have you try it both ways so you can feel the difference when someone tries to push you. The better your angle, the less muscle and energy will be required to defend against the pushing. The better you get, the more exhausted the aggressor (or your training partner) will be.

Scalability

Scalability refers to the range of responses and the range of doing harm to your opponent. This concept is another key component of jiu-jitsu that makes this martial art especially suited to trauma healing. Jiu-Jitsu has been referred to as the gentle art for a reason. To restrain or defend against an attacker without having to harm them can take trauma healing to the next level; therefore, it has the power to interrupt intergenerational trauma transmission.

Allow us to provide a simple example: a friend and training mate of Anna's got into a crowded elevator and asked a lady, a stranger, closest to the buttons if she could please hit 8. The women angrily swore and yelled at her to hit her own &$%@ buttons. Anna's friend did not allow herself to become infused with the violent poisonous verbal attack; she simply said with the utmost compassion, "I hope you have a better day." In that moment, by not becoming venomous in return, she became a mirror for the other woman. She chose not to engage. Her response helped prevent her from sinking to that level. She was able to avoid spending her own energy on something unworthy of it. Not only did she avoid wasting energy, she also avoided the unnecessary overflow of adrenaline and cortisol that erodes our bodies and often chronically pumps in complex trauma survivors. She de-escalated and shut the potentially traumatic incident down. This in turn prevented the event from invading her entire day. Had she taken the bait offered and engaged in continued or escalated negative verbal interactions, this could have left her with intrusive thoughts and adrenaline in her body throughout the day, or it could have even led to physical violence.

We've both had our own experiences with life moments like these and have walked away feeling invigorated. Not engaging in verbal violence filled us with a sense of accomplishment and left us respectively elevated and happy. We could reflect with kindness and then remove ourselves from the stress of the situation. That is a big deal for us and for most survivors of complex trauma (described more in Chapter 2). There is power in not getting hooked into the fight. When you are offered bait for a fight and shut it down with confidence, firmness, kindness, and gentleness, you are giving the antagonist the exact opposite of what they were fishing for. It's the ultimate win. For trauma survivors, the potential additional layer of triggering in this moment makes this a superhero feat. For many of us, it means overcoming all the years of brain wiring and the chemicals that are potentially flooding our body to signal it to react or freeze. After daily training practice, rehearsing over and over again, taking care of your sparring or training partner, and learning to keep yourself calm and not react but instead stay in your body, unaffected by another's aggressions, you are not only able to consciously control your emotional and physical reaction in very emotionally difficult scenarios, but you may even be able to enjoy the experience. In our experience, combat and conflict actually move from being scary, to being tolerable, to sometimes being enjoyable.

We contend that jiu-jitsu is the best possible martial art for facilitating these benefits and an overall sense of transformation for survivors of trauma and any individual on a healing journey. Our contention is made both as holistic clinical professionals who specialize in trauma and as jiu-jitsu practitioners ourselves. The chapters of this book will further reveal why we fell in love with the practice both personally and professionally. Both of us are survivors of long-term complex and developmental trauma and were exposed to an array of body-centered, holistic, and effective practices for healing trauma throughout our lives. Yet there was something about jiu-jitsu that was a game changer. Jiu-Jitsu filled in the necessary missing pieces for bringing about a sense of greater self-confidence and empowerment within ourselves, which inevitably translated into how we interact with the world.

How to Use This Book

This book is written for three primary audiences: trauma survivors seeking new options for healing and recovery, mental health clinicians seeking to expand their knowledge of embodied recovery options, and jiu-jitsu instructors seeking to be more trauma-responsive in their approach both for the purpose of referral and to expand their own skillsets. Certain sections, especially in the latter part of the book, may apply to you, and others may not feel as relevant. You are invited to take what you need to from this book and leave the rest. However, we hope to bridge the gap between different audiences that desperately need to work together for the magnificent potential of this healing art to be further unleashed. You may benefit from learning about this issue through various angles regardless of your role, so we do encourage you to read every chapter. If you are a trauma survivor, reading the chapter to instructors can give you even more of an idea of the qualities to look for in a solidly trauma-informed school. If you are an instructor or a clinician/educator, reading the chapter to survivors can better assist you in stepping into their shoes. If you are a survivor or an instructor, the chapter to clinicians and educators can give you an idea of what to look for in a helper, or it can assist you in getting the most out of your current therapeutic experience if you do see a professional. A principle of trauma-informed care is the emphasis on creating and engaging with collaborative opportunities in the community; we all have something to offer each other.

As part of this collaborative intention, we have included the voices of many jiu-jitsu practitioners in this book. Over a period of several months, we conducted interviews with practitioners with various levels of physical skill and from different backgrounds and walks of life. You will hear from jiu-jitsu legends like Guilherme (Gui) Valente, Eve Torres Gracie, and Nick "Chewy" Albin, as well as folks we know from our local gyms who have a great deal to share about how jiu-jitsu changed their lives. We hope that this sharing of lived experience will help the content from our research, study, and trauma knowledge come to life!

If you have not done so already, we encourage you to take a look at the glossary before reading the remainder of this book if you are unfamiliar with jiu-jitsu so you'll have a better understanding of the material as you read. You can reference the glossary as you need to while reading the book, especially if terminology is confusing or new. Following this introduction, in Chapters 2 and 3, we dive more deeply into the material you will need on the fundamentals of both trauma and jiu-jitsu to fully understand the rest of this work. In Chapter 4 we fully explore what it means to make your jiu-jitsu practice trauma sensitive and lay out a plan of action. Chapters 5 and 6 specifically address survivors of trauma or people who think they may have been affected by trauma in any way and who are seeking some sort of solutions for recovery. We outline the challenges that trauma survivors may face in approaching jiu-jitsu and highlight practical solutions for addressing those challenges, including preparation strategies in the areas of yoga and mindfulness and how to seek out an ideal training environment for learning jiu-jitsu. We wrote Chapter 7 specifically for clinicians, therapists, and educators who want to expand their somatic healing options and provide guidance on how to do that in a trauma-informed manner; we provide ideas for making referrals and even integrating some elements of jiu-jitsu philosophy into your own practices. Chapter 8 targets existing jiu-jitsu instructors; we explain trauma's impact and offer ideas on how to better assist survivors in learning the art of jiu-jitsu. Chapter 9 offers a grand synthesis, tying together all of the voices, knowledge, and ideas we present in this book.

Throughout the book we include "Try This" practices to build upon the foundational "Getting Up in Base and Defense against Pushing" practice that we covered in this opening chapter. We write from a blend of our own lived experience (personal and professional), and we are also happy to feature the lived experiences of other practitioners and instructors. Our work is informed by our own research in this area. We also worked tirelessly in preparing this book by visiting a variety of schools and talking to practitioners from a variety of backgrounds. Although we are primarily Gracie Jiu-Jitsu practitioners, we honor and respect the other traditions and lineages that fall under the umbrella of what is generally called jiu-jitsu and seek to highlight a variety of voices and lineages. Chapter 3 goes into some of the particular distinctions about the history and the lineages/traditions. We believe that all manifestations of jiu-jitsu provide an outlet for healing, and instructors in all traditions must equip themselves in being trauma informed to serve a diverse world that may desperately need jiu-jitsu as a transformative, healing path.

We've elected to simply use *jiu-jitsu* in the title of the book, and this choice has allowed us to be more inclusive. Even though Westerners, particularly Americans, are most familiar with Brazilian Jiu-Jitsu in modern times, it is important to note that the practice did not begin with Helio

Gracie in the 1920s. A long Eastern tradition of philosophy, meditation, and martial arts practice is the foundation of Brazilian Jiu-Jitsu. Connecting to these Eastern roots, we believe, is where the real gold can be mined for trauma survivors seeking to translate the lessons that they learn in jiu-jitsu training into the arena of life, with all of its triggers and stressors.

Jiu-Jitsu can be for everyone. Even if you are an individual with limited physical mobility, the right instructor is out there (in-person or online) who is willing to work with you on modifications and on being able to use skills appropriate to your body. Even if your body mobility is significantly limited for whatever reason, so much of jiu-jitsu is mental and philosophical—the principles are there for your consideration and adoption if they feel relevant to your journey.

You know the feeling that when something really changes your life, you want to shout its benefits from the rooftops for all to hear? That's us! We've both learned that we are stronger than we once gave ourselves credit for through the non-striving power of leverage. How we use our bodies and minds, often moving them in creative ways, allows us to be effective. Trying too hard rarely works.

Speaking to the practices of getting up in base, defending against pushing, and scalability offered in this chapter, Jamie's coach Micah gave her a powerful phrase during training: *embrace the suck*. In some jiu-jitsu maneuvers, you may want to pull away, like when an aggressor grabs your wrists. Yet this act can create more tension and the sense of fight. However, by learning to step into the aggressor with your body leverage, and by engaging in the release technique, you can make getting away easier. And the process can help you lean into your truth and your power.

When Jamie first learned this move, she protested, "What! You want me to step into it?"

"Yes," he said, "I know it's scary, yet it's what will get you out."

We are both amazed to see how the principle of *leaning in* and indeed *embracing the suck* apply to so much in jiu-jitsu, and this can inevitably translate to life mastery. The parallels to mindfulness and yoga practice are numerous. What we resist will likely persist, yet being with something, calmly and with breath, will help us move through it. Even the bad stuff.

No practice taught us this quite like jiu-jitsu, and the impact of it has made us both more effective meditators and practitioners of life. The potential the practice holds to serve survivors of trauma and anyone seeking to improve their lives is massive. We are committed to making the practice as accessible as possible for the most people and hope that this book offers an important step toward our universal mission.

Two

Trauma and Embodiment

Your whole body, all the way down to your individual cells, is in constant motion.

—THE VALENTE BROTHERS, *THE 753 CODE*

When Ayesha Kamal, a complex trauma survivor who has struggled with anxiety throughout her life, took her first jiu-jitsu class in 2013, she didn't think it would be a good fit . . . especially because she viewed herself as nonathletic *and* a germophobe! She initially began training with her husband, which was, and continues to be, helpful for her when her anxiety is high. Jiu-Jitsu eventually allowed her to step away from being self-conscious, and it has helped her immensely with boundaries. Now a purple belt and a *Women Empowered* instructor herself, Ayesha shares the life insights she's gained from jiu-jitsu on her own blog. Already holding a doctorate in her field (English), she was inspired to return to school to study clinical counseling. For her, the lessons that she's learned through jiu-jitsu, especially the common jiu-jitsu teaching *manage the distance, manage the damage,* have translated beautifully into her own life. For example, surviving the loss of her brother has been a painful process for her, yet she notes that this teaching in particular has helped to make working through those emotions more tolerable.

Ayesha is glad that she stayed around jiu-jitsu long enough to find the magic in her own body. Traumatic recovery specialists are continually pointing to the imperative of working with the body and its wisdom if meaningful healing is going to result. Because of the way that unhealed trauma impacts the brain, simply talking through the trauma over and over again will bring about little lasting help. Rather, survivors must find ways to safely acquaint or reacquaint themselves with the body. This process might be easier said than done because of the disconnection a trauma survivor may feel from their body, due to either addiction and dissociation, or a fear of feeling things fully at the level of the body because it just may hurt too much. This chapter goes into detail about the fundamentals of trauma, how it can manifest in life, and why embodied and holistic approaches to healing are essential.

For Ayesha, practicing jiu-jitsu helps her find the magic in her own body. This process happened because jiu-jitsu practice invited Ayesha to step away from self-consciousness. She then tapped into the present moment and responded to stressors on the mat accordingly. All of these skills now serve her in life off of the mat. Jiu-Jitsu teaches trauma survivors life lessons in an embodied way that we as therapists cannot always show in the confines of an office. As the chapter evolves, we will continue to explain the importance of embodied, experiential, healthy healing options and how jiu-jitsu can factor in for others similar to how it impacted Ayesha, both of us, and other folks that we've interviewed in preparing this book.

Finding the Magic in a Wounded Body-Mind Complex

To fully explore why we must engage the body in trauma recovery, we must first go through some of the fundamentals of trauma and how unhealed trauma impacts the body. The English word *trauma* comes from the Greek word meaning "wound." Although definitions for trauma abound in clinical textbooks and trainings, if we're truly keeping it simple, we can define trauma as *any unhealed human wound*. These wounds can be physical, emotional, sexual, verbal, spiritual, or financial in nature. Throughout this section, we explain how the body receives and processes traumatic experiences and go over what can happen when a person is unable—or does not have the opportunity—to process an experience. We also cover what the field has learned about best practices for healing. Yet before we go into all of this detail, please feel free to come back to this basic teaching anytime you feel overwhelmed with the content—trauma is any unhealed human wound.

Trauma as a Wound

Let's bring in the body right away—consider everything that you're learned in your life so far about physical healing following an injury. For instance, wounds and injuries can come in all shapes and sizes. Even those that may seem innocuous on the surface, like a scrape or simple cut, do require treatment. That treatment may simply be giving the wound some time and space to breathe while it scabs over, protecting the body as the body engages in the natural process of full healing from the inside out. Some wounds and injuries may require professional intervention to assist in this healing process. The natural constitution of a person and their overall health may determine how efficiently the healing process may flow. Throughout the COVID-19 pandemic, we've all learned how individuals who are immunocompromised are more susceptible to being harmed by the disease. The same applies for any wound or injury—deficiencies in the system, whether acquired or inborn, can make the healing process more complicated for some than it is for others.

Using a purely athletic example, let's say that any athlete gets cut on the field of play and is bleeding. What could happen if they go back into the game? Or in the case of jiu-jitsu, go back on to the mat? Several things could happen. Opponents might try to take advantage of the fact that the player is injured. The player could also put others at significant risk because, let's face it, open blood sores are not considered safe and can contaminate the space for others. Or the player could go back in and nothing could happen, which is often expected in certain elements of sporting culture. The player might even accomplish a glorious feat of athleticism, drawing praise, all the while needing care. For many athletes, the adrenaline pushes them through during the game or match, and it's not until afterward that they realize they are injured and are in need of care. And even if we notice injury later, some of us still respond to old programming to push through no matter what. In society, we tend to praise this ability to rise to the occasion while hurt—yet we criticize those who may need to stop and to ask for help.

Here's one more example of this metaphor we'd like you to consider. Some physical injuries or wounds may never truly heal. Think of someone who is born with a chronic illness, or perhaps someone who is missing a limb. Healing for them will never have a connotation of being restored to the state in which there is no chronic illness or missing limb. And yet they can learn to adapt and thrive. Especially if they are afforded appropriate resources and shown the skills for *how* they can adapt and thrive. As an example, someone who was born with one leg, or who perhaps lost it through combat or an accident, can learn to adapt and thrive by first having access to the technology that they need (e.g., prosthetics, others assistive devices). Physical therapy or other embodied practices, good coping tools, and a support system can be other pieces of the proverbial puzzle. Yet think of how many people in life who endure such physical trauma do not have access to such resources and/or are not shown how to use them.

We hope that this *trauma as wound* metaphor is making sense to you. The reality is that wounding is a complex phenomenon, and this metaphor is meant only to be a starting point to invite you into critical thinking about this complexity. After all, everything you know and realize about physical injury has an emotional parallel where other types of trauma are experienced. Yet for the traumas that do not leave a physical imprint, like a severed limb, a visible scar, or any other obvious sign of injury, the pain of recovery may be brutal because there isn't outward evidence that something is wrong. In so many cultures, emotional injury is not taken as seriously as physical injury. This reality can add to the stigma and shame experienced by a survivor, especially when cruel comments like "There's nothing wrong with you," or "Why aren't you over it already?" get pelted at survivors. Yet on the other side of this coin, many individuals deal with chronic physical illness, injury, or disability, which can come with another layer of shaming and stigma from societal forces. Whether it's outright discrimination or ableist barriers constantly showing up as a factor, or the tendency society has to show such individuals unhelpful pity, the chances of being wounded are numerous. Very often, people learn to internalize this shame, compounding the physical and emotional wounding fusion even further.

As we will explore in the sections that follow, the body-mind complex is all one. When the body suffers, so can the mind. And when the mind is troubled, distress is likely to manifest in our bodies, in our emotional state, and in our overall spirit. Yet we've also seen, time and time again, that when we as individuals accept the challenge to embrace healing in one channel of experience, because we are holistic beings, healing can inevitably show up in the other aspects of our being and our lives.

This Is Your Brain on Trauma

Have you ever tried to talk reason to someone who is activated or otherwise in crisis? Perhaps you've tried to de-escalate an altercation with words alone and your intentions fell flat. Maybe you have even tried to talk sense into someone who is zoned out as a response to being overwhelmed and you wonder why they can't hear you. These experiences can be commonly shared by jiu-jitsu instructors, therapists, human services professionals, educators, and members of the general public. And as it turns out, there is a good reason why talking reason, or trying to get a person to just talk about what happened to them, is rarely effective.

Even among mental health professionals and academics, many models abound to elucidate the neurobiology and help ordinary people better understand why the impact of unhealed trauma is not just all in their heads. Certain biochemical responses ignite the system when a traumatic experience happens, and if these are not neutralized or processed, long-term damage can result. Because this is not a science textbook, we will not go into every little detail about how the brain works. Such an approach would be like getting under the hood of the car and going over every little switch, socket, and gadget. Important, yes. Yet to truly drive the car, you need to know more basic mechanics than that—where is the wheel, for instance, or the transmission or clutch, the windshield wipers, the breaks, the speedometer, and the warning lights? In this section, we are imparting to you that level of mechanical detail so that no matter how you serve (as a clinician, a human services professional, an educator, or a jiu-jitsu instructor), you will have the basics that you need to navigate more smoothly in working with all people, not just those impacted by trauma. If you are a survivor of trauma, we hope that this information can put your experience into perspective and perhaps help you see a way forward.

THE HAND MODEL OF THE HUMAN BRAIN

In the past decade, trauma experts have embraced Dan Siegel's hand model of the human brain. This model provides a cursory overview of how the human brain is structured and offers a relatively easy metaphor (e.g., the hand) for most clients to understand. Originally based on the work of Paul MacLean and other neuropsychiatrists, this model (sometimes called the *triune brain model*) is sometimes criticized for being overly simplistic and not sufficiently comprehensive in its explanation of evolutionary neurobiology. We do feel that the model suffices in teaching the basics of what therapists, educators, jiu-jitsu instructors, and anyone who works with the public may need to know, especially when it comes to informing their approaches to reaching people who are distressed or activated.

Here are the basics of what you must know about each component of the brain as shown in the hand model:

- The *brainstem* (sometimes called the reptilian brain, although brainstem is more correct) includes the cerebellum; controls instinctual survival behaviors, muscle control, balance, breathing, and heartbeat; is very reactive to direct stimuli; and is most associated with the freeze response and dissociative experiences.

- The *limbic brain* (sometimes called the mammalian brain, the learning brain, or the heart brain) contains the amygdala, hypothalamus, hippocampus, and nucleus accumbens (responsible for dopamine release). The limbic system is the source of emotions and instincts within the brain and is responsible for fight-or-flight responses. Emotion is activated by input in this brain. Everything in the limbic system is either agreeable (pleasure) or disagreeable (pain). Survival is based on the avoidance of pain and the recurrence of pleasure.

- The *neocortex* (or cerebral cortex) is unique to primates and some other highly evolved species like dolphins and orcas. This newest region of the brain regulates our executive functioning—which can include higher-order thinking skills, reason, speech, and sapience (i.e., wisdom, calling upon experience). The limbic system needs to interact with the neocortex in order to process emotions. When the limbic system is overactivated, this process can prove difficult.

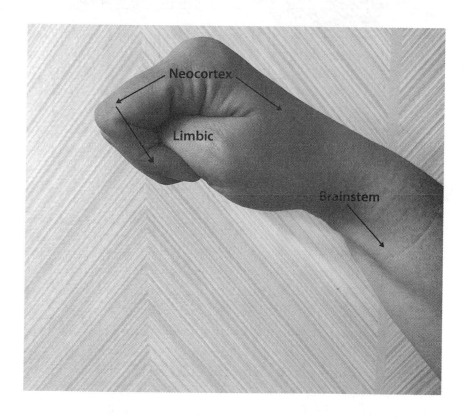

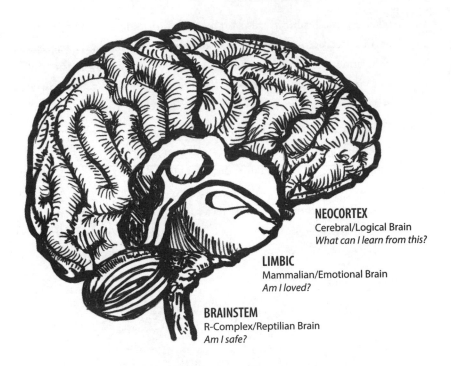

NEOCORTEX
Cerebral/Logical Brain
What can I learn from this?

LIMBIC
Mammalian/Emotional Brain
Am I loved?

BRAINSTEM
R-Complex/Reptilian Brain
Am I safe?

So how does all of this relate to trauma and how people show up in life? In humans and, indeed, in all mammals, the limbic system serves as a central processing unit for incoming information. That information can be taken in through any of our major senses; the limbic system is there to act as a filter. The limbic system does not operate on the same time scale that we associate with the neocortex, or the higher brain that regulates speech, thinking, reason, and yes . . . our sense of time and chronology. The amygdala, a major component of the limbic system, determines if incoming input is dangerous or not. If the amygdala codes the information as nonthreatening, the information can process through to the neocortex and integrate with other data that have been acquired over the years (both useful and useless). In essence, the information integrates into our existing experience without fallout.

If the amygdala codes the information as threatening, that is a different story. When information is deemed a threat, other areas of the brain will illuminate, specifically the survival-driven thalamus. This illumination can trigger one of three reactions, assisted by the brainstem: the fight response, the flight response, or the freeze response. Other responses that look similar to freeze, such as fawn (often described as the tendency to submit without question) or the varieties of dissociative responses, are covered in greater detail later in this chapter. When these responses are activated, the body does whatever these parts of the brain tell it to do, regardless of what rational thought might be saying. Even after the danger has passed in actuality, the thalamus remains on high alert, signaling the same responses if anything reminiscent of the original danger happens again. The thalamus and the reptilian brain work together, on overdrive, to prevent the threat from happening again. Some behaviors that are well known to us, such as drinking too much, eating too much, or engaging in other pleasurable behaviors that may become problematic, are designed to numb the system and prevent against further danger responses.

In his landmark work *The Body Keeps the Score*, Bessel van der Kolk declares that in healing trauma, for real change to take place, "the body needs to learn that the danger has passed and to live in the reality of the present."[1] The encoded threat responses live in the limbic system, so we must work with the limbic system and the brainstem if we truly want to heal where these responses are stuck or to assist others in their healing. We often get asked why two people can go through similar traumatic experiences and one person turns out to be okay and another suffers greatly. Sometimes, the person who seems to be alright may just be masking it well—please be advised of this before you make too many judgment calls without the full story. Most likely, the individual who was able to learn that the danger had passed closer to the time of the traumatic experience had support and resources in place to help them process and heal. According to Earl Grey, a psychotherapist and trauma specialist who writes about the brain for the general public in simple language, for many people who go through experiences where threat or danger is signaled, receiving help, support, or validation in as timely a manner as possible assists them with the process of integration. Thus, the chances of long-term consequences resulting from PTSD and related problems associated with trauma diminish.[2]

Validation is a powerful intervention, which speaks to the relational nature of the limbic system. Although this book focuses on this phenomenon in human-to-human intervention, we can learn a great deal from animals about the power of relationship and presence—two important aspects of validation—in general. (If you are not an animal lover or do not own a pet, this point may not resonate with your experience, but perhaps you know an animal lover and that person can operate as your frame of reference.) Consider your dog, cat, horse, or any other mammal in your life or one in the life of someone you know. Their timescales are likely very different than yours; they are very responsive to direct stimuli, and, perhaps most importantly, they are capable of forging relationships and connections. The animals in our lives have taught us both so much about empathy, loyalty, and energetic connection . . . and no words even have to be exchanged. The healing that our animals can bring us is through the power of connection. Imagine if we could meet our fellow human beings on this level, validating their experiences instead of forcing them into action constantly, or shutting down their experiences and emotions all together.

As we work to develop trauma-informed solutions that can help people heal, a common question that we get from non-therapists is "Why can't people just live in the present?" Although learning to be more present is a goal of mindfulness, jiu-jitsu, and other conscious practices, expecting someone with unhealed trauma to do that right away is unrealistic because the limbic system has no real rational sense of time. We try to approach our clients and students in this manner: How can we help you to learn to be more present? We recognize that it may be easier said than done if you've been numbing out or dissociating for so long. The most insensitive thing you can say to a trauma survivor is "That happened twenty years ago . . . just get over it." If the limbic system is still registering threat because of unhealed or unprocessed trauma, the impact of the event can still feel very present in the individual's body and mind.

Another very important reality to understand about the limbic system is that during a traumatic experience, or when someone is being reminded directly or indirectly of its impact, blood flow suspends (to some degree) to their left prefrontal cortex. Have you ever heard that saying *their blood is up* when someone is having a rage response? More accurately, the blood flow is actually cut off to the area of their brain that they need to process or make sense of an experience. Blood is still reaching the right prefrontal cortex, however, so they are aware of what is going on. Yet with limited ability to process or make sense of it, an individual can stay stuck. This phenomenon explains why you cannot talk reason when someone is in crisis. And if you try, you may make matters worse because a person is aware that you're trying to "fix" the situation, but their brain just will not allow it in that moment. Validation, presence, and grounding—many skills that we cover throughout the book—are key in crisis management. Being able to manage triggers and intense emotions is an important *base* (using the language of jiu-jitsu) that one must learn before moving deeper into the healing process.

THE ADAPTIVE INFORMATION PROCESSING MODEL

One of the leading treatments available today for PTSD and other trauma-related issues is called eye movement desensitization and reprocessing (EMDR) therapy. Jamie is an internationally recognized trainer and author in this area, and she regularly draws from a concept in EMDR therapy—the adaptive informational processing model—in teaching general courses on the impact of trauma on the human experience. Francine Shapiro, the founder of EMDR therapy, developed the model based on learning theory. Although we teach a more detailed version of the model in EMDR therapy training, the main points are as follows:

- The human brain is hardwired to process information and make sense of experiences.

- Experiences, both adaptive and maladaptive, are stored in the brain in a way that plays out in the body.

- Past experiences shape present realities.

- Trauma, which can include events that qualify someone for a formal PTSD diagnosis, causes memories to be dysfunctionally stored in the brain.

- Not all experiences of trauma necessarily qualify for a PTSD diagnosis. Experiences of abuse, neglect, or abandonment that impact people in the realms of responsibility, safety, and choice also qualify.

- This dysfunctionally stored information, especially when accompanied by a visceral or implicit charge or activation, can cause similar experiences that filter through the limbic brain to be experienced in the same way.

- This charge keeps the brain from being able to connect to positive or adaptive learning about self or the world.

- Continuing experiences in this realm compile on top of each other, causing or worsening symptoms of PTSD, other disorders, or general impairment in life.

- Comprehensive processing that involves all of the senses and the whole range of human experience is needed to shift how memories are stored in the brain.

- Once this shift happens from more of an implicit or visceral level storage to more of an explicit level storage, the negative symptoms that do not serve the individual fall away.

- Individuals feel better as a result in ways that include a shift of symptoms, improvements in beliefs about self and the world, and greater ability to conceptualize time and age (e.g., "This happened in the past. I am safe now.")

We can simplify the model even further to say that we learn things about ourselves and the world as a result of traumatic experience, and some of that learning messes us up. Until we shift what we learn and/or learn new things about ourselves and the world, we stay stuck. Much more on what *comprehensive processing*, the element required to facilitate this shift, will follow.

A major lesson from developments around EMDR and similar therapies is that trauma is more than just the PTSD diagnosis. You may be a member of the general public who only associates PTSD with war, combat, natural disasters, or life-altering accidents. Yet our study and scholarship of trauma since the Vietnam War has taught us that trauma does not have to be threatening to physical life. Life-altering events or experiences qualify. Anything that makes you feel less safe in your body or safe in the world might be a factor. Divorce, relationship troubles, death of a loved one, major life changes, neglect, instability, bullying in its various forms, being put down for who you are or who you love . . . these *all* qualify. When you consider that trauma is really and truly just any series of unhealed human wounds, you can start to realize that we've all been affected by trauma in some way. No human being gets out of this life without being wounded. Simply embracing this understanding can help us to be less fearful of trauma survivors whose symptoms or clinical manifestations may feel overwhelming to us. Or reading this far in the chapter may be giving you increased insight into what may be keeping you stuck in life.

Clinical Manifestations

The general public is most likely to associate the idea of trauma with the post-traumatic stress disorder (PTSD) diagnosis. Although PTSD was not a new concept at the time of the Vietnam war, the political maneuvering that followed Vietnam allowed for its formal introduction into the *Diagnostic and Statistical Manual of Mental Disorders* (DSM) in 1980. The diagnosis has gone through several updates since. Although going into the fine points of the diagnosis extends beyond the scope of this book, we feel that it's important to at least give you a cursory overview of what meets the clinical criteria for a PTSD diagnosis:[3]

- Exposure to actual or threatened a) death, b) serious injury, or c) sexual violation: directly experiencing, witnessing (Criterion A)

- Intrusion symptoms (Criterion B): some examples include flashbacks, nightmares, invasive thoughts, unexplained physical or emotional distress

- Avoidance of stimuli associated with the trauma (Criterion C): can manifest in a variety of ways, such as isolating, avoiding triggers in a way that interferes with life (e.g., not getting back into a car after an accident), substance use or other addictive behavior to block emotional impact

- Cognitions and mood—negative alterations (Criterion D): include potentially blocking out memories of event, increasingly negative emotional states that may look similar to depression, and negative beliefs developed about oneself and the world (e.g., "I am defective," "I cannot trust anyone")

- Arousal and reactivity symptoms (Criterion E): most common examples include hypervigilance and the heighted startle response; can also include problems falling or staying asleep, self-destructive behavior, problems concentrating, and sudden angry outbursts
- Duration of symptoms longer than one month
- Some degree of functional impairment due to disturbances

We specifically cover how some of these symptoms may manifest in all areas of life (Chapter 4) and specifically in jiu-jitsu training (Chapters 5–6) as the book progresses.

Many survivors of trauma, especially veterans, do not like the "D" (disorder) label in the PTSD diagnosis yet will verify that post-traumatic stress impacts them. Many providers of veteran mental healthcare have changed their language to reflect this destigmatizing preference. Also note that other diagnoses can result from unhealed trauma. The fifth edition of the DSM, published in 2013, even went as far as to add a chapter specific to trauma- and stressor-related disorders. While PTSD is a part of this chapter, other diagnoses that suggest traumatic causality may include acute stress disorder (when the symptoms of PTSD show up within the first month), adjustment disorders (as the name suggests, generally involved impairment due to life stressors that may not seem as large as PTSD on the surface), and reactive attachment or disinhibited social engagement disorder (diagnoses in children under 18, related to attachment trauma that occurred before the age of 5).

One of the criticisms of the traditional PTSD diagnosis and many of these other diagnoses is that they are very event-centric. They do not adequately account for the impact of trauma over time, especially at developmentally vulnerable ages or when specifically experienced at the hands of caretakers. In 1992, Dr. Judith Herman coined a term called *complex PTSD* to begin a conversation around this phenomenon. The following is a succinct definition from Courtois and Ford on the types of trauma that are more complex in nature.[4] They

- Are repetitive or prolonged
- Involve direct harm and/or neglect or abandonment by caregivers or an ostensibly responsible adult

- Occur at developmentally vulnerable times in the victim's life, such as early childhood

- Have great potential to severely compromise a child's development

While the International Classification of Diseases (ICD) manual has added complex PTSD to its system as of 2019, the DSM has not yet caught up with the progression of trauma scholarship around complex PTSD. We are hopeful that they will in future editions.

Wider embrace of the complex trauma concept helps us to see that many other diagnoses that people receive, from simple depressive disorders, to substance abuse or addictive disorders, to conditions like bipolar disorder or attention deficit and hyperactivity disorder (ADHD), may be better explained by the legacy of unhealed trauma. Even if trauma does not appear to be a direct cause of these conditions, exposure to trauma can certainly be an exacerbating factor in what makes them worse. People who get diagnosed with what are called personality disorders (e.g., borderline personality disorder, antisocial personality disorder) are likely in need of complex trauma treatment. Such conditions do not develop in a vacuum; they typically result from the impact of unhealed trauma and dissociation during these very developmentally vulnerable periods (e.g., before the age of 8). Dissociative disorders, which appear as their own chapter category in the DSM, are also clearly connected to trauma. Dissociation is such a widely missed and overlooked component of trauma, even among professionals, that we've devoted an entire section to it.

Dissociation

Dissociation means to sever or to separate. Dissociation is an inherent mechanism of the human brain—specifically the primitively driven brainstem— that is designed to keep us safe, especially in preverbal times when we don't yet have the verbal capacity to express ourselves. When the brain signals danger or even discomfort, we have the capacity to separate, whether from the present moment or from aspects of ourselves. Dissociation is a normal part of the human experience; we guarantee you've all done it. Daydreaming, zoning or checking out, not making eye contact when it's appropriate within your cultural norms, or taking escape from your surroundings using something like your smartphone are all forms of dissociation. Many humans dissociate and it's rather innocuous. In fact, it can even be adaptive or protective. All dissociation generally occurs to protect the core self or to get a need met.

Yet dissociation becomes problematic when it so pervasively keeps us from being present; when this happens, we may put ourselves or others in harm's way. In more intense forms of dissociation, some folks report blacking out or blocking out time, almost as if they are under the influence of a substance. Indeed, Jamie and another colleague have developed a model and are currently working on more research that directly describes addiction as dissociation.[5] When young people dissociate enough as a response to complex trauma in their setting, the brain can become so used to or bonded to the dissociative state that when pleasurable substances or behaviors enter the picture later in life, they amplify the intensity of something already familiar. Dissociation can generally be described as a continuum phenomenon—on one end, it is a very normal response to life's distresses and traumas. On the other, manifestations that can cause harm may result. Jamie, an individual who is publicly out as having a dissociative disorder, finds the continuum description a bit limited. In describing the continuum, many describe the extreme other end of the continuum as containing the "problematic" diagnoses like dissociative identity disorder (formerly called multiple personality disorder).

To be clear, many people who have a dissociative identity disorder—where several distinct parts of self may show up in the world—are able to lead full and adaptive lives if the sources of trauma that led to this severing are healed. And despite the myths, this healing can happen whether or not a person ever "integrates" their personality into what society sees as one cohesive whole. We must note that parts can be present in so many different kinds of human beings, not just those with dissociative identity disorder. Many survivors of simple or complex PTSD report having parts or aspects of self, and even those of you reading this without a known clinical diagnosis may relate. Think of it this way: Do you ever feel like you have an inner child that can get so easily wounded, even when your rational, adult self feels calm and in control? Do you relate to the experience of having a Dr. Jekyll and Mr. Hyde within, or perhaps Bruce Banner, who shows himself to the world, and the Hulk, who can pop out whenever Bruce's system gets too activated? Does it ever feel as if you have so many aspects and sides of yourself that just can't get along?

This is how normal it can be to dissociate and to have parts. Consider that for people with unhealed trauma of various kinds, the levels of separation—either from the present moment or the self—may be more pronounced. Jiu-Jitsu can be both the trigger and the resource for those who dissociate. The practices of jiu-jitsu teach you high degrees of presence, and being present with your body in an experience can be necessary to productive, safe practice. Yet for people who have spent so much of their lives checked out and disembodied, too much exposure to direct stimuli in jiu-jitsu can overwhelm the system, causing further dissociation. Both of us, and many of the survivors that we interviewed for this book, report experiences of dissociating during jiu-jitsu practice. While that might seem frightening to you, we must reiterate how dissociating does not mean you've done anything wrong, nor does it mean that you will become an incapacitated mess. Yes, the experience can be normal, yet how it's handled is vital in the healing process. Much of our teaching emphasizes that fear of dissociation is one of the greatest barriers that we experience to working with it effectively. In the chapters that follow, we endeavor to give you, as survivors, solutions for working with your dissociative tendencies, and to empower instructors, therapists, and educators with the skills that they need to be with a person who is struggling with dissociating while it is happening.

Learning to be more present with your whole self and in your body is key to recovering from maladaptive or unhealthy manifestations of dissociation. Yet people who have become so used to dissociating can become "phobic" of mindful presence, in the words of dissociation scholar Christine Forner.[6] As is the case in working with any phobia, the answer is safe exposure to the thing that scares you—in this case, being fully present and embodied. Throughout the book, we will share many suggestions for how survivors, clinicians, other human services professionals, and jiu-jitsu instructors can know dissociative responses when they see them and respond in a way that is grounding and potentially reparative. Not responding effectively may cause the student further damage and further fear of being in their body.

Healing the Traumatized Brain

So how do traumatized bodies learn that the danger has passed, making it more possible to live in the present? While a variety of evidence-based practices are research tested to specifically treat PTSD and other trauma manifestations, the general consensus that the field has reached is that we must first help people manage day-to-day stressors and body responses. Once they have achieved an adequate degree of stabilization or preparation, then people can engage in some deeper work to heal the sources of their traumatic responses. Finally, they will need periods of adjustment and integration to test out their healing gains in real life. Traumatic stress professionals disagree on whether or not a person can ever truly stabilize until they heal the source of their wounding. Anna and Jamie both see examples of clients and clinicians alike who are hesitant to "go there" with the deep work out of fear that they (or the people they serve) cannot adequately handle what might emerge in the therapy. So of course it's a delicate balance in these general tasks of trauma healing. We constantly work in a process often called *titration* with our clients—this involves preparing them with resources. Then we guide them into the source of their wounding to a certain degree, all the while letting them know that at any time they can turn back and take refuge in one of their healing resources. Once many people realize they can do this, they feel stronger about returning to the arena of that deeper work.

Both of us have seen this play out on jiu-jitsu mats—for ourselves and for those that we serve. Jiu-Jitsu has been a form of exposure therapy, of sorts, to the triggers that can scare us the most. Facing these triggers elevated our personal recoveries to more profound levels of healing, especially in our bodies. Yet when the process feels as if it may become overwhelming, we have the power to step back, to ask for a break, to literally reattune to our breath and the present moment. We will teach you all of the skills that we have for facilitating this process in the chapters that follow.

We are adamant believers that working with the body is essential to the most complete trauma healing possible. Human beings are a body-mind complex, and working with just one while ignoring the other is ineffective. We've already mentioned that Bessel van der Kolk's *The Body Keeps the Score* has become a modern classic among trauma specialists, yet so many others in the field of trauma recovery published books even earlier that addressed the body imperative in trauma and its healing: *The Body Remembers* (Babette Rothschild, 2000), *The Body Bears the Burden* (Robert Scaer, 2014), *The Body Never Lies* (Alice Miller, 2005) . . . and this is a short list. The basics that we gave you in this section, and some more advanced content on the brain in the sections to follow, hopefully make this connection clear.

In healing the traumatized brain, van der Kolk emphasizes three major tasks that must take place—all of which align with the hand model of the brain already presented:

- Top down (neocortex level): Learning new things/psychoeducation, connecting with others, insight-oriented work

- Technology or outside interventions (limbic level): Can include medications or other therapies specifically designed to activate the limbic system and help the brain reorganize or shift how information is stored

- Bottom up (brainstem): Allows people to have visceral and embodied experiences that *contradict* or override the rage or the helplessness that may have resulted from the trauma; jiu-jitsu and other martial arts most definitely fit into this category.

All of the tasks are important. And yet if we only engage healing from the top down, it would be like bandaging a wound over and over again. Although some healing may result over time from this stabilization process, the deepest healing generally occurs from the inside out (i.e., or from the bottom up).

In both of our journeys, we needed a variety of interventions to heal the brain holistically and completely—at all of these different levels. Traditional talk therapy and participation in experiences like twelve-step recovery were essential for top-down healing, especially to begin our journeys. Other office-based therapies like EMDR assisted us with shifting how information is stored in our brains. Yet the embodied practices like yoga, dance, and eventually jiu-jitsu were vital in attending to the bottom-up healing experience.

Working the Edge and Other Essential Knowledge

You will often hear teachers of yoga and embodied practices, including martial arts, use a term called *the edge*. A teacher may say something like "Notice when you've reached your edge," or "When you've reached your edge, you have complete permission to back off. You can always reset the pose or the move with this new awareness." In the yogic traditions that Jamie studies, the edge is generally referred to as that place, that sweet spot even, where you can safely practice yet still feel yourself being challenged. If we practice under our edge, we may receive some benefits, yet the potential for growth is limited. If we push ourselves or someone else pushes us too far past our edge, negative consequences can ensue. The concept of the edge can be useful for trauma survivors, clinicians, human services professionals of all kinds, educators, and jiu-jitsu (and other martial arts) instructors. The edge closely relates to an important concept in the field of trauma studies called the *affective window of tolerance*.

Affective Window of Tolerance

The practices that can help us to heal can also overwhelm our systems, especially if we are not used to connecting with our bodies. Trauma specialists have widely embraced the window of tolerance model (developed by psychiatrist Dan Siegel) to help them guide clients in what may be *too much* in the way of intensity. The model generally states that a healthy nervous system maintains an appropriate degree of sympathetic (arousal) and parasympathetic (rest and digest) balance to allow an individual to manage the emotional ups and downs, ebbs and flows of life. Being in the "window" that allows for this experience is referred to as *calm arousal*, where a person is emotionally regulated and able to self-soothe. When someone is in this window, they have better interaction in relationships, and a greater ability to be psychologically flexible, or meet challenges that life may bring.

The greater the degree of unhealed trauma a person's brain is trying to manage, the more likely it can be for this balance to be disturbed. An excess of sympathetic activation can cause a person to go over their affective window of tolerance into a state that is generally called *hyperarousal*—commonly associated with the flight/fight response. Common signs that a person is hyperaroused include being anxious, easily overwhelmed, easily angered, or prone to outbursts or aggression. Other signs that an individual is hyperaroused can include acting-out behaviors (e.g., drinking, drug use, eating), mental rigidity, or obsessive-compulsive thoughts and behaviors. Think of some of the people that you serve, or reflect on some of your own tendencies—do these sound familiar?

When a person is triggered or out of balance, other responses that indicate more hypoarousal (excess parasympathetic activation) can occur. We tend to associate these responses with freezing, fawning, or otherwise shutting down. Examples include depressive tendencies or flat affect, memory loss, disconnection, operating on auto pilot, or feeling separated from the self or otherwise not present. Once more, we invite you to notice if any of these sound familiar. Some of the scholars working in the arena of somatic psychology with the affective window concept use the metaphor of a light switch. Hyperarousal responses are like having a light switch constantly on, and hypoarousal is being stuck with the switch off. A healthy system needs a balance of the two, and unhealed trauma can make living in this balance difficult.

In the chapters that follow, especially Chapters 4 and 5, we will equip you with plenty of strategies for helping yourselves and the people you serve to live more frequently in this balance. Or if you should be knocked out of your window with responses that indicate hyperarousal, hypoarousal, or some mixture of the two (which is possible the more complex the trauma), you will learn how to come back into the window. You will learn a very practical tool called *scaling* that allows you to monitor where you are in this process.

Clinicians often discuss with their clients the importance of widening the affective window of tolerance, or at least working to creating a healthier balance in the nervous system. To put it simply, you can work on being able to take on more in the way of stimulation or challenge without harming yourself. For those of us who specialize in trauma, helping people widen their affective windows of tolerance is a necessary first step to prepare them for the larger journey. The *no pain, no gain* mentality that is often promoted in fitness cultures will not be productive in jiu-jitsu or any other embodied practice that you are aligning as a tool in your recovery process. In your path toward trauma recovery, you may have the goal or intention of healing your nervous system. If you push the system too hard, especially at first, the healing process may shut down altogether.

Lessons from Polyvagal Theory

Polyvagal theory, the work of neuroscience researcher Stephen Porges, informs how many trauma therapists assist their clients to more effectively heal their nervous systems. Porges explains, "Mammals . . . evolved in a hostile environment in which survival was dependent on their ability to down regulate states of defense with states of safety and trust, states that supported cooperative behavior and health."[7] In a world that is seemingly becoming more hostile, especially if you are a vulnerable individual, mental flexibility is required. Yet the corroborative impact of unhealed trauma can make us more rigid, less flexible, and less likely to respond to life from that calm window.

Many of us working in clinical, medical, and other wellness professions are familiar with the vagus nerve—the long nerve canal that extends from the brain, down the spine, linking the brain to our vital organs. *Vagus* comes from the Latin word meaning to wander or to travel, and working with something so vitally connective is an imperative in healing trauma or taking any student through an embodied process. While polyvagal theory can be seen as scientifically complex, many clinicians are applying its principles to their work with trauma survivors and anyone presenting for help to deal with life stress. Clinical social worker Deb Dana breaks down the three main components of polyvagal theory as such:[8]

- Autonomic hierarchy (e.g., the organization of the nervous system from oldest to newest); dorsal vagal (formed 500 million years ago in earliest animals; responsible for mobilization strategies and part of the parasympathetic nervous system); the sympathetic nervous system (formed 400 million years ago; responsible for fight and flight); and ventral vagal (formed 200 million years ago; responsible for social engagement and part of the parasympathetic nervous system). Dana explains that when our ventral vagal state is activated, our body-mind complex is most receptive to healing and change.

- *Neuroception* suggests that the body can work below the level of awareness to give us information at an implicit level. Jamie has long told her clients, "Your body will alert you to what's going on ten steps before you even realize that anything is the matter." This teaching exemplifies neuroception.

- *Coregulation* teaches that all mammals are in the best position to stay regulated and balanced when they have consistently engaged in this behavior with others. We, as people and as mammals, attune to each other's nervous systems. This is why you can have a very meaningful relationship with your pet—without ever having to exchange any words. A major reason that trauma therapists speak to the power of the calming presence is that such a presence can be a healing intervention in and of itself, explained by coregulation.

If you are new to your healing journey, it may feel like your nervous system is all over the place, and hopefully this model gives you some explanation to frame that. As people who serve the public, whether as therapists, human services professionals, educators, or jiu-jitsu instructors, it's important to recognize when a person is outside of their affective window of tolerance, likely in a heightened dorsal vagal (hypoarousal) or sympathetic (hyperarousal) state. In the experience of registered nurse, holistic health coach, jiu-jitsu brown belt, and breath specialist Marty Josey, "most of our society is in a state of sympathetic dominance." Josey notes that breath is one of the simplest ways to be able to decompress and tap into the parasympathetic nervous system. Also, recognize that one can take actionable measures for returning to a ventral vagal space. Begin the process by making sure that you keep the calming presence—stay grounded, breathe evenly, and speak in an even (sometimes call prosodic) voice. In our experience, the more you've practiced the grounding and embodiment skills that can keep you settled in your body-mind complex, the more you'll be able to set the stage—through your presence, modeling, and direct teaching—for others as well. If, as an instructor or even as a therapist, you can model solid and full breathing, it will inevitably impact the people you serve.

Jiu-Jitsu is uniquely suited to help in the process of bringing the nervous system into balance because the practice works with techniques that are traditionally associated with heightening parasympathetic stimulation (i.e., breathing) while also working with traditionally sympathetic, fight-based responses. Jiu-Jitsu teaches people how to sink into calm, even in situations in which they would ordinarily be activated. Jamie's colleague, somatic psychologist and complex PTSD expert Arielle Schwartz, has written extensively on the polyvagal theory in psychotherapy. She states that

> The goal of regulating emotions is not to make feelings go away. Rather, the aim is to help clients build their capacity to ride the waves of big emotions and sensations. Initially, this occurs because they know that we are willing to join them in these difficult moments. In time, this process helps them learn that temporary experiences of contraction can resolve into a natural expansion of positive emotions such as relief, gratitude, empowerment, or joy.[9]

This is sage wisdom that embodied trauma therapists take to heart. Throughout the book, we hope to show jiu-jitsu instructors and educators how to put some of the same skills into action with students and to inspire clinicians and human services professionals to deepen their practices. If you are a trauma survivor reading this book for your own healing, seek those experiences that can promote the type of healthy connection that allows you to ride these proverbial waves of emotion in as safe and supported a way as possible.

Lessons from Somatic Psychotherapies

Many approaches in the human service professions identify themselves with the concept of *somatics* (being in the body) or body-based psychotherapy—

dance/movement therapy, expressive arts therapies, Gestalt therapy, Sensorimotor Psychotherapy, and Somatic Experiencing. Even therapies like EMDR bring in a strong body-based component, with practitioners like Jamie (with training in other more somatic approaches) choosing to highlight these somatic elements further. If you get a group of professionals practicing in these modalities together, you will hear the general consensus that it's not sufficient to just talk about the trauma—you must get into the body where the maladaptive or negative effects of it are stored. Getting into the body also encourages survivors to tap into their natural ability to be resilient and heal. As the adaptive information processing model covered earlier suggests, when a person realizes that they can link up the maladaptive material with the more resilient, adaptive material, meaningful shifts can happen. Yes, *the body keeps the score* when it comes to trauma; yet consider that *the body keeps the score* on the positive connections we've made as well. You can try it right now—bring something pleasant from your life into your awareness—what are you noticing in your body?

For both of us, and indeed for many practitioners of jiu-jitsu, the practice allows for experiences of strength and empowerment that create new, more adaptive imprints in the body-mind complex. The more adaptive networks and associations we build, the more we are setting the brain up for further success, whether that is in formal therapy or in practices like jiu-jitsu that give us a live-action way of seeing new solutions. Because jiu-jitsu is such a psychically dynamic process, it can also offer people chances to shake off and move through stress at the level of the body, allowing for dynamic transformations of how certain memories may be stored in the brain.

Peter Levine, creator of Somatic Experiencing, is known in the psychotherapy professions for showing a video during his trainings of a shaking tiger that had recently been shot. In this video, the tiger shakes for an extended period of time to literally "shake off" the impact of the assault and bring his nervous system to a place of equilibrium. Levine explains that memories need to experience a completion or resolution, and shaking is an innate way for this process to run its course. For instance, if you survived an attack in which you froze when you wanted to stand up and defend yourself, the body may need to complete those desired motions while the body-mind complex addresses the memory in question. Trauma survivors need to feel activation and energy in the muscles in order to move the stuck material (i.e., memories) through to an adaptive resolution. In Somatic Experiencing, trauma survivors are invited to feel gentle vibrating or trembling sensations to assist in the letting go, much like the tiger shook itself. Such experiences are signs of nervous system state change. This phenomenon also offers people a way to transform maladaptive procedural or body memories.

According to Ramona Skriiko, a trauma therapist and Somatic Experiencing practitioner who has some experience training in jiu-jitsu, the various practices of jiu-jitsu—even something as simple as learning to get up in base—can help people move their bodies in a way that feels safer. In her experience training with Jamie's coach Micah Bender, she experienced the necessary coregulation to be able to *let the beast out* in a way that didn't overwhelm her nervous system. Ramona explained, "You want to work with what's happening in the body, especially flight or fight, without sending the nervous system into overwhelm, especially freeze." The various somatic trauma therapies clearly emphasize this necessity, and throughout the book, we hope to make a case for how jiu-jitsu instructors and practitioners alike can embrace this wisdom.

What Jiu-Jitsu Offers Survivors of Trauma

Moving the body in a dynamic, perhaps specifically in a bilateral or side-to-side, way (like we do in EMDR[10] or Somatic Experiencing) looks to be a vital component in how memories can shift from primary limbic activation to storage in the neocortex, which is more efficient for long-term storage of memories. Jamie has spent thousands of clinical hours with EMDR patients and trainees, watching them move their eyes back and forth or tap their bodies side-to-side, observing powerful movement that would take ages to get to in talk therapy, if it could even be gotten to at all that way. Perhaps this is why Jamie was overcome with chills and tears when she and Anna spoke with Guilherme (Gui) Valente, a multi-degree black belt instructor and son of grandmaster Dr. Pedro Valente Sr. about how he raised his children. Gui explained that grandmaster Valente was insistent that his children train in three practices—jiu-jitsu, swimming, and horseback riding. He saw all three skills as vital to human survival, which makes sense when you consider how they can all help you get away from a dangerous situation. Jamie resonated so strongly with this belief because all three skills work with bilateral stimulation—moving the body and thus engaging the hemispheres of the brain in a back-and-forth way. This process, regardless of how we engage it, appears to be a major component in how the body can bring its nervous system back into balance and shift how memories are stored in the brain.

For Gwendolyn Samuels, a professional Equine Bodyworker and adult amateur rider who trains in jiu-jitsu, the parallels are clear. She notes that the mindfulness you need when you practice jiu-jitsu is the same mindfulness you need when you ride a horse. She notes, "The breathing techniques that you need in jiu-jitsu, not to go into the fight or flight reflex, is the same breathing that you need when you're on the horse so that the horse can keep you safe." Gwendolyn also notes how body awareness is important in both practices. Adding in another piece of the larger embodiment conversation, Gwendolyn became interested in jiu-jitsu when a yoga studio she practiced at offered a women's self-defense class taught by Micah, her now long-time instructor. Mindfulness of breath and body is clearly a thread that runs through jiu-jitsu, yoga, horseback riding, and many other healing arts. As van der Kolk and other trauma specialists teach, properly guided mindfulness can help trauma survivors widen their tolerance for affect and other sensory experiences. And consistent mindfulness practice can lighten the load of the amygdala, decreasing the intensity of fear-based responses. Mindfulness is not all about sitting on a cushion and being still—it can be practiced in more actively physical ways that may be optimal for trauma survivors who struggle to sit still. *Mindfulness* is the art of remaining in the present moment or returning to the present moment once your attention drifts or distress causes you to dissociate from the here and now. There are a variety of approaches to cultivate this skill of being more present, with many specific ideas to follow in later chapters.

While the focus of this book is specifically on jiu-jitsu, we hope that you are already starting to see how jiu-jitsu fits into the larger conversation about embodiment, healing the brain, and recovering from trauma. Especially when jiu-jitsu is presented in a safe and responsible, yet challenging and engaging manner, the possibilities for healing and dynamic exploration of life lessons are innumerable. For this book, we had the privilege of interviewing a whole host of jiu-jitsu practitioners who identify as trauma survivors or who have been exposed to trauma, in addition to the instructors who work with them. Yes, we can make proposals based on a theory about why jiu-jitsu can help in trauma healing, and certainly we can share from our lived experiences, yet these nuggets of wisdom we've received from those willing to share their stories with us further answer the question—why jiu-jitsu?

For purple belt jiu-jitsu instructor, professional weapons instructor, and Marine veteran Brian Needham, jiu-jitsu teaches the brain how to explore solutions. The more you train, the more these solutions on the mat and in life appear to you, whether you're looking for them or not. The brain is hard-wired for resolution and seeks it—this is an excellent way to summarize the adaptive information processing model covered earlier. Direct processing, which can happen through the various practices of jiu-jitsu, can allow the human body-mind complex to experience this resolution. Many of the folks we interviewed shared direct experience of how practicing jiu-jitsu helped them put these pieces together.

Katie Maloney is a complex trauma survivor who has worked in various aspects of the fitness industry throughout her adult life; she's been a personal trainer, has taught CrossFit, and has even taught self-defense classes based on other methods. Katie was sexually abused by both of her parents (an experience she writes about in her memoir *From Cake Pops to Coffee: A New Conversation about Trauma*). Dissociation was a significant part of her struggle, a common phenomenon for complex trauma survivors. She felt that jiu-jitsu, which immediately felt different than some of the other self-defense training she received and taught, offered her something different. In her interview with us, Katie explained

> You don't really have the option to zone out . . . that aspect is helpful with dissociation and working through triggers. Jiu-Jitsu requires my brain and my body to work together—that's why I'm able to stay embodied. Even with yoga, the mind can wander more . . .

Many other female survivors of trauma we spoke with share similar connections, and both of us relate to this experience in our own training.

Clearly jiu-jitsu can be a healing balm for veterans of all genders as well as survivors of sexual assault and other interpersonal trauma. Jiu-Jitsu can also be an option in helping traumatized children heal and/or in allowing the developing brain learn vital life lessons about connection, self-esteem, and fairness. Jamie first got interested in jiu-jitsu through watching her stepson Brendan train. Her former husband enrolled the boys in jiu-jitsu when Brendan, himself a survivor of multiple childhood traumas, was going through behavioral difficulties at school. Several of the women interviewed for this project, including Staci May, Jami Jeffcoat, and Katie Gollan, were also inspired to try out the practice by first watching their children take lessons. All three women are now instructors or assistant instructors themselves, enthusiastically testifying to how much jiu-jitsu changed their lives.

In the words of black belt instructor Alex Ueda, who specializes in teaching children and who is also quite masterful at working with adults, "The whole practice of jiu-jitsu is a very interesting lens through which we can discover humanity and self-love." Alex goes on to offer even more insight into what makes jiu-jitsu so special as a healing art, both for adults and children. He explains that the practices of jiu-jitsu can short-circuit the survival-driven inner critic: "When you practice it enough in a controlled environment, you realize you will survive and you develop an analytical approach to the things that would make you normally panic outright." Through consistent practice of this process, according to Alex, you can learn the most important lesson of all—you were always worth defending.

You are worth defending.

I am worth defending.

Trauma therapists seek to help the people they serve embrace such positive cognitions or beliefs about self at a truly holistic or total level. Sure, you can know in your rational mind that "I am worth it," especially if you've previously received more cognitively driven therapy. Yet there is often something unhealed in the limbic system that prevents you from totally embracing these beliefs.

We asked everyone that we interviewed what the top five to ten lessons that they learned from jiu-jitsu were, whether they were techniques for protecting themselves or the elements of jiu-jitsu philosophy that most resonated. When Gwendolyn Samuels answered the question, she simply stated with a conviction that represents a major shift from the demur, repressed manner in which she was raised: "I am capable." For ourselves personally, for the women we had the privilege of researching, and for many of the people we interviewed, jiu-jitsu was and continues to be a major factor in allowing these shifts in perception and experience to happen.

We had the privilege of speaking with Dr. Gino Collura, multi-stripe jiu-jitsu blue belt and practitioner of several martial arts, whose newer research on veteran reassimilation through jiu-jitsu caught our attention in researching this book. Gino's passion for jiu-jitsu comes from a personal connection with the practice; it has helped him to build self-confidence, even though he has training in many other martial arts and formerly worked in executive protection. Gino credits the technique and strategy of jiu-jitsu as components in explaining what makes it special, and he notes the entire practice can give people, especially veterans, a chance to reset their nervous systems. All of these components make jiu-jitsu an ideal practice for learning adaptation and working on your identity and how you relate to the world. For veterans, Gino says, jiu-jitsu teaches that it's permissible to still be a warrior and to still be connected to something larger than yourself, especially if you are training in community. Jiu-Jitsu allows veterans to hold onto what serves them about this military identity while realizing that it is not all they are, and that having a warrior mentality can be practiced differently and healthfully upon their transition back to civilian life. As defined by the adaptative information processing model, what Gino describes is the essence of adaptation.

If you are reading this book as an existing practitioner of jiu-jitsu, what positive beliefs about yourself and the world have you been able to more fully embrace through your practice? If you are picking up this book as someone who has yet to try jiu-jitsu and are perhaps curious about how it can help you, we invite you to put the book down for a moment and scan your body. Ask yourself: What are the beliefs in my life—whether they are about myself, others, or the world—that are getting in the way of me living my life to the fullest? Do these beliefs seem to exist because of traumas or wounds that I experienced in the past?

Now please do yourself a favor and take a breath, especially if you engaged in this inquiry very deeply and fully. As you read on, we hope to provide you with a wide variety of solutions, both within the practice of jiu-jitsu and in other healing arts, including professional therapy, that may be able to assist you in moving through these blocks. Just as you are worth defending, you are also worthy of the gifts that total healing can bring.

TRY THIS STOP!

According to our instructor, Eve Torres Gracie, one of the most powerful moments she witnesses as a teacher is when women find their voice. A feature of the *Women Empowered* curriculum is a practice called "STOP! Block. Frame." where women are literally invited to proclaim the word *stop* assertively, accompanied by a gesture. This practice is reminiscent of Gestalt therapy and other somatic psychotherapy approaches. You can try a version of the practice here. This presentation is similar to what we might show clients in our therapy offices as it is ultimately a lesson in setting boundaries. If you end up training at a jiu-jitsu school, it's very likely that you will learn a similar practice as part of a self-defense curriculum.

1. Begin by finding your base. For the purposes of this exercise, place the leg that you perceive to be on your weaker side in front of you, and place the other stronger leg behind you. Place the legs far enough apart that you experience a strong sense of base and not too far apart that you feel unstable.

2. Hold your hand out in front of you in a gesture that for you represents "Stop," traditionally, palm out toward your would-be attacker.

3. Once you feel the stance in your body, boldly declare, "Stop!" Do not be afraid to use the fullness of your voice.

4. Repeat as many times as necessary until it feels natural.

5. If you have the chance to do this with a practice partner, engage them in the drill. Try to make eye contact if possible. Then, get feedback from them about the strength they perceived in your voice. If they suggest that the "Stop!" wasn't as convincing as possible, make some adjustments and try again.

6. You may also consider trying this with the other foot forward and investigate whether or not you notice anything different.

7. If it's not possible for you to stand up, please engage in this exercise sitting down, feeling into the source of your voice and moving your arm or arms in whatever way is appropriate to set the boundary.

Three

An Expanded History of Jiu-Jitsu and Jiu-Jitsu Philosophy

Whatever be the object, it can best be achieved by the highest or the maximum efficient use of mental and physical energy directed to that purpose or aim.

—JIGORO KANO, *KODOKAN JUDO*

As is the case with the practice of yoga or other Eastern forms of conscious meditation, the wisdom of jiu-jitsu philosophy can have an impact on survivors of trauma whether or not they ever have a chance to train on a mat. Some of these life lessons from jiu-jitsu philosophy are highlighted within this chapter and within the context of jiu-jitsu history. Tracing the roots of jiu-jitsu can be a highly contentious endeavor. Like with all study of history, interpretation is variable and sources must be considered. To fully develop this chapter, we conducted interviews with several authorities on the topic. We present this history through our interpretive lens as trauma clinicians. Hopefully this chapter will come alive with meaning for trauma survivors and for those who seek to help them, whether they are clinicians or jiu-jitsu instructors.

A Brief History of Jiu-Jitsu

Guilherme (Gui) Valente, son of Pedro Valente Sr., explains how there is a great deal of exaggeration in many historical representations of the origin of jiu-jitsu. In an interview given to Anna and Jamie, he explained that three generations of his family trained with Helio Gracie in Brazil for a span of sixty-seven years. Gui's grandfather Dr. Syllo, his father Pedro Sr. who became a grandmaster, Gui himself, and his two brothers Pedro and Joaquim all had many years of direct instruction from Helio Gracie and other top experts in judo and boxing. Gui Valente shared how his family was given a copy of all of the newspaper articles that Helio Gracie had collected documenting the specifics of fight matches, dates, times, weights, and other details. From those articles, his family has worked to put together as accurate a history as possible in their publications.

Other authors agree with the complexity of the history and note that telling an accurate narrative may prove challenging. In his book *Japanese Jiu-Jitsu: Secret Techniques of Self-Defense*, author Darrell Max Craig offers wisdom from Sensei G. Koizumi, Kodokan 7th Dan in judo. There is a great deal of speculation on where *jūjutsu* (jiu-jitsu) was born. Koizumi paints a picture of numerous sources of inspiration over many years and many countries. He explains that much of what is out there is simple conjecture from stories related to the creation of certain schools or from "some incidental records or illustrations found in the ancient manuscripts not only in Japan but in China, Persia, Germany, and Egypt."[1]

There is no foolproof way to define the exact roots of jiu-jitsu, especially when we recognize that the impact of commercialism and Westernization affected how the original practices were disseminated. What we practice now may seem watered down to the earliest practitioners of these arts, yet there is also a chance that they might also view what has evolved, especially in the wake of Imperialism, as being quite interesting and even necessary to preserve the art form. We do believe it's important for instructors of jiu-jitsu to have a working understanding of these general origins and how they developed so they share jiu-jitsu as respectfully as possible.

Koizumi hypothesized that since the beginning of human kind, people have most likely instinctively been working on skills related to self-preservation, including the ability to fight. Koizumi describes that "the development may have taken various courses according to the condition of life or tribal circumstance, but the object and mechanics of the body being common, the results could not have been so very different from each other."[2] Given these limitations of the human body in its ability to fight, it is no wonder that there are so many commonalities within fighting arts across the world.

The Valente brothers, Pedro, Gui, and Joaquim, sons of Pedro Sr., highlight a Babylonian sculpture from BCE in which two men are shown in a position in which they appear to be grabbing each other by the hips in an effort to unbalance the other.[3] Some sources trace the origins of jiu-jitsu to the mountains of India 2,500 years ago, and then have it move into China 400 years ago.[4] Other sources credit the origins of all martial arts much further back in the Chinese antiquity. According to legend, Huang Di, also known as the Yellow Emperor (2697–2597 BCE), is said to be the founder of the martial arts. He defeated would-be emperors who were coming at him and his army from all directions because of his ability to gain advantages, even in adversity.[5]

Even though there is a lack of consensus as to when and where jiu-jitsu was first shaped and from what origins, numerous martial arts and studies in self-defense are credited as having led to the development of jiu-jitsu. According to Nihongo Master, a Japanese online dictionary, *Chikara-Kurabe*, translates to "a contest or trial of strength."[6] According to Judo Info (described as an online dojo), *Chikara-Kuirabe* was held in the seventh year of the Emperor Suinin, 230 BCE.[7] This tournament might have led to the development of sumo wrestling, and sumo wrestling in turn might have had an impact on jiu-jitsu. According to another online source, influences can be traced to Japan during the Samurai years (as early as the twelfth century CE).[8] If Samurai, typically battling on horseback, were to find themselves disarmed and on foot, they would use ground techniques they referred to as *ju-jitsu*. Given their heavy armor and lack of mobility, strikes were less effective than throws, chokes, and joint locks, which are characteristic of jiu-jitsu.[9]

In *Asian Fighting Arts*, authors Donn Draeger and Robert Smith share that the Emperor Nimmyo (794–1185 CE) endorsed Sumo as a military strength. They explain that a shift then occurred in the Kama-Kura period (1185–1333) in which sumo was transformed by the "development and perfection of grappling skills."[10] George Kirby goes on to explain that the Daito-ryu Aiki jiu-jitsu school was formed in 880 CE by Prince Sadagami.[11] According to an article by Team BJJ Hashashin (that explains some of the differences between jiu-jitsu and judo), this school was founded on the secret teachings of the Shukendo (*shu* meaning "search," *ken* meaning "power," *do* meaning "way"). They explain that the *jutsu* in *jūjutsu* is focused on "defeating an opponent," while the *do* in judo implies a focus on defeating one's self. The authors suggest that the jiu-jitsu they know incorporates both.[12]

Empty Hand: The Essence of Budo Karate by Kenei Mabuni credits a man named Chin Gempin with bringing Confucian, Buddhist, and Taoist influences to the art of jiu-jitsu in the Edo period (1603–1868). Mabuni explains that "Fukuno Masakatsu Shichirouemon and Ibaragi Sensai developed the *Kito* style of Japanese jiu-jitsu after having been instructed by Chin Gempin."[13] On their website, the Valente brothers credit these Chinese belief systems as the philosophical base for the art of jiu-jitsu. They go on to emphasize jiu-jitsu concepts that they feel were pulled directly from the *Tao Te Ching*, a classic of Chinese antiquity. They describe these concepts as *soft overcoming hard, yielding rather than resisting.*[14] The *Tao Te Ching*, the work of teacher Lao Tzu, is described by translator Charles Muller as offering a way of living that brings us back into the harmonious flow of the natural. "Nothing in the world is softer than water, Yet nothing is better at overcoming the hard and strong."[15]

According to a 1990 column in *Black Belt Magazine*, the "first officially recognized martial arts in Okinawa was simply known as *te*, meaning hand."[16] According to this article, the martial art had developed in response to a ban on weapons in the late 1500s. Although karate is not noted often as having connections to jiu-jitsu, it is notable that the shift away from weapons spurred the need for other solutions for defense. Changes in culture, away from weapons and toward nonviolence, can be seen sprinkled throughout the origins of jiu-jitsu.

Many credit Helio Gracie with transformations to jiu-jitsu that made it the Brazilian Jiu-Jitsu we know today, especially in the West. The book *Gracie Jiu-Jitsu* explains that the Gracie family traces their roots to George Gracie from Scotland.[17] George arrived in Brazil by 1801. One of George's grandchildren, Gastão, was raised to be a diplomat, studying German and seven other languages. But Gastão ended his diplomatic pursuits and turned to a career in business. Helio was Gastão's son. Yet while the Gracie family was emigrating to Brazil, jiu-jitsu and judo were still evolving in other parts of the world.

The Kodokan

According to the Martial Arts International Federation (MAIF), Jigoro Kano (1860–1939) founded a martial arts school known as Kodokan Judo. Kano is credited across many sources as having a significant impact on jiu-jitsu as we know it today.[18] According to the United States Jiu-Jitsu Federation, Kano studied both Tenshin Shin'yo and Kito Ryu, which is said to have led to the many throwing techniques of judo.[19] In *The Way of Judo: A Portrait of Jigoro Kano and His Students*, author John Stevens describes Kano as seeking guidance from both sumo wrestlers and the books on Western wrestling.[20] The book goes on to suggest that this inspiration was then incorporated in new techniques. Some of these techniques were throws and holds that Kano used against stronger opponents.

In *The Historical Sociology of Japanese Martial Arts*, Raul Sanchez Garcia describes numerous periods of backlash and difficulty among samurai.[21] According to the Valente brothers, similar discord surrounding the jiu-jitsu community influenced Kano to separate his trainings from these negative connotations by incorporating a spiritual aspect. The Valentes describe how he rebranded his martial art to incorporate "way or doctrine" (*dō*). They detail how safety, morality, and positivity in the training environment were new priorities. This can be seen in MAIF's explanation that "the ultimate aim of Judo is to perfect yourself and to contribute to the well-being of mankind."[22]

John Stevens contends that the spiritual elements and other changes Kano made helped his martial art program eventually gain acceptance and incorporation into the public school systems as physical education. Stevens describes an 1886 Tokyo Police tournament in which Kodokan practitioners won almost all of the matches. This success caught the attention of military and law enforcement, who then adopted it as part of their training regime.[23] The Valente brothers highlight that Kano's pedagogy was based on three principal objectives: self-defense education (*shobuho*), physical education (*reshinho*), and moral education (*shushinho*).[24]

Mataemon Tanabe developed a system of jiu-jitsu called *fusen-ryu*, which emphasized ground fighting. One of Tanabe's students defeated a Kano student in the Kodokan vs. Fusen Ryu bouts in 1891. The authors of a popular martial arts blog called *Combat Otaku* speculate that Kano might have invited Tanabe to teach at the Kodokan school, and therefore introduced his ground fighting influence.[25]

In *The Way of Judo*, John Stevens maintains that Kano is said to have struggled with the changes in a martial art switching from self-defense to competition. He took issue with the focus on quickly winning. He is quoted as saying, "I instituted formal competition not to show a student how to win at any cost but how to lose with grace and humility."[26] Several of the people we interviewed noted that competition and sport jiu-jitsu, in their assessment, potentially degrade the *art* of the martial art. Does the sporting mentality cause practitioners to lose sight of judo and jiu-jitsu's focus on self-defense and moral principles? Some of these same questions are being asked in jiu-jitsu communities over a century later.

From the Kodokan to the Rest of the World

Numerous Japanese jiu-jitsu masters are credited across sources as having traveled the world to share jiu-jitsu as a new martial art. The Valente brothers credit Yukio Tani, Sada Uyenishi, Taro Miyaki, Mitsuyo Maeda, Tokugoru Ito, Soshihiro Satake, Akitaro Ono, and Geo Omori with traveling the world to promote jiu-jitsu in the nineteenth century. Various marketing and teaching efforts were employed, including fight demonstrations given in every possible outlet: theatres, stadiums, circuses, and fairs.

Mitsuyo Maeda (1878–1941), specifically, has been identified as a top student at Kodokan, having expertise in both traditional jiu-jitsu and judo.[27]

Thomas Green and Joseph Svinth, in *Martial Arts of the World*, give lengthy details of Maeda's world travels to Belgium, Scotland, Spain, Cuba, Mexico, the United States, Brazil, and many more places globally.[28] Numerous sources describe Maeda and Satake, another top practitioner, as both having traveled to Brazil in 1914 and founded the first Judo school in Brazil. In their book *The Toughest Man Who Ever Lived*, Nori Bunasawa and John Murray explain that Maeda was said to have participated in no-rules matches in an effort to share the efficacy of jiu-jitsu.[29] The *Gracie Jiu-Jitsu* book details a connection between Maeda and Gastão Gracie and that Maeda was the one who taught Gastão's son, Carlos Gracie (Helio's brother).[30]

Several resources, including "The True History of Brazilian Jiu-Jitsu," a blog by Evan Meehan, debate how much time (if any) Carlos actually spent training with Maeda. Meehan suggests that Carlos received much or all of his training under Donato Pires dos Reis, the only Brazilian Maeda-certified instructor, and that Donato had invited Carlos to be his assistant in teaching jiu-jitsu when he opened a jiu-jitsu academy called Academia de Jiu-Jitsu.[31] In their history blog, the Valente brothers share a history that describes the Gracie brothers as having had a falling out with Donato in 1932 and that they kept the academy when Donato moved away, rebranding the facility as the Gracie Academy of Jiu-Jitsu.[32]

Many other blogs and websites, the modern carriers of the oral traditions, give other accounts of the history. They explain that Carlos, the oldest of eight Gracie boys, opened his own school in 1925 in Rio de Janeiro and brought his brothers, Oswaldo, George, Gastao, and Helio, to help him run it. Carlos is credited as having had a big impact on the preservation and promotion of the art.[33] The Valente brothers describe him as a philosopher; he was said to study extensively across the fields of exercise, hygiene, nutrition, spirituality, and marketing.

Helio Gracie's Contribution

Gracie Jiu-Jitsu and many other sources describe Carlos's brother Helio (1913–2009) as having had difficulty executing Mistuyo's techniques due to lack of strength and health issues. Helio is said to have watched the classes without participating for several years. In his blog titled "Top 30 Myths and

Misconceptions about Brazilian Jiu-Jitsu," Roberto Pedreira contests Helio being sickly and shares that Carlos is noted as stating that his brother Helio was a champion swimmer before 1930 when he began training in jiu-jitsu.[34] Strong swimming skills are congruent with later reports that he saved a man from drowning in shark-infested waters.

According to *Gracie Jiu-Jitsu*, Helio accidentally ended up teaching jiu-jitsu one day when his brothers were delayed. Students enjoyed the class with him and requested more. The book describes how Helio then began adjusting the techniques so that they worked with his weak disposition, making them effective regardless of size or strength. These adjustments were made as a result of simple trial and error using leverage. Authors have often heard in class from Gracie instructors about Helio's discoveries. They describe how he found that if you put your torso, arms, and legs in particular positions based on your opponent's attack, you can defend against and even take dominance over an opponent. The *Gracie Jiu-Jitsu* book clarifies that he continued to refine techniques to use the least amount of strength and energy to make them effective. These refinements have become known in many circles as Brazilian Jiu-Jitsu (BJJ) or Gracie Jiu-Jitsu (GJJ).[35]

Jeff Reese explains that "the survival mindset" is the most significant difference between Gracie Jiu-Jitsu and Japanese jiu-jitsu/*jūjutsu*.[36] Many argue that when you are fighting against an opponent who is significantly bigger or more athletic, the survival mindset is the only option. The essence of this philosophy is to stay focused on staying safe, not on dominating or injuring the attacker. Anna, your author with the more advanced practice that includes sparring, knows firsthand that if you move to attack your opponent in advanced classes (also known as *master-cycle classes*), you often leave yourself open to attacks; defense is the goal. If you are lucky enough to exhaust your attacker, then a moment of offense may eventually open itself to you. However, on the streets with a real attacker, and especially one who is bigger or more athletic than you, if you are not severely injured, you win.

If you survive, you win.

Gracie Jiu-Jitsu describes how the techniques were further refined and tested through challenge matches. *Fight Sports and American Masculinity* by Christopher David Thrasher described these matches as *Vale Tudo*. *Vale Tudo*, translated from Portuguese, is "anything goes."[37] Many years later, Victor Cesar Bota made a documentary about the UFC Ultimate Fighting Championship titled "The Gracies and the Birth of *Vale Tudo*." In these unsanctioned matches, there were no rules, no gloves, no weight classes, and no time limit. Groin shots, elbows, eye gouging, and head-butts were allowed.[38]

Lute Livre, Portuguese for "free fight," is another influence. Many sources detail how *Lute Livre* became a rival of Brazilian Jiu-Jitsu, further influencing the evolution of jiu-jitsu techniques. The Valente brothers' history shares how differing philosophies even grew within the Gracie family.[39] George was said to pursue professional fighting, which often came with a focus on entertainment and money. Carlos and Helio were said to focus on self-defense in real fights, therefore refusing fights with points or judges. The Valente's history also describes that although the Gracie family had established a reputation as powerful fighters, Helio's successes, while weighing only approximately 143 pounds, highlighted the huge weight and strength discrepancy between him and his opponents, helping him attract people as students from across the country.[40]

Roberto Pedreira, one of the leading critics of the Gracie mythology, gives a different account of the weight discrepancies, stating that there were actually no weigh-ins at the time and everything was simply a guess. He also disputes the national sports heroism of Helio as a myth. He highlights numerous sports awards and honors given in Brazil, none of which were awarded to Helio.[41] We've included some of Pedreira's challenges to the traditionally accepted Gracie history throughout this chapter.

Gracie Jiu-Jitsu describes Helio's seventeen fights. The book reports exceptionally long fights, with opponents weighing significantly more and often taking place while he was injured or out of training. One match, against 192-pound wrestling champion Fred Ebert, lasted 140 minutes.[42] The book also states that a match against 234-pound wrestling champion Wladek Zbyszko ended when Zbyszko declined a third, 10-minute round.[43] In *Gracie Jiu-Jitsu*, Helio describes that despite his broken rib going into a fight with Kato, the second-ranked jiu-jitsu fighter in the world, the fight ended in a draw, and the second fight ended with Helio choking Kato unconscious. In his blog, Roberto Pedreira contests Kato's description as

Japanese jiu-jitsu champion and says that, "He was a young inexperienced regional judo competitor with some successes but not the vice-champion of anything."[44]

Gracie Jiu-Jitsu emphasizes a specific moment in the fight with 200-pound Japanese fighter Masahiko Kimura in which, unbeknownst to Kimura, Helio had actually lost consciousness.[45] Kimura, unaware of the unconsciousness and thinking his move was unsuccessful, moved to a different assault and the fight continued as Helio awoke to the next attack. The book shares that at thirteen minutes in, the match ended as Carlos threw in the towel fearing Helio would receive serious injury in what is known as the "Kimura Lock." Roberto Pedreira states that "Years later Kimura said he felt like he lost, which was half Japanese modesty but possibly also suggested that Helio's defense on the ground did surprise him. Credit where it's due. Helio had a good defense."[46]

Other Gracie Family Contributions

According to *Gracie Jiu-Jitsu*, Helio's son Rorion immigrated to the United States in the 1970s and began sharing the techniques from his garage. Rorion continued the tradition of challenge matches and quickly gained the respect of the community. Many of Rorion's brothers also began making significant contributions to the growth and sustainability of jiu-jitsu in the United States.

In 1988 Rorion created and released a video of the no holds barred fights in Brazil: *Gracie Jiu-Jitsu in Action*. A shift had begun as people now witnessed real fights without limits and the effectiveness of jiu-jitsu within. The video details other efforts as Relson opened a jiu-jitsu school in Hawaii and Rickson, Royler, Royce, and Rorion worked together to open the Gracie Jiu-Jitsu Academy in Torrance, California, in 1989. *Gracie Jiu-Jitsu* describes efforts to prove Brazilian Jiu-Jitsu's effectiveness to the world as Rorion founded the Ultimate Fighting Championship in November 1993. The story is told that although Rorion and his brother Rickson were perfectly capable of fighting in this event, Rorion had his younger brother Royce represent jiu-jitsu to emphasize that a smaller, slender-build participant could defeat larger opponents. Jiu-Jitsu has been an important part of MMA ever since.

The Takeaway from History

There is disagreement on and debate over the exact history of the origins of jiu-jitsu as we know it today in the West. It is clear that the practices connect to the Japanese and Chinese arts from which they descended, and in the richness of this philosophical tradition rests much of the benefit for trauma survivors. As the goal of this book is to assist trauma survivors in their healing journey, we felt compelled to give a brief overview from as many sources as possible. These sources include the many blogs that jiu-jitsu enthusiasts and instructors write on the topic, a modern-day method for documenting oral history and oral tradition. Even though oral tradition serves as a primary source of information in passing down any practice with several centuries of history, problems can naturally emerge with accuracy and interpretation. We want to allow readers to make up their own minds on what they believe is both important and true. We have a secondary intent in giving the variety of opinions—to combat what could be described as a cult-like mysticism around the prominent players in the jiu-jitsu world, many of whom are often viewed as god-like idols.

Anna remembers waiting for class to start one day early in her training, when a new person sitting next to her asked if she knew if they would actually be able to see Rener Gracie, grandson of Helio and son of Rorion, teaching on the mat that day. Anna came to jiu-jitsu with no awareness of Rener's celebrity status and responded that he was there almost every time she trained. The person exclaimed their excitement that they might be able to see him and instructed Anna that she should feel very fortunate indeed to have such an amazing opportunity. Anna remembers thinking that she found Rener to be helpful and supportive and an all-around solid instructor and good guy. That night she remembers doing a quick search of the web to see just how famous he was and was shocked to find his 78,000 followers on Facebook. Anna, who has never been impressed by celebrity and actually finds it to be a thing to avoid, found the new information to be less than helpful. She had already felt lucky to have his instruction, and now that it was pressed upon her to do so, because of his celebrity, she found herself irritated by the imposition. Rener was still the same supportive instructor and human, with both strengths and weaknesses, that day on the mats.

Anna continues to feel deep gratitude for the instruction she has received from him and his brother, and at the same time, recognizes that they are human beings like anyone else. As therapists, we believe that the majority of this world is neither good nor bad; rather, beauty and reality exist in the shades of gray. Our job, as humans, is to find the good intent and hold boundaries with the rest. According to the Valente brothers, Carlos and Helio were both known for being idealists and teaching an art that could transform lives for the better. Regardless of any human flaws in many of the leaders of this industry, we both believe in and can find evidence of the good intent.

The mysticism and cult-like following of Gracie Jiu-Jitsu and other celebrity martial artists have the potential to lead some survivors to difficult places and potential for further traumas. We want survivors to remember that people are people and businesses market. Just because a facility is run by someone popular or well known does not necessarily mean they are the best teachers. In addition, although we can find, perhaps, a stretching of the truth or excessive marketing tactics at some facilities, we encourage you not to discard the good aspects when you're sorting through the bad. If these same people have created programming in which great benefits are being realized for trauma survivors, we want to give them the credit they are due.

Jiu-Jitsu Philosophy and Approaches to Life

Philosophy is a common area of interest among jiu-jitsu practitioners. We have often heard jiu-jitsu instructors explain that they don't want students memorizing techniques. Instead, they want students to become masters of principles and philosophy. In this section we aim to answer a few questions:

- What are some of the primary goals and tenants in jiu-jitsu?

- Why are those important to trauma survivors?

- What kind of messaging should you expect to see in a trauma-informed school in how they convey philosophical principles?

Tony White, a purple belt and now an assistant instructor, trained for many years off and on in martial arts. As he came to find a strong connection to jiu-jitsu, he discovered a shift in himself. In the past he was "learning to fight," now he was "learning how to live." Similar statements were made in our research study of *Women Empowered* students. Students recognize profound life impacts on and off the jiu-jitsu mats. We believe that how a particular facility conveys jiu-jitsu philosophy can be a key factor in making it safe for survivors to train. Such commitment also translates to the potential for jiu-jitsu practices to have a healing impact.

These are some examples of core principles of jiu-jitsu philosophy that are taught on jiu-jitsu mats across the world. As we explore the meaning of each, you will hopefully garner insight into how each has the ability to translate to life off the mat.

- Safety First

- Control

- Don't Count on Kicking and Punching

- Be Aware of and Regulate Your Emotions

- Find Comfort in Uncomfortable Situations

- Be Energy Efficient

- Position before Submission

- Fail Forward

- Have Conviction

- Keep It Playful

- Keep a Beginner's Mind

- The Warrior Archetype

Safety First

Often people will associate "self-defense" with defense against punches (punch protection) and trying to stay away from dangerous situations or aggressive people (distance management). That is only a small part of the story in jiu-jitsu. When practicing jiu-jitsu, our mind is focused on defense first. How do I stay safe? I need to figure out what my opponent's objective is and how I can neutralize it. A second safety focus when you practice techniques that involve submissions (armlocks for example) is the importance of tapping early. Never wait until your arm is fully extended to tap. Third, self-defense is being patient; it's waiting for your opponent to open an opportunity via their errors, versus trying to lead the fight in a direction you want it to go (e.g., "I'm going to triangle you"). Remember the focus on defense first, exhaust the opponent, and then submit if needed.

Emotion regulation skills help us to not overreact or underreact. Not only are survivors who practice jiu-jitsu reporting that they are less likely to withdraw from disagreement and more easily able to face conflict, they also report a newfound ability to not cause or exacerbate one. At Anna's training center, students are told that there *should be nothing anyone can say to you that would cause you to fight.* This directive may seem like a tall order if you are a survivor of trauma. Consider, though, that you may realize, over time, that you don't have anything you need to prove to anyone else. Your self-esteem is now internalized; you do not need validation from and are not threatened by others. You know who you are and what physical defense and control you are capable of if you need it. You can use that confidence to walk away.

Numerous online videos showcase jiu-jitsu practitioners on the street who often say to an aggressive person that they "don't want to fight" or "there is no need to fight." This approach is parallel to what Sun Tzu advises in the time-honored *Art of War.* Anna and Jamie were both trained to walk away or run away if possible. If you are present during a robbery (no matter what belt rank you are), give the robber your wallet, phone, car keys, and anything else they want. Just get home safely. If, however, you are faced with an attempted abduction, fight with everything you've got not to be taken to a secondary location. This teaching makes us both think of a specific technique we learn while standing and responding to a person who is walking toward us aggressively. One of our options, for example, if we are in a crowded space where we can't run, is to turn and step toward them putting our forearms across their biceps, with our hands resting on top and asking, "Can I help you?" We are using our words to attempt to diffuse the issue at hand. If done correctly, it becomes very difficult for the aggressor to land a punch with our hands on their arms should they decide to try.

Control

Unlike many other martial arts where injuring an opponent with strikes is the main goal, in jiu-jitsu, a main principle is to gain control over your opponent. Jiu-Jitsu teaches you to use your opponent's aggression and energy against them and gain a dominant and safe position. You then stay in control, wearing them out until you can either escape to safety or submit them (breaking joints by applying locking pressure to a joint or choking by cutting off blood to the brain) if you need to. Again, once they are worn out and you are safe to escape, submission is an option that you may not have to choose and therefore not cause any lasting harm. A variety of circumstances call for a variety of responses. If you are out in a general public space and are able to run to safety, submission may not be necessary. You are gaining control versus being controlled, and you get to make choices instead of choices being made for you. This paradigm shift is massively important for trauma survivors.

As a trauma survivor, Anna explains that her brain often flashes back to times in which she could have used many of these skills she has since learned and how powerless she felt on those occasions. Anna says, "I was either out-of-control explosively violent in response to violence or withdrawing and unable to do anything. Other options were not available to me back then." Jiu-Jitsu has given Anna a new sense of control over herself and her opponents. "I have hundreds of options now, whereas I had only two in the past."

Don't Count on Kicking and Punching

There is a significant issue with relying on strikes to defend yourself. For starters, if you are close enough to throw a punch, so is your opponent. Jiu-Jitsu teaches us to carefully manage the distance between ourselves and an attacker for this reason instead of relying on striking or punching. Jiu-Jitsu player and Gracie *Women Empowered* instructor Jami Jeffcoat shares this: *Manage the distance, manage the damage* was actually my cover picture right after my husband and I separated." This saying helped her to hold a boundary.

In addition, striking defenses hold an underlying assumption that the pain will get the attacker to stop or comply. If the attacker's physical stature is significantly larger and/or the attacker is high on drugs and not registering pain, then pain compliance through strikes will be ineffective. Again, the main goal of jiu-jitsu is to survive and escape and, if you need to, apply a submission. Remember, *submission* is done by applying locking pressure to a joint or by cutting off blood to a part of the body. Submissions have the potential to break joints, and some have the potential to be lethal. At our schools, we have been taught to use the least aggressive option possible in defending against an attack. We have also been told that if someone is attempting to forcefully take us to a secondary location where our chances of survival decline significantly, we should use whatever means necessary to get away, and this could include submissions. On certain occasions, it is also possible to hold the person in the submission position and apply pressure in order to restrain them, without causing them lasting physical harm. One goal of submissions is to leave the attacker less able or unable to attack anyone. If, for example, I break your arm using jiu-jitsu, then you are not able to punch me or hold me with that arm anymore regardless of whether or not you feel the pain. As survivors, this made a great deal of sense to both Jamie and Anna. Anna reflects:

> Most of my trauma was inflected by people bigger, stronger, and/
> or intoxicated. I had also sometimes been drinking myself. It makes
> me laugh to think of it now, because my body reflexes have grown
> so strong that I have to now work to not use them if someone walks
> toward me or touches me. Not in a hypervigilant way, but more so in
> a playful way. I have often found myself hugging a friend or family
> member and resisting the urge to use the body fold technique to take
> them to the ground. I don't drink anymore, but I imagine if I did,
> that I could be a real hazard to any attackers even while drinking.
> My body knows what to do, even when my brain doesn't.

Although striking defenses are often taught as part of the jiu-jitsu curriculum, they are generally not the emphasis. And if taught, the emphasis is on control and on using your body leverage effectively, not flailing and punching in a way that can escalate the situation. For Jamie, learning a series of these simple strikes (for example, slapping the ear coming out of another move to knock the aggressor off balance) was imperative and helped her to work through many of her blocks about being ladylike and restrained. Yet even she realized that they were only a small part of the puzzle.

Be Aware of and Regulate Your Thoughts and Emotions

A key principle of jiu-jitsu is staying in control of your own emotions during an altercation. If you are staying calm, your brain will be better able to recall what to do to stay safe and not expose your body to high-intensity punches, chokes, and more. For a trauma survivor who might be triggered by the prospect of a physical altercation, this is a skill that may take some time to develop. Learning to regulate your emotions while participating in jiu-jitsu, which is potentially highly triggering, can be a significant life-altering skill to develop. Many trauma survivors in our study indicated that there were profound and unexpected changes in other parts of their lives after they started to train. After having had to face situations that would normally leave us in fight, flight, or freeze responses, through jiu-jitsu, we have found that other everyday-life stressors tend to become smaller. Everyday conflicts at work or home became less intimidating, and trauma survivors feel more confident and more assertive in other areas of their lives. Survivors noted having a newfound ability to set boundaries. This in turn helped to break the cycle in which trauma survivors are more likely than others to be attacked again.

Anna personally relates to thought and emotion regulation challenges and her journey of building awareness and tools. She explains

> Over all the years of trauma, I believe I had developed into quite the adrenaline junkie, always seeking another hazard to conquer from mountain biking spines to skiing triple black diamond chutes, to getting my motorcycle license. I often found myself walking up to the biggest toughest guy I could find on the mats in the beginning. However, even my "adrenaline junky" habits have been changed by my jiu-jitsu experience. I volunteered to assist at a law enforcement training event. I was told by many others that at this event, they did not train the way we do and were not always as aware of protecting their partners as we are at my school. I disregarded their warnings and did it anyway. Unfortunately, after many other extreme

sport injuries to my head, ribs, wrists, knee, fingers, I got injured in a way that would sideline me for a whole year. In one swift side-crushing takedown from a 250-pound partner, I switched the title of "bulging disks" in my lower neck to now officially herniated with a painful pinched nerve down my arm to boot. This injury left me in excruciating pain for six weeks, unable to train for six months, and restricted from sparring for another six months. What I have learned over the course of this time while sidelined is that I love my time on the mats so much that I am not willing to risk a permanent injury anymore. I want to participate as long as I possibly can, and keeping myself physically whole is required. This led me to explore why I'm drawn to adrenaline-producing activities. During further exploration I could tie my behavior back to trauma.

Much like the differences between fight, flight, and freeze reactions to trauma as it happens, sometimes a pattern in the nature of our long-term responses to trauma triggers afterward. Some survivors withdraw or recoil (flight, freeze) from situations that induce fear, while other survivors walk straight toward the danger (fight). I discovered that my attraction to adrenaline-producing activities is often fueled by an unconscious need to re-create the traumatic experience, fight it, hopefully win, and finally master whatever threat I had connected it to. Jiu-Jitsu has taught me to instead pause, slow down, and carefully consider what my training intent is. It has taught me to stay aware of myself and be able to spot when I'm triggered. It has given me countless opportunities to simply stay present in difficult positions, sense that I am safe, and extinguish the need for fight, flight, freeze, and reckless adrenaline junkie behaviors.

Others we interviewed also described a development and enhancement of emotional regulation skills. Tony White describes how jiu-jitsu skills apply in his everyday, real life. He states that "things feel clearer after sparring. It all melts away for a while. Being in the bottom of mount [lying on the ground with someone sitting on top of you] can be crappy. Dealing with my dad one day can be crappy too, but not like the intensity and difficulty of being on the bottom of the mount." Tony expressed gratitude for his training, punctuating, "It helps me stay out of arguments."

Finding Comfort in Uncomfortable Situations

Finding comfort in uncomfortable situations is key to anyone's success in jiu-jitsu. With or without trauma history, it can feel uncomfortable at first to be at the bottom of the mount with someone sitting on your stomach. Numerous positions in jiu-jitsu offer the opportunity to build tolerance for discomfort. In turn, this exposure teaches us the ability to stay calm and stay in our frontal lobes where real strategic thought can happen and it prevents us from sinking into our more reactive brain. When you are beneath someone, the normal human inclination is to try to escape immediately, yet that can actually potentially increase your chances of getting hurt. The first task at hand is to stay safe.

Matthew Lee, a purple belt at Gracie University, describes how jiu-jitsu stands out from other martial arts. He explains that jiu-jitsu reminds him of Jungian philosophy in which you directly face your shadow parts.

> You don't try to dodge or deny them. In other martial arts you are taught to bob and weave and dodge the punch or kick. In jiu-jitsu, if the fight is unavoidable, you confront it directly. You deal with the fight. You actually run towards the punches and deal with the attacker head on in a move often seen in professional boxing called the clinch. Although it seems counterintuitive, you are actually safer as you hug the attacker close because their punches become ineffective.

Anna has heard in her studies that most street fights aren't likely to last more than one or two minutes. Louis Martin describes his research in watching street fight videos, stating that "Fights rarely last more than a minute."[47] Tony White explains from his lived experience and from what he's heard from other coaches that the typical fight is short, usually lasting no longer than twenty seconds. He states that it's rare for it to last any length of time at all. Maybe five to ten seconds before people dive on top. Fights only last as long as it takes for people to break them up. That said, he suspects that if an attacker is attempting to isolate a woman in an area without people to jump in, it could take longer. So getting comfortable with the uncomfortable for a minimum of a few minutes helps you to stay safe. In mainstream psychotherapy, we call this skill *distress tolerance*. For Jamie, who was skittish to even start jiu-jitsu because of her hesitancy to fight in the first place, approaching the skills she learned as vehicles for sharpening her distress tolerance was of optimal impact to her trauma recovery and wellness.

When Jamie first began training, a meme that she found on social media quoting Rickson Gracie, Helio's son, spoke to her. This well-known teaching of Rickson's declares, "You have to find comfort in uncomfortable situations. You have to be able to live your worst nightmare." Interestingly, most Gracie Jiu-Jitsu instructors will tell the tale that when Rickson was a child, he suffered from severe claustrophobia, and it was only by rolling himself up in a carpet over time that he got over it through this progressive exposure. For Jamie, approaching jiu-jitsu practice was frightening at first, and it felt like she was rolling herself up in a carpet, even though she was safely guided by Micah, her instructor. The point is clear though—exposure and practicing distress tolerance in a safe enough space can be a vital component for healing that jiu-jitsu provides.

Nick "Chewy" Albin, a third-degree black belt instructor in Louisville, Kentucky (also described in a Google search as the BJJ World's Most Popular YouTuber and podcaster), emphasizes the importance of becoming comfortable and learning to survive first. This *survival first* mentality takes precedence over technique mastery. He shares that we need to desensitize to the stress so that we can instead have situational awareness. He offers the metaphor that "you can have the most amazing fighter jet, but if the pilot is panicking, they can't fly the thing."

Energy Efficiency

We are often told that we don't defeat our opponent, they defeat themselves. One of the key principles in jiu-jitsu is to exhaust the opponent's energy while keeping yourself safe and then wait for the right moment to apply a submission if you need to. The goal in a fight is simply to stay as safe as possible. When you are trapped, your entire goal is to observe, identify, and defend against their attacks. The goal is not to defeat someone. Helio Gracie worked to make moves in a way that conserved energy by using leverage versus muscle activity and strength.

Once you have nullified their attempts, not only have you caused them to lose confidence and energy, but you have set the stage for a more efficient and safer escape. Another important way to see this is that no one can control you *and* attack you at the same time. Think of the process in terms of steps:

- Be patient (emotional regulation is key)

- Neutralize

- Seize the opportunity

Micah Bender, former MMA fighter, jiu-jitsu black belt, and Jamie's primary teacher and mentor throughout her training, explains his approach to conserving energy use using a simple acronym: SEE (simple, effective, and efficient). He is concerned when certain approaches to self-defense teach so many steps that they can become easy to forget, especially when your adrenaline is up and your brain is entering a free response. Micah notes, "You ought to have no more than three or four components to executing a move effectively, because when you're in a situation or a fight, your body may only remember one or two." Micah and many other skilled instructors like him epitomize the wisdom of *less is more*.

Position before Submission

The right move at the wrong time is the wrong move is a teaching often shared at Gracie University. Anna often explains to her clinical clients that timing is everything. If they try to work on something with a family member at the wrong time, then the outcome could be the opposite of what they intended. Anna knows, for example, that her significant other is not a morning person and if she wants to discuss ways to improve their interactions in the morning, she ought to choose another time of day to address it with him. The same is true of jiu-jitsu. If we want to use the rear takedown on our opponent but we are facing them, we will need to move behind them before we can attempt it. Sometime the slightest change in position will open up all new kinds of possibilities. Position dictates what is available.

Anna shares candidly:

> There have been many times where I was in a rush with an agenda to accomplish a particular move and failed because I had not put myself in the best body position for success. I was once working to get a triangle, a submission choke using my legs from the guard in which my opponent is already in-between my legs. I ended up leaving myself open to punches and losing the guard control (control of their body using my arms legs; please see the appendix for more) because I had not established the best body position prior to giving away to my partner what I was trying to accomplish.

If you become rigid in your pursuit of a particular submission like a triangle, you can miss the potential opportunity for an armbar. It's important to stay fluid and have the confidence that an opportunity for a submission will present itself eventually, and potentially even the one you originally shot for. If you remain intentional but unattached, you gain the flexibility to reach your goals through as-yet unforeseen means, and you remain open to doing things better than your original aims.

Fail Forward

We often hear our instructors emphasize failed attempts as a key to progress. We've both heard black belts share the hundreds of times they went for a particular move without success and then finally, on a particular day, it worked for the first time. Being okay with mistakes and failure is a common challenge for many of our clients. The struggle is staying positive and keeping tenacity alive in the face of numerous mistakes. We both collect inspirational affirmations to help ourselves and our clients fail forward. A few of our favorites that help us with training and in life, from both jiu-jitsu and other sources, include these:

- *You need to learn to fail or fail to learn. Losing is where the learning happens.* (Matthew Lee, purple belt)

- *Find something you love and fail until you are good at it.*

- *Give yourself permission to write a shitty first draft.*

- *Live in the process, not the perfection.*

And the list goes on . . . Feel free to add any of your favorites to this collection. Affirmations tied to the concept of failing forward and other jiu-jitsu philosophies help students remember and internalize the concepts. They can bring comfort and peace to uncomfortable processes on and off the mats. And the impact of these practices for trauma survivors rests in that translation to life off of the mat.

Becoming comfortable with failure and viewing it as an opportunity for growth and not as a proverbial death sentence is another life lesson that jiu-jitsu fosters. In citing a teaching that he learned from Rener Gracie, Micah Bender shares that you can learn to look at a larger, perhaps more skilled opponent and say, "Isn't this interesting?" For many jiu-jitsu practitioners, that is the takeaway—an ability to reframe how we look at challenges. That includes the challenges that trauma triggers may bring our way.

Conviction

Conviction can be defined as "a firmly held belief or opinion" by several standard dictionary sources. Survivors of trauma can often feel unsure about so many things that others take for granted in daily life. Belief or confidence in themselves has often been eroded by trauma and especially by complex trauma that has been inflicted over a period of years by the very people who should have been instilling confidence in them as children. This, in turn, damages self-esteem and the ability to put themselves out there in the world. In the end, lack of conviction can cut survivors off from opportunities. Tony

White gives an example of how, in his experience with basketball as a kid, lack of conviction prevented him from presenting his best self:

> In my driveway as a kid, I had awesome moves. But I didn't bring my moves to the game. I didn't want to try my fancy moves and fail. I didn't believe I was good enough in the moment and had a crippling fear of mistakes that stopped me from doing it. In jiu-jitsu I had to be willing to put my moves to test. It demanded an act of courage and you never know unless you try. If you don't believe at half speed you have already lost it. Better off going in with 100 percent conviction and 50 percent technique than the reverse. Try hard enough to fail, and if you don't fail, you're not trying hard enough.

Conviction or a trust in your ability to execute is a factor in your success in jiu-jitsu. Anna has experienced instructors advising her to not hold back in her conviction in executing a move. She remembers that holding back often came from both a lack of confidence in herself and a fear of not wanting to hurt her training partner. She felt tentative and unsure and didn't want to commit to pushing into her partner. Many techniques require an opposing force to work against. A counterpressure and leverage applied by the practitioner against the aggressor's force is what makes jiu-jitsu work. A lack of conviction while executing some techniques could actually be a hazard to your training partner. Over time you learn to trust the techniques as you realize that you can have conviction and stay safe. For a trauma survivor, trust and belief in their ability to stay safe is exactly what has been stolen in the traumatic experience. Clinicians actively work to assess for trust issues and work to provide corrective experiences for trauma survivors. Self-trust and conviction are often understandably hard earned after trauma. When life-threatening situations have stolen our trust, our brain is often not readily impressed by the small positive moments in correcting beliefs about a dangerous world. A phenomenal aspect of jiu-jitsu is that belief in oneself is sometimes quicker to correct.

Lack of conviction or belief in oneself is often one of the most difficult aspects to repair in talk therapy. Our brains and bodies are not easily convinced via words that we can be safe. Our bodies need to physically feel the sensations. Imagine, for example, you are held down on the ground in an attack. Now you learn and even execute, on the same day, the reversal of this position. You have caused your brain to wake up and pay attention to something positive. The brain is potentially triggered with adrenaline and cortisol as you are held down in the starting position. Old ideas, memories, and thoughts of danger and hypervigilance may surface. All of the old information that erodes conviction and self-trust has come online. You have awakened sections of the brain that do not like to open to therapeutic conversations about healing. Then your brain gets to observe the situation being corrected in a split second; the incident and lack of possibilities it once experienced are being rewritten. As you practice, you imprint the brain with new corrective information . . . over and over and over again, rewiring this neuronal recording. You then build belief and conviction in yourself. As time goes by and you master techniques, you reestablish conviction and trust. Often the belt test is a true test of not only technique but also whether our minds have more fully recovered from the trauma.

One caveat to this positive experience is our readiness for it. Hopefully what you are seeing and will continue to see throughout this book is the need to do your homework first. Part of that homework is taking the necessary steps to first be aware of your triggers and your stress responses. Second, build and practice your own emotion regulation tools, and third, make sure you have support in place in case things get too heavy; if you don't, you could be setting yourself up for potential retraumatization. We cover much more on putting these principles into action in the chapters that follow.

Keep It Playful

Jami Jeffcoat, a practitioner and assistant jiu-jitsu instructor in South Carolina, reports that "without the playful, I couldn't imagine being there still." We agree that playfulness is a critical part in being able to be patient enough to develop jiu-jitsu skills; being calm and playful will allow you to be more aware and able to pick the right moment to execute on a specific technique.

Anna reflects that small windows of the sensation of play gradually opened up to her when her concerns about safety abated. The more these concerns consistently dissipated both on and off the mats through jiu-jitsu training, the more frequent and longer the windows of fun and joy on the mats became. "After three years in training, I was no longer attending class to learn how to be safe. Now I come to have fun and sharpen my skills," she says.

Mark Barentine self-describes as a "reluctant brown belt" who began consistently training in 2009. When he reflects on the playfulness of jiu-jitsu, he recalls memories of wrestling with his dad as a kid. "I'm getting tossed around while laughing. I'm getting picked up and dropped into the couch. It's funny and no one's getting hurt. There is no goal other than just to have fun."

For Mark, jiu-jitsu provides that same sensation of fun. He shares that it's not about going for the kill, it's about exploring, being curious, collaborating, and even building community. Mark describes how people are silly and goofy on the mats. Sparring is specifically like a science experiment. You are testing hypotheses. If I do this, what will he do? Mark described the humble and playful banter that keep it fun.

Once, when he was a purple belt, he got tapped by a combatives belt (a much lower belt in the Gracie system). He recalls that the combatives belt said, "You gave that to me." And Mark said, "No. You got me. Good job and you won't ever get me that way again." Mark experiences an excitement and joy in the surprises that are discovered during sparring when someone accomplishes something new on him. Anna relates to this feeling and says it's like Christmas. "Who-hoo, I've learned a new trick!" She reflects that if you were fortunate enough to have fun wrestling with your parents as a kid like Mark did, you know the joy in those interactions. The sensation of getting thrown in the air safely onto the couch is something your body might happily remember. Unfortunately, some cultural norms prevent little girls from having the same experience. For those who did, the question is: When was the last time you were able to actually wrestle with your parents? Did it stop as a teenager? Every day Mark steps on the mats he gets to play in this way with his friends again.

Playfulness can be natural healing medicine for a trauma survivor. We understand that it can take some time, practice, and desensitization to get to the point you feel playful. Feeling playful is the exact opposite of being vigilant and scared. Every step we can take to train in places that support playfulness and pick partners who bring that out in us is setting the stage for a long, empowering, and fun jiu-jitsu journey.

Keeping a playful mindset also reminds Anna of the vast space between play and violence. Jiu-Jitsu enables the practitioner to decide how violent they need to be and if they even need to be violent at all. In the *Gracie Jiu-Jitsu* book, jiu-jitsu is described as the "humane approach."[48] Humanity is accentuated in that jiu-jitsu "enables its practitioners to control an attacker without hurting them." We can indeed keep it as playful as we like. The more playful we feel in practice, the more we can bring that mindset to the streets if we need to defend ourselves.

Tony White explains that keeping a fun vibe facilitates learning. He explains that jiu-jitsu is not fighting, but more of a process of exploring how bodies connect, without being married to an outcome. It's okay to lose because losing means you are learning. He explains that the vibe is set by jiu-jitsu instructors who explicitly state in a straightforward manner that *we are here to help each other.* The message is intentional: practice in a way so that everyone has fun and no one gets hurt. Many jiu-jitsu practitioners, including purple belt Staci May, refer to themselves as "jiu-jitsu players" instead of jiu-jitsu practitioners, and Jamie's coach Micah routinely refers to their training sessions as "play time." This mindset certainly reveals much about how they approach and benefit from jiu-jitsu.

In Jamie's assessment, this emphasis on playfulness may be the truly unique Brazilian contribution to the evolution of jiu-jitsu. An avid dancer who often teaches to Brazilian audiences, Jamie has long been impressed by the joy for life and spirit of dance that Brazilians seem to bring to their approach to life. For instance, Brazilian football (soccer) players are known for bringing the spirit of dance and the samba to how they approach the game, and many commentators note that this can get driven out of them when they go to play in more technically focused European leagues. As Jamie often notes in her teachings, jiu-jitsu has become one more way that she dances mindfully.

Beginner's Mind

One of the concepts of Buddhist mindfulness is called *beginner's mind*, a spiritual practice and approach to life that shows up in many global faith traditions. Approaching any new practice with the curiosity and spirit of a child is imperative for conscious development and growth, and jiu-jitsu offers many opportunities for that. Many other concepts relate to beginner's mind, such as failing forward, covered earlier in this section. Beginner's mind teaches us that we can always begin again and that we can be met where we *are* when we are learning new challenges on the mat or in life. Jamie's coach Micah makes the comparison to teaching new life skills to his young sons. "I'm not going to get frustrated with them just because they're not learning something the first time. It will take some time and repetition to get it."

Many of us, including Jamie and Anna, can arrive on jiu-jitsu mats beaten down by societal pressure to be perfect and master something immediately. Jiu-Jitsu encourages us to approach learning new things as a child would; this approach also taps into the philosophy of keeping it playful. Jamie recalls learning this powerful lesson firsthand when she had a chance to train several times with her stepson Ethan, who was twelve years old at that time. She recalls:

> Because I didn't want to hurt him, especially because I was much larger, I was able to move more gingerly, more gracefully, and with less sense of striving. This helped to slow me down and ultimately improved my approach to jiu-jitsu.

Later that fall Jamie had the occasion to take a seminar with Grand Master Pedro Sauer, one of the top teachers in the Gracie system. In that seminar, he mentioned how important it can be for adults to train as if they were training with small children.

Another concept that beginner's mind relates to, specific to jiu-jitsu, is a mantra or saying that you will hear from many jiu-jitsu practitioners: *Slow is smooth, and smooth is fast.* We force and push when we strive, which can include trying to move too quickly. In this fast-paced mindset, which can be promoted by modern Western life, we can lose the technique and our connection with the essence of how such an approach can help us. Throughout both of our training, we were taught about the importance of going slowly, especially at the beginning. Although it may sound like an oxymoron on the surface, you can get to where you are going much more efficiently (and yes, even quickly) by maintaining good breath quality and not rushing. This teaching is one of the many parallels between jiu-jitsu practice and classical mindfulness practice. The lessons we learn on the mat or on the cushion can be translated to living a more effective life.

The Warrior Archetype

Nick Albin (Chewy), BJJ World's Most Popular YouTuber, describes his fascination with the innate warrior archetype. He explains that our society often works to extinguish this fire inside us. If we come off strong as a woman, we are a bitch. If we are a man, we are toxic. Chewy doesn't view it that way. He uses the metaphor of fire to describe our innate human ability to fight and engage our warrior self and its spectrum of usefulness.

> If the fire is dead and down to embers, it's not useful to us. Alternatively, if it's uncontrolled, it can destroy and burn down everything. A raging fire we don't control is reckless aggression that does harm without a clear goal in mind. If, however, it's contained and harnessed in the right way, it can heat a home, and it can cook food. Fire within our control can be employed for a specific and directed purpose.

Jamie has long used a similar metaphor in her writing on trauma and emotional management.

Chewy shares his experience of witnessing new students arrive with either embers or an out-of-control fire. He suggests that people can work to access that fire in a safe training environment and learn how to control it to turn it up or down. He relates his own experience as a kid without an outlet for his fire; he would oscillate between a "temper that would flare out" and an inability to assert himself as he was being picked on. Then he described the moment he knew that a shift had taken place. After a season in wrestling training, he was getting picked on and a trigger was flipped; instead of backing down, he simply double-legged the guy. The guy looked up at him with fear, and Chewy said to himself, "Oh, this is neat!" From that moment on, he had a new level of confidence and starting walking places he had avoided. His takeaway from this experience over the years was "With the right training and preparation, if I trust in myself, good things will happen."

Jamie's jiu-jitsu practice also helped her to tap into an inner sense of warrior in a way she had never experienced before. She reflects:

> I did so many warrior yoga poses before coming to jiu-jitsu, and I even spent a lot of time dancing to songs such as *Live Like a Warrior*. Yet there was something about training in jiu-jitsu, feeling the intensity of that inner fire and allowing it to purify me, that helped me to realize my warrior strength in a new way. In yoga, fire is used as a metaphor for purification or cleansing, and I found that jiu-jitsu brought that teaching full circle for me. Not only did the practices of jiu-jitsu teach me that I can get out of unsafe or unhealthy situations, they cultivated a sense within me that I can stand up for myself and I can live from the fullness of my expression and voice. I literally walk taller because of my time spent training in jiu-jitsu, and I hear this from many women who were at first reluctant to step on a mat.

When Jamie first began practicing jiu-jitsu, she noticed that her coach Micah Bender had the word *Bushido* tattooed on the top of his chest. When she asked him about it, Micah recalled getting it when he was about nineteen and a young, arrogant fighter. Generally translated as "the way of the warrior" or thought of as the warrior code of the Samurai, the word *Bushido* has come to mean so much more to Micah. Now, reflecting on the meaning of Bushido as a man of thirty-five, he says, "For me, Bushido is honor, respect, and dignity—and if you're doing something, to give it 100 percent." Inspired by one of his favorite movies, *The Last Samurai*, Micah says that living the Bushido code for him is not just about how you approach battle; it's how you make your tea, how you appreciate nature, how you appreciate the breath of life. Indeed, practicing mindfulness in every experience of human life and tapping into the potential of those experiences and that energy to hone one's inner warrior is the essence of what that code and the entire warrior archetype means to us. And this is a gift that we endeavor every day to bring to our clients.

TRY THIS The 753 Code

The Valente brothers, whose work we cite heavily throughout this book because of their outstanding reputation as teachers and guardians of jiu-jitsu history and philosophy, are known for a system they call *The 753 Code.*[49] This system represents their synthesis of jiu-jitsu (or *jūjutsu*—they prefer the more traditional spelling) lifestyle and philosophy. The holistic system contains seven elements related to spirit, five to body, and three to mind.

Consider scanning each area of the code and either meditating on or journaling about what each element means to you. What areas feel like they can be more consistently integrated into your daily lifestyle through consistent practice in jiu-jitsu or any other conscious practice? How might each element of "the code" connect to trauma recovery and overall mental health?

Spirit	Body	Mind
Rectitude	Exercise	Awareness
Courage	Nutrition	Balance
Benevolence	Rest	Flow
Respect	Hygiene	
Honesty	Positivity	
Honor		
Loyalty		

Four

Trauma-Sensitive Jiu-Jitsu— Yes, It's a Thing

Respect your needs.

—EVE TORRES GRACIE

This chapter defines the concept of *trauma-sensitive jiu-jitsu*. When a practice, teacher, clinician, or program is trauma sensitive (sometimes used interchangeably with trauma informed), that entity recognizes the knowledge of the trauma and translates that knowledge into implementation and practice. Like yoga, jiu-jitsu is uniquely suited to assist the healing process for trauma survivors because of its dual attention to embodiment and working to cultivate mental awareness. However, certain precautions will likely need to be in place for the greatest number of people to be served and to benefit.

We've both heard the potential concerns from the public, especially from women, about the struggles of accessing jiu-jitsu in a safe manner, and this also emerged as a theme in our research. In this chapter, we lay out a plan for trauma-informing the practice of jiu-jitsu, and we begin to discuss the complementarity of jiu-jitsu practice with psychotherapy and other healing arts. We deliver more insights gained from our grounded theory research on using jiu-jitsu with female survivors and our lived experience cowriting and consulting with jiu-jitsu instructors on making jiu-jitsu more trauma sensitive and accessible. We continue to share elements of our personal practices of what has worked for us to help us embrace the practice of jiu-jitsu instead of being scared of or shut down by it. The hope is that these insights will inspire everyone drawn to this book—trauma survivors, clinicians, and jiu-jitsu instructors.

What Is Trauma-Sensitive Jiu-Jitsu?

We often talk about the healing aspects of jiu-jitsu with colleagues, friends, and clients. Their faces usually register confusion if we don't explain the how and why of it all. Many people in North America and the West in general have come to know jiu-jitsu as a martial art used in the Ultimate Fighting Championship (UFC), in which opponents are often violently attacked and left with significant injuries. To help reframe the association, we offer something like this: imagine that a person was held down on the ground and attacked as part of a traumatic experience. Now imagine that same person finds themselves in a safe, empowering, friendly, and gentle training facility. Imagine them with a person holding them on the ground, whom they can learn to quickly flip for their advantage. They are now on top of and controlling the "attacker." This is the ultimate corrective experience as the body now gets to change the story it has about being held down.

The key ingredients offered in this example are the adjectives that describe trauma-sensitive jiu-jitsu: safe, empowering, friendly, gentle, and focused on self-defense. Trauma-sensitive jiu-jitsu exists on a spectrum. Some facilities offer none of these qualities, and we would deem them contraindicated for trauma survivors because of their potential to exacerbate already existing physical and mental wounds. Other facilities are attempting to be more sensitive to survivors. Despite their good intent, they may often have unknowingly done exactly the opposite of what is needed. There are facilities that have worked to be more trauma informed, specifically training their staff and offering as much accommodation as possible in group and individual settings. Some facilities are now beginning to take it a step further and are offering lessons, classes, or workshops in conjunction with therapists. The therapists and instructors work side by side to assist in a customized, client-specific systematic desensitization process. Just as the facilities range in terms of their trauma sensitivity, participants also range in terms of how much assistance they need to work through the process. It may take some exploration to figure out what you as a survivor will need. If you are a clinician or an instructor, the same exploration will be necessary. Preliminary research and our interviews with jiu-jitsu practitioners offer some guidance on the basics of trauma-informed jiu-jitsu instruction delivery and what participants can consider as they make choices in training (e.g., location, teachers, style of jiu-jitsu). More of these details are explored fully in the coming chapters, yet in this section we offer a general profile for what makes any embodied practice more trauma informed, with specific examples provided for jiu-jitsu.

Language

One of the hallmarks of trauma-informing any practice is being mindful of the language that you choose. Sometimes a simple change in words can make all of the difference between a person feeling invited to try something out and feeling commanded to do so. Commands have a tendency to shut people down, especially people who are relatively raw in their experience of trauma recovery and have not yet realized the power of choice. In Jamie's work in both trauma-informed yoga and trauma-informed addiction recovery approaches, she challenges people to reevaluate the impact of how they say or teach certain things.

We've learned it's no different with jiu-jitsu. Language is key. If instructors demonstrate respect and humility in their choice of words and tone, they create a space of empowerment. When Jamie started working with her coach Micah Bender, he immediately decided to use the language of aggressor or assailant instead of opponent. That simple switch-up helped Jamie realize that the focus of their training was on self-defense and not getting good at a sport, especially a sport that she saw as *brutal* before she began training. We go into much more detail on these specifics in Chapter 8, geared toward jiu-jitsu instructors.

In addition, language can empower or stigmatize. *Survivor* versus *victim* is just one example highlighted in the literature;[1] in our research, *survivor* was reported to empower, whereas *victim* left participants feeling disempowered. This language choice is emphasized in other facets of trauma-informed discourse. In Anna's own story, which served as the pilot case for our larger research inquiry, she notes that jiu-jitsu, specifically her experience in the trauma-informed *Women Empowered* program, turns the victim into a warrior.

The trauma community generally accepts that people may first need to identify as a victim to realize and to admit that they were violated. There is certainly nothing wrong with using this word, depending on where someone is in their journey. Yet fundamentally there is great power in moving people to the mentality of survivor/thriver, and ultimately, perhaps, to that of warrior. As trauma-informed practitioners, we generally use the default language of *survivor* to model this idea and then give people power to choose their identification from there.

Content

Content is another important factor emphasized in our research and our interviews with practitioners. Knowing what is going to be taught in advance allows participants to prepare themselves for the types of physical contact they will be engaged in, and this preparedness helps people avoid or at least manage jolting surprises. Instructors who explain why a given technique has been chosen to be on the curriculum can enhance participant learning and make the practice more personal for them. For example, "sport" jiu-jitsu techniques can be very different from "street" or self-defense jiu-jitsu techniques. Street techniques are specifically designed to be used in a fight on the street, without time limits, referees, and rules that prevent punching. You can use these techniques to defend yourself from an average attacker in any avenue of real life. Sport techniques, on the other hand, are not always viable on the street and can often leave you open to significant strikes (punches) from an attacker. Other schools take it a step further and provide gender-specific rape and abduction prevention techniques in the curriculum for women based on guidance from law enforcement on how these assaults are committed. We can best speak for the *Women Empowered* program since that is the basis of our experience;

in this program, nonbinary individuals are welcome and space is created to discuss modifications and adaptations based on lived experience. In our formal interview with Eve Torres Gracie (which followed both of us having direct interactions with her as a teacher), we were very impressed by her awareness of needed accommodations for nonbinary and transgender practitioners, and her presence on social media is one of unapologetic welcome for all women and members of the LGBTQ+ community.

A fundamental of trauma-informed care is to give people a general idea of what to expect at a macro and micro level. We've established that many schools do this at a macro level by making the curriculum known for students to review ahead of time, yet small steps at a micro level can also be taken within a lesson. For instance, in much of her other writing on trauma-informing yoga and therapeutic practice, Jamie emphasizes the importance of letting people know what to expect and, if possible, letting people know how long a certain exercise is going to last.[2] Even a simple announcement of, "One more minute" from an instructor lets a survivor know that whatever they are working on will not last forever. When students know that these breaks are in place, they are generally willing to try out more and take appropriate risks. Trauma is often experienced in a way in which the start or end of the difficult experience is unknown. This not knowing is a piece of what makes trauma so difficult. We are asking trauma survivors to get uncomfortable. Knowing that it will be brief and will end helps provide some comfort in the discomfort.

Choice

When practitioners are given a choice of whether to participate or not, this can be a corrective and important experience in and of itself. When instructors explain that it is not a problem and even good to sometimes opt out of practicing a particular technique until practitioners are ready, they may be offering a first-time experience for survivors in hearing someone remind them they have a choice. This is the exact opposite of traumatic experience that has been inflicted without choice. Instructors can demonstrate the value of choice into action in two major ways: by giving participants the choice to opt out and observe only or to step out and take a break if they need one, *and* by highlighting opportunities for choice within the practices. Jamie remembers that at several points in her jiu-jitsu journey, especially when she was transitioning to taking group classes, she needed to sit out and just observe her training mates try out a new technique. This prevented her from getting too flooded with emotion and blown outside of her affective window of tolerance, and it made her more likely to give a technique a try during the next round of training or during the next repetition of the drill in the same class.

Here are some other general best practices for amplifying the element of choice in jiu-jitsu practice:

FOR INSTRUCTORS

- Make all participants feel that they can come and go as they need to. Feeling trapped is not something that should be reinforced.

- Instructors can also advise their students to start slowly and gently. As a key example, critical techniques can involve defending against someone choking you with their hands. The first time this particular technique is practiced, instructors can advise that partners don't even put the hands on the neck at all and simply start from gently, without pressure, putting their hands on their partner's shoulders to practice. As students get more advanced and comfortable, they can then ask their training partner to put the hands on the neck, and at some point actually put pressure on their neck and eventually even try to resist the good guy's defense technique.

FOR PARTICIPANTS

- Simply watching the move being executed either on video or in person may be enough to get you in the yellow zone, as described in the scaling exercise that appears later in the chapter (see "Scaling: Self-Awareness as a First Step"). It is perfectly okay to watch and opt out of physical contact if you need to.

- Practicing the move alone, simply through body movements without a partner "attacking," can be a great starting place for learning to move your body in the best way.

- You can then move on to practicing the move with a partner by only being the bad guy, or aggressor, if you wish to use more gender-neutral language. For some participants, being the aggressor is a very foreign and unusual thing to experience. For many, the perspective shift can not only help with their training, but help with their individualized processing of a troubling or traumatic experience.

- Practicing the move as the good guy often means you start as the person being attacked. In more advanced ground techniques, this might mean you are lying on the ground and the bad guy is on top (so you are the bottom of the mount or guard). We understand that some trauma survivors may want to work up to the ability to participate in this way.

These six examples are based on technique-specific training. In more advanced stages of training, you may feel prepared to transition into sparring. *Sparring* is when you are now allowed to practice whatever you know with a partner, sometimes for three to five minutes at a time. Think of it as a freestyle flow. Sparring with someone when you are new to jiu-jitsu is not recommended. Before you are allowed to spar, you should master a number of basic techniques, especially if you are a trauma survivor. If you do not, you are at a significant risk of being retraumatized. A typical 60-minute class contains numerous moments of language, interaction, and content involve the instructor's ability to offer choice and to explain how students keep each other feeling physically and mentally safe as they participate. We expound upon these concepts further in Chapter 7 for instructors and hope we also give survivors and clinicians more insights on working with the power of choice in the chapters written specifically for them.

Preparing Ourselves for Jiu-Jitsu as Survivors of Trauma

In Jamie's early training as a trauma-informed yoga teacher, she heard a saying from Mark Lilly, the founder of the nonprofit *Street Yoga* that changed her life: *yoga can be both a trigger and a resource.* Survivors can find a vast number of skills within yoga helpful and even healing, and the same general concept applies to jiu-jitsu and the martial arts. And yet learning these new skills can be challenging and even triggering before they become resources. So how can we help our clients, students, and anyone we work with ease into a practice so that it can become a resource and at least minimize the potential for unhelpful triggering?

Avoiding triggers completely is not a component of trauma-informed care. After all, life is one big trigger potential when you're a survivor of trauma, and it's not realistic to cultivate a life that is completely trigger free. While we can do our best to minimize retraumatization, as guides through a healing process (whether as jiu-jitsu instructors or clinicians), it becomes even more important that we equip people with skills that they can use should they become triggered. As therapists, we both say that if a person is going to be triggered, this experience can be used in the therapeutic process and can even serve as a corrective experience if it's well handled.

Building a Toolbox

In this section, we teach you how to build an emotional regulation toolbox. What we present parallels a term often used in jiu-jitsu training: prep drill. *Prep drills* are microskills that are taught before the main skill or technique to further break it down. We introduce these skills for building your toolbox as their own variety of prep drills. They are ideas inspired by our larger work around trauma-informed care that we think survivors may find especially helpful to try out before they even approach a public jiu-jitsu class. These skills can be your safeguards, the proverbial ounce of prevention that is worth the pound of cure. If you are an instructor, having these skills on hand can be helpful in trauma-informing your ability to give students extra help before, during, or after class. As a clinician or educator, these skills are generally universal and can be integrated into your practice at any juncture.

If we were going to explore underwater caves, we would want the right equipment and training to keep ourselves safe. The same is true here. As we dive deeper into the challenges of self-defense training and healing from trauma, we will have a better chance of staying calm and tolerating distress if we know that we have safety tools. Anna likes to allow at least a week to thirty days of daily practice with one newly learned tool before moving to the next. Anna and Jamie both emphasize consistency—find the practice that you are going to be most likely to do *first*, and then commit to doing it in a time frame you can manage consistently each day, even if it's just three to five minutes. As with many aspects of trauma-informed work, honoring variation in practice is important, so keep an open mind that what may work for you may not work for someone else; you can apply this logic to working with clients and students as well.

It is essential that you master each tool so that they are easily available to you when you need them. Learning the new tool or skill may not feel natural at first. This is a normal part of growth and the change process. Do your best to stick with it consistently and notice what happens. We recommend having a mini-sketchbook or journal to track how you are using the tools. The four key tools to begin with are scaling, grounding, breath and yoga strategies, and the creative and expressive arts. While it may surprise you to see so many references to yoga and expressive arts in a book on jiu-jitsu, we invite you to consider the natural fusion that can exist between these approaches, as they all have the potential to teach people how to befriend their bodies. Moreover, we consider jiu-jitsu and all martial arts to be expressive practices. Although we break down each of these tools to explore the possibilities, we also feature another skill that is applicable across the healing arts, for the "Try This" feature for this chapter: progressive muscle relaxation.

Scaling: Self-Awareness as a First Step

Knowing how you are feeling on a scale from 0 to 10 (where 0 is calm, at ease, or neutral, and 10 is emotionally excruciating) is important. You may have encountered a 0 to 10 scale like this to describe pain in a medical setting. Mental health therapists often use such a scale to gauge emotional pain or distress. We often find clients are unaware of where they are mentally, and this can foster a great sense of confusion or disorientation with life. For the sake of clarity, here is a general guide to navigating the scale that we present:

- Green zone: (0–3) You are calm, cool, at ease.
- Yellow zone: (4–6) You are now getting uncomfortable; you are "lifting the emotional weight."

- Orange zone (7): You are now at your edge of tolerance; this is a boundary between where your skills may seem to work and where they become inaccessible.

- Red zone (8–10): You are feeling what seems to be extremely unmanageable emotion (e.g., anger, pain, frustration, rage, sadness).

Consider, however, how many trauma survivors spend their lives living in the 8 to 10 range, which was never intended to be maintained (biologically speaking) long term. Traumatized brains, or those that have not been given the chance to adequately heal or process the impact of unhealed trauma, are very likely to overreact to everyday events as if they were emergencies. Like many things in life, the earlier we recognize we are in a trauma trigger, the more effective we are in regulating it. Therefore, knowing your number is crucial to having the ability to effectively use tools in the 4 to 6 range and, ultimately, get back to 1 to 3.

When you begin your jiu-jitsu journey, knowing your "number" can help you understand when it is time to push into more discomfort and when it is not. Optimally you want to train in both the green (1, 2, 3) and the yellow (4, 5, 6). The corrective work really begins when you carefully push into the discomfort zone and up to your edges. We can face the fear and lift the weight but also stay out of the red (8, 9, 10); in the red, we are retraumatizing ourselves and flooding our bodies with adrenaline again. To use an analogy, this is similar to pressing the accelerator (gas pedal) down so quickly in a car that the RPMs go into the red. High RPMs can cause engine damage, and running your car engine that way is nicknamed *redlining*. Another example can be found in weightlifting. If you have never lifted weights in a gym, most personal trainers would not ask you to come in and immediately lift 200 pounds. You would likely begin with much lighter weights, say 5 to 20 pounds, and begin your repetitions there. You would have to push into discomfort to continue to progress, but this would happen over time. You pick up weights that make you exert yourself and lift the weights for eight to twelve reps and repeat three times. Most people then take a period of rest, perhaps a day or two, before returning to lift again in the same way. In a week to three weeks, you might master that weight and then begin adding more in the same gradual process. It is possible that you could actually pick up the entire 200 pounds on the first day, especially if an emergency made it so you needed to. But at what cost? Your body might have been able to lift the weight, but if you're like many, you will pay a significant price in potential pulled muscles, torn ligaments, and/or complete exhaustion. We like to think of our brains as working in the same way. We prepare in the mental gym. We acquire and practice safety tools to use if we need them, and then we begin the process of lifting the emotion weight, growing stronger each time.

People who have been through traumatic experiences are often so dissociated that they cannot even sense what their number might be. Getting back into your body after such an experience can feel unsafe. So scaling is not as easy a task as it may seem. In cases of severe trauma and dissociation, it can be important to have a mental health professional assist you in this process. They can help you gain awareness of your number and help you build a mental/emotional weightlifting plan. Developing such a plan involves the survivor describing and processing their prior trauma experiences and identifying what types of touch might be particularly triggering with the help of their therapist. Once the person identifies such triggers, a plan can be created to gradually expose oneself while staying in the yellow (4, 5, 6) and approaching the edge.

So what does a 2 or a 5 or a 7 feel like? How do we begin to know what our number is, as it varies widely from person to person? Anna has her clients examine their number throughout the day for a few days in a row or even for a week. It can be interesting to notice how the number might be different on weekends versus weekdays, for example. The work is to simply try to notice how you are doing, give it a number, and begin to practice checking in with yourself. As you do this, you may discover things that indicate you are in the green (1, 2, 3), for example. Maybe you are simply happy it's Friday night! You might also discover that certain people, places, things, or situations move the number up. Or perhaps certain people help you feel calm or bring you joy and laughter. Maybe other people are more challenging and leave you feeling increasingly stressed. Perhaps certain places or things also affect your number. People are often surprised when they begin to notice what is challenging for them and what puts them at ease.

For instance, we both know that we are in the green zone by the language we use. We might find ourselves talking to someone about our gratitude for something, or we might feel joy when referencing an exhilarating experience. We know that we are moving into the yellow when our language becomes more negative. Talking about our frustrations in a productive manner with the intent of looking for solutions and continuing to feel understanding and kindness for others is a good indication that we are in the yellow. If, however, our focus is no longer productive, or the negative talk is excessive, we might be traveling into the higher ranges of the scale.

Noticing ourselves and what our specific behaviors and sensations are as we travel up the scale is an individualized process. Some things that might indicate that you have traveled into the red are the following:

- Dissociation: A feeling that you are not in your body anymore, or that you have drifted away. This can feel like you are "zoning out," and in more extreme cases, you might have a full-on flashback or a feeling that you are back in the scene of a trigger or a trauma.

- Freezing: Feeling like you can't move.

- Increased startle response—being jumpy: For example, when someone you are not expecting comes around a corner and you jump or are startled more so than the circumstances may require.

- Body posture changes: This is highly individualized. For some this can look or feel like your shoulders are moving up and your chest and body are curling inward; for others it may involve curling into a ball or making some other retreating posture.

- Accelerated breathing or heart rate: Feeling like you can't breathe or can't catch your breath

- Above normal sweating: More sweating than the current situation may warrant

- Widening eyes when faced with panic

- Fidgeting/difficulty staying still

- Difficulty concentrating: Inability to hear or understand instructions

- Hypervigilance: An extra sensitivity to your environment

- Hypervigilant hearing: A symptom sometimes found in complex trauma survivors in which their brains have learned from childhood trauma that the tone of a person's voice is more key to survival than the content of what they are saying. The brain will then tune out from the words and only pay attention to the tone.

Regularly engaging in the scaling practice is an excellent way to build self-awareness. Consider tracking what you find in the notebook or journal that you may have set aside for this inquiry. As we move on to exploring some other practices in the rest of this chapter, use your scaling tool to help you gauge if certain practices may temporarily increase distress, or if they may immediately help you experience relief. It is completely normal, in the process of learning something new, for your levels of anxiety to go up on this scale. Consider if that is about self-judgment or fear that you are not doing it right; this happens quite a bit with our clients, and we've even been prone to it from time to time.

Grounding

Grounding is a process of getting yourself present. The practice invites us to use any available sensory channels and experiences to come into the here and now. Grounding is an imperative skill for trauma survivors and ought to be developed before they work on any additional skills, even breath-deepening techniques. If we feel unsafe exploring any of the skills that follow or in diving deeper into jiu-jitsu practice, knowing that we can find or return to our ground can be the ultimate safeguard. In many cases, the reason we are getting stressed is that we are thinking about something from the past or the future. If we can get ourselves to just be present, it often helps. We know, much easier said than done!

Think about it this way: if we were in a room with a hungry lion, it would make sense that we wouldn't care or notice if our hands or feet got scratched. We would be too worried about getting out safely to care about the scratches. So it makes sense that when we are stressed, our hands and our feet are the first things we lose touch with. If we manage to notice (get back into) our hands and feet, our brain will also take notice and be able to slow the adrenaline release. So let's practice!

Finding Your Feet

Although this can be done sitting or standing, allowing your body to sit is sometimes preferable. Lift and place each foot on the ground once. After doing so, notice the bottom of your feet connecting to the surface below them. Notice the ball of your foot and the heel of your foot. Now try to notice (without looking) your smallest toe on your right foot. And then the one next to it, and the one in the middle, and the one after that, and so on until you have found each toe on both feet. The middle toes are often the hardest to feel by themselves. You may have to wiggle them a bit to try to find them. If you are able to find your toes, your brain will also notice and slow the adrenaline release. If there was truly a lion in the room, of course, you would most likely not be able to do this. Unfortunately, our brains can often make everyday events into "lions in the room."

Scan the Room with Your Senses and Anchor Objects

In whatever room or space you may currently find yourself, start taking a look around the room and notice what you see. Observe and describe it without getting too caught up in analyzing what you see. Perhaps you notice an object in your scan that especially resonates with you. Maybe it's a clock, or perhaps it's a plant, a statue, or a certain color pattern on a set of curtains. It's personal for each individual. Then consider recruiting that object of your attention as an anchor object. In other words, whenever you feel shaky or are not sure where you are, you can look at that anchor object and have the assurance that you are here, now, and present.

You can continue this process of scanning with your other senses. Notice what you hear in your space (or maybe there is an absence of sound), what you smell when you take a breath. Maybe there's even a taste in your mouth. For the sense of touch or sensation, perhaps touch your clothes, touch the floor, or make contact with your fingers and whatever surface on which you are sitting. Any of these other sensory experiences may work even better for you as a grounding anchor, especially if your primary channel is not visual.

Taking Space

Taking space can mean anything from actually removing your body from a location to mentally checking out of a conversation. While some may judge this as maladaptively dissociative, consider how it may be a vital skill to have in your toolbox when you are learning something new. Often many survivors of trauma were not allowed the choice to remove themselves or stop a toxic verbal exchange. The simple act of being able to choose to remove yourself, regulate your emotions, and then return when and if you want to, can potentially be a liberating, corrective experience. Often the language involved in being able to leave a room in a polite and respectful manner is a new skill. I often offer that the very simple statement of "I'm going to take space" can be all that is needed.

TRY THIS Progressive Muscle Relaxation

The human body likes to hold tension in specific areas and, over time, significant physical issues can result. Often, we are not aware that we are holding tension in our bodies. Progressive muscle relaxation can help us find and release tension. This technique is used in classical hypnotherapy and in many schools of yoga nidra. For the extended investigation of the body that we take you through in this exercise, try to allot twenty minutes to work with the whole physical body. You may sit or lie down. You are invited to move from the top of your head to the bottom of your feet and isolate a particular muscle group. Hold just that group for ten seconds while relaxing all of your other muscles to the best of your ability. And then relax that muscle group for twenty seconds. It may help to shake things out after tensing to really allow the muscles to release. Please be careful not to do this exercise on any areas in which you have any injuries, soreness, or medical issues. As you tense different muscle groups, you may feel a little uncomfortable.

- Face: Start with your face muscles. Close and crunch your eyelids shut and hold shut and crunched for ten to twenty seconds. Then allow them to relax, get heavy, and be completely at ease.

- Jaw: Hold your jaw open as wide as possible for ten to twenty seconds. Then allow it to relax, get heavy, and be completely at ease.

- Neck: Look upward for ten to twenty seconds. Then allow your neck to relax, get heavy, and be completely at ease.

- Shoulders: Tense them up high. Hold for ten to twenty seconds. Then allow them to relax, get heavy, and be completely at ease.

- Arms: Hold your arms out straight. Tighten your triceps on the back of your arms. Hold for ten to twenty seconds. Then allow them to relax, get heavy, and be completely at ease.

- Fists: Clench your fists tightly without putting pressure into the rest of the arms. Hold for ten to twenty seconds. Then allow them to relax, get heavy, and be completely at ease.

- Fingers: Spread your fingers wide, as widely as they can move away from each other, and then hold for ten to twenty seconds. Then allow them to relax and move back to their natural placement.

- Back: Arch your lower back and hold for ten to twenty seconds. Then allow it to relax, get heavy, and be completely at ease.

- Glutes: Tighten your glute muscles and hold for ten to twenty seconds. Then allow them to relax, get heavy, and be completely at ease.

- Upper Legs: Hold one leg out at a time and tense your quad muscle for ten to twenty seconds. Then allow it to relax, get heavy, and be completely at ease. Repeat with the other leg.

- Lower Legs: Let your leg lie out straight, resting on the floor (both legs or one at a time), and tighten your calf muscle(s) by arching your feet back toward your body for ten to twenty seconds. Aim your toes up and back toward you. Then allow them to relax, get heavy, and be completely at ease.

- Toes: Curl your toes tightly for ten to twenty seconds. Then allow them to relax, get heavy, and be completely at ease.

Some muscle groups are easier to tighten and relax in public than others. Allowing your jaw to just hang open is, for example, something that you might not want to do in public in the middle of class or at a work meeting. But clenching your fists or tightening your glutes could potentially be done without drawing attention to yourself. Experiment and explore in this investigation of discovering what works for you.

Breath Strategies

Once you are aware that you have become emotionally uncomfortable (increased your number to 4–7) or ungrounded, check your breathing. One of the first things to change when we are upset is our breathing. As our breaths become shallower and faster, the brain responds by sending even more adrenaline. If we work to regulate our breathing, the brain receives the message that breathing has slowed and therefore it cannot be a true emergency. The brain then responds by cutting back the adrenaline. It can often take a minimum of three breaths for this to begin to work. Ask yourself to notice your number before you work on your breathing, and then check what the number is afterward to see if you have noticed any difference. Even if it only moves from 6 to 5.50, it is working. Any decrease in the number is better than none.

Some people get overwhelmed by breathing because they feel they have to breathe deeply in order to feel an effect. We've seen many survivors get overwhelmed by trying to take too many deep breaths too quickly. A simple practice of breath tracking might actually be an optimal start, with the knowledge of your grounding anchor(s).

Pay attention to your normal breathing for thirty seconds to a minute. If your mind starts to wander, it's all right. Invite the focus back to your breath. Start slowly and be gentle with yourself. If you need the extra help, consider using this classic teaching from Buddhist tradition as a guide, saying to yourself: "As I breathe in, I know I'm breathing in—as I breathe out, I know I'm breathing out." A simple "in-out" will also do.

Once you feel confident with this process, you can move along to diaphragmatic breathing, the classic breath strategy known to many professionals in the healing arts.

1. Breathe in through your nose and out through your mouth or nose, focusing on the rise and fall of the upper belly and the extension it creates around your entire midsection. This will help you notice the diaphragmatic muscle (the dome-shape muscle at the bottom of your rib cage) as the source of deeper breathing.

2. Expand your belly as far as it will go (without forcing or striving) as you inhale. As you exhale, release the air and notice the belly pull back in toward your center.

3. If it will help you, put one or both hands on your stomach to concentrate on this rise and fall motion.

4. Keep the inhales and exhales even when you begin, although you may eventually notice that a longer exhale may feel better in the body.

5. If at any point this practice becomes overwhelming for you, return to grounding, specifically one of your anchor objects or experiences.

An advanced breathing strategy, and one of Jamie's personal favorites that got her through initial hurdles with freeze responses in jiu-jitsu, is called *ujjayi* breathing. It's sometimes called Ocean Breathing or Darth Vader breathing because of the sound element that can be accessed by the breath. While there are different ways to master the technique, the essential idea is to breathe in through your nose and out through your nose with a bit of force, with the intention of making a sound. Keep the mouth closed, if possible, and let your nose do the work. If you can make a little constriction in the back of your throat, like you would do if you were fogging a mirror, you will be able to tap into even more sound. Try this technique three times and then check in. Some people can get a bit overwhelmed or lightheaded at first when trying this breath because it is so powerfully oxygenating. Again, what can make the breath helpful may make it overwhelming at first, so go slowly. In yoga philosophy, this breath has long been taught as *the* technique for getting you out of a flight, fight, or freeze response. We now know this happens because this strategy so powerfully works with the vagus nerve, helping to increase parasympathetic, or the *rest and digest*, response. Jamie makes sure that all of her trauma therapy trainees are aware of this breath for this very powerful reason, and she finds its application to jiu-jitsu to be marvelous.

Another powerful variation on both diaphragmatic and *ujjayi* breath that you can try is to pucker the mouth as though you are exhaling through a straw. This variation, called *sheetali* breath, is also a powerful vagus nerve stimulator as the very act of puckering the lips, even without special attention to the breath, can increase a parasympathetic response. While this variation may or may not work during your training itself, you may discover that using this strategy before you train, after you train, or when you need to take breaks is a game changer for you.

The more we practice breath strategies, the more likely they will be there for us to access, especially when we are in distress. Having solid use of them before beginning a jiu-jitsu practice can help you feel more prepared. After you have mastered scaling, grounding, breath awareness, and diaphragmatic breathing, the next things to add to your toolbox can be any healthy coping strategies that you already have or want to invest in learning. The possibilities are endless, and we offer you just a few examples in the section that follows from areas that are very near and dear to our own hearts.

Yoga

In our grounded theory investigation of female practitioners of jiu-jitsu in the *Women Empowered* program, over half reported being exposed to yoga and meditation either before their exposure to jiu-jitsu or during it. While many participants in the study felt that the pace of yoga and meditation was too slow for them and that the pacing of jiu-jitsu was more ideal, many noted how the two can work in concert. One participant described that yoga calms her anxiety while jiu-jitsu increases her sense of inner confidence.

We've obviously made many references and drawn many parallels to yoga in this book because many of the same trauma-informed principles yoga teachers and clinicians who use yoga have become familiar with also apply to jiu-jitsu. Moreover, both yoga and jiu-jitsu derive from Eastern practices. Although jiu-jitsu is traditionally seen as Japanese, note the history that we covered in the previous chapter about evidence of origins in India. While the finessed differences between cultures and ethnic groups can certainly be appreciated, a common denominator that we find in our study of Eastern practices in general, compared to those modalities of Western psychotherapy, is emphasis on bodily experience and being in process without forcing an outcome. There is a greater implication here, too; many of the skills and approaches taught in yoga can help trauma survivors prepare the base from which to approach jiu-jitsu. We've covered some of the connections to yogic breath strategies; the physical elements that work with posture, stretch, alignment, and flexibility can also be useful.

While we both recommend that studying with a trauma-informed teacher in your community or establishing a mentorship with a clinician who can competently introduce you to the fundamentals of yoga is ideal, many of the basics can be explored on your own. Jamie's resources website, www.traumamadesimple.com, gives you video instruction through many of these basics in a trauma-informed way. We highly recommend that you at least have some experience practicing what is called mountain pose. Not only does it closely relate to the concept of base as covered in jiu-jitsu, it can also be a powerful strategy in its own right to help you feel into a greater sense of grounding before class, after class, or if you have to take a break. Here are steps to take you through mountain pose. (Contrary to popular belief you do not need a yoga mat to try out yoga poses; they can be done wherever you find yourself, most especially this pose.)

1. Keep your feet together. If this puts too much pressure on your knees or hips, step the feet apart slightly at whatever distance you feel the greatest sense of balance.

2. Press down into your feet and extend up through the crown (top) of your head. Keep your eyes open and look straight ahead.

3. Fold your hands in front of your chest if you'd like, or gently keep them at your side, palms facing to the front of you. To receive the energetic benefit of the pose even more, become firm through your buttocks and inner thighs and drop the tailbone.

4. As you inhale, extend your arms straight overhead, interlacing your fingers into a temple-style position if possible. If this is not available in your body, keep the arms straight overhead, palms facing each other, shoulder distance apart. Do your best to keep the arms alongside your ears and slightly back. Keep breathing.

5. Use your breath to help you support the holding of the pose. This hold is not intended as a feat of strength or a timed endurance test. When you first notice that you want to come out of it, challenge yourself to use your breath and other tools you now have to help you sustain the pose. The hold invites you to use breath skills to help you be more comfortable in a potentially uncomfortable position.

6. Reset and try again, if possible, until you feel a sense of strength and restfulness in the body.

To modify, you are free to use the wall or a chair for support if you need to. You may stand up and back up against the wall for that extra support. If using a chair, you may stand behind it and hold on to it with one hand; do your best to use the other hand and arm for the overhead component of the pose. Feel free to use Figure 4.1 as a guide.

Figure 4.1: Mountain pose.

Creative and Expressive Arts

Because Jamie is an expressive arts therapist (an approach to healing that is ultimately multimodal, bringing in the fusion of visual art, dance/movement, music, and other creative forms) and Anna is an art therapist, skills in this realm appeal a great deal to us. While such a section may seem like a stretch in a book on jiu-jitsu, we don't see it that way. Some people come to regard the natural flow of jiu-jitsu as an expressive arts form, and we want to equip you with as many embodied skills as possible that can supplement your trauma recovery journey. Whether a specific art medium has the power to calm varies greatly from person to person, so naturally a great deal of trial and error may be involved. Because of their focus on action and process, any of the creative or expressive arts can be a powerful component in healing trauma or in supporting survivors throughout the process of healing.

For many of you who have not experimented with an expressive arts form for years (or possibly ever), you may have some homework and exploration to do. Because there are so many different types of art making, there is bound to be something for each of you if you are willing to try. A quick internet search can provide you with numerous mediums and methods. Jamie has written an entire collection of these expressive practices called *Process Not Perfection: Expressive Arts Solutions for Trauma Recovery*, and she has included many free resources, especially in the movement realm, which are available at www.traumamadesimple.com and www.dancingmindfulness.com. Anna's Instagram page annas_art_therapy also provides plenty of free suggestions and her eBook *12 Creative Experiences for Personal Growth in Recovery* is also available. We encourage you to go explore and see what might work for you. Some of Anna's clients enjoy activities like ZenTangle, a practice of tracing your hand and filling it in with lines and doodles. Knitting and crocheting, coloring, and creating repetitive signature shapes or drawings are other favorites.

In her clinical practice, Jamie also assigns clients the task of compiling a driving-home-from-therapy playlist. This way if an individual feels a little unsteady after a session, they have a preselected series of songs that they've already identified as being ones that will help them stay alert and awake on a drive home. A similar playlist can also work to get a person in a motivated space before therapy. In her own training, Jamie used a similar strategy when driving to and from jiu-jitsu training, as music has long had the capacity to soothe her and elevate her mood. Consider adopting such a strategy if you are a trauma survivor who is feeling shaky about going into a public space for lesson or classes. If you are an instructor, feel free to use this suggestion with your group.

In your explorations, you may discover that the creative or expressive arts especially speak to you, and it may feel like a worthwhile endeavor to seek out a specifically credentialed professional in one of the creative or expressive arts forms. Please know that art and expression are for everyone, so this type of formal engagement is not necessarily required for art and creativity to support and assist your healing process with jiu-jitsu or any other healing endeavor.

Applying the Toolbox in Jiu-Jitsu and in Life

Imagine that you are driving a car in a rainstorm; you turn on the windshield wipers to see better. In case you need to park on a hillside, you have an emergency brake. Your car has seat belts to protect you in case of accidents. We can use all these things in more urgent situations and preventatively. However, if you want your car to stay in good working condition, it needs maintenance: tire rotations, oil changes, and parts replaced. If you don't take care of maintenance, you might run into more urgent problems, and your emergency precautions may not work properly or be enough to avoid danger.

Anna has a bad habit of not paying attention to her windshield wipers because southern California doesn't get a lot of rain (a problem that Jamie in Ohio cannot relate to). Unfortunately, the California sun disintegrates them, so they rot away and need to be replaced often. Then, on the rare occasion that it actually rains, Anna finds herself with nonfunctional windshield wipers, unable to see the road clearly, which leaves her more vulnerable to dangerous situations. Maintenance is important if we want our tools to be available and work when we need them. In addition, if our car breaks down, we need to be able to open up the hood and take a closer look at what the problem might be. We might even bring in an expert mechanic to help us examine our car and examine our options.

Our mental health works in a similar way. We need to have fast-acting emotional regulation tools available to us in case of an urgent situation, and we need to do proper maintenance so that we are spending most of our time in the green (1, 2, 3) and staying out of the red except in emergencies.

If something doesn't seem to be working in our relationships or our work life, we can examine our thinking to make things more efficient and functional. In other words, we need to look under the hood to understand what's happening. Sometimes we need clinical expertise to help us build the urgent tools for repair, set a plan for maintenance, and examine deeper challenges. Many times, we can do all of that on our own. Either way there are three types of mental health tools: urgent, maintenance, and examination.

Reflecting again on the car metaphor, if you do not need to go anywhere, say in the middle of a pandemic, you might store your car away in the garage. Stowed in this manner, it requires less gasoline, oil, and maintenance. Similarly, when we are at home, we have much less chance of needing jiu-jitsu to defend ourselves. If, however, we suddenly need to start travelling via car and haven't driven in a while, our defensive driving skills might be rusty. As all experienced drivers know, there are many dangers on the road, and less time on the road may cause our driving skills to be diminished. Jiu-Jitsu skills are similar in that they require maintenance. The more often you practice; the more readily these skills are available to you in muscle memory.

For trauma survivors, their trauma is much like a car collision—unexpected, unwanted, and causing damage. After the collision, there may be physical and mental injury. The vehicle may require repair, causing the owner to drive less often to fewer places, or the owner may stop venturing out altogether. Smaller accidents may require simple body work; more serious ones may require specialized frame work. After trauma, survivors often have new fears and distrust in being in a variety of places or around people. Some trauma survivors can lose hope, as the repairs to their psyche seem insurmountable, and they "total their cars." They might do this by completely avoiding any experiences that can trigger their trauma again. Research into the effects of the *Women Empowered* jiu-jitsu training program revealed that after jiu-jitsu training, many trauma survivors became more confident to venture back out into the world post trauma, became more trusting in themselves and others, and became more able to assert themselves and speak up. There was a special type of repair that they had not gotten through traditional therapies, yoga, or other martial arts. Jiu-Jitsu was the framework repair that the other therapies couldn't deliver. Jiu-Jitsu may have the potential to heal people in a way that conventional mental health treatments or traditional coping skills just cannot touch. However, preparation is required. You need to look for training facilities that seem to promote many of the qualities we described at the beginning of the chapter. We offer much more guidance on this matter in the chapter to follow, which is written specifically for survivors of trauma. Even if you are fortunate to find the ideal training facility, we still recommend that you build this toolbox and practice the skills within it. Practice the skills that seem to work the best for you in crisis so they are easily available. Do the maintenance so you are ready for what life throws at you, and examine and find solutions as the challenges arise.

Although the ideal situation would be for you, as a survivor of trauma, to work on building these tools first and then seeking out a jiu-jitsu training program, the opposite may happen. You may elect to begin a jiu-jitsu training experience (or perhaps you already have) and then find yourself overwhelmed and flooded. That's okay. Feel free to step back and know that not all hope is lost. Work with the toolbox, and perhaps let your instructor know about your plan to stay as safe as possible. If you are an instructor or clinician serving in the community and you endeavor to serve the public in the most trauma-informed way possible, have working competence of the skills we've covered in this chapter. Regardless of where you stop on your jiu-jitsu journey, none of the time or effort will be wasted. The mental health tools and mental strength you have built will be there to benefit you in other areas of your life.

When Anna stepped onto the mats at her first jiu-jitsu training, she arrived in a "semi-repaired commuter car with structural damage." Like many complex trauma survivors, she still had healing work to do despite the wide variety of therapy she had tried. The *Women Empowered* jiu-jitsu training provided the specialized trauma healing that allowed Anna to hit the road again with more trust and less redlining into flight, fight, or freeze.

But the benefits went beyond healing the trauma. For Anna, jiu-jitsu unknowingly upgraded her commuter car to an off-road stick-shift Jeep. In master cycle, where she was given the opportunity to free spar and learn varied techniques with numerous body shapes, sizes, and abilities, her skills were upgraded and opened up roads that had been unavailable to her before. This expansion brought her new levels of joy and excitement. The redlining was gone, the yellow zone of discomfort was less pronounced, and the sparring allowed Anna to enter moments of green-zone playfulness that she hadn't experienced before on or off the mats. Pre jiu-jitsu, Anna's hyper-vigilant traumatized brain scanned the room for threats. After learning to spar in jiu-jitsu, Anna now scans the room for fun. She says, "it's like a strategy game" to match techniques with varying effectiveness on differing sizes and shapes of people. The same is true for difficult people in her work environment. They are no longer emotionally charged threats to her career success. They are now playmates. Their difficult behaviors offer a fun game that Anna wants to see if she can diffuse, find solutions for, and enjoy the challenge of using her verbal jiu-jitsu skills. To be clear, sparring is not for everyone, just as off-roading in a Jeep is not for everyone. Jamie and Anna agree that the opportunity to decrease and stop the redlining via skill-building in technique-only classes with no sparring is the therapeutic healing we want to shine the light on in this book. More information about the differences between technique-only and sparring and sport jiu-jitsu will be outlined in the next chapter.

Five

For Trauma Survivors: Defining Trauma-Sensitive Jiu-Jitsu

If you feel like you have to "survive" your school, you're at the wrong school.

—RENER GRACIE

U nder the right instructor's care and in the right training community, jiu-jitsu can be a life-changing and empowering experience for trauma survivors. Jiu-Jitsu also has the potential to retraumatize survivors if conditions are not ideal and if instructors are not mindful and conscious. Anna and Jamie are advocates and protectors at heart. We are eager to share all that we know and hopeful that we can answer your questions and cultivate awareness to prevent unnecessary injury. There were so many things we wouldn't have even known to ask at the beginning of our journey.

Before finding jiu-jitsu, Anna was a fan of MMA and the UFC, and yet she wasn't really aware of the techniques and skills involved. On the day that she signed up for self-defense training, she had absolutely no clue that she would be learning the very skills used by the top fighters in the world. Or that she would have something so powerful sparked inside of her from day one, or that she would return for more over the next several years. Anna was lucky enough to have stumbled into a program that prides itself on being as trauma informed as possible. Even though Jamie began her training in another part of the United States at a gym that was not specifically trauma informed, she had the good fortune to be able to find a trauma-informed instructor, as she shares in Chapter 2. Through the years, both Anna and Jamie have met many people of all genders who have been injured physically and mentally by their experiences in other gyms or with careless instructors.

This chapter is a natural extension of Chapter 4, where we set a preliminary definition of trauma-sensitive jiu-jitsu and gave both survivors and instructors preliminary prep drills and toolboxes they can use to ensure success. Survivors can practice these skills on their own in preparation, and instructors can have them on hand for their classes and schools, especially if they notice that students may be struggling. In this chapter, we go a step further by equipping survivors with more of the inside knowledge we wish we had at the beginning of our respective jiu-jitsu experiences. We give survivors guidance on how to best do their homework to find a training environment and instructor(s) that can set them up for success from the beginning. We include an overview of questions you can ask a potential school (sometimes called a *dojo* or *training academy*) to assess what is a good fit for you. We also include descriptions of some basic and key techniques that you are likely to learn on any beginner's track at a school so you have an idea of what to expect.

Finding the Right Environment

Nowadays, especially in major urban areas, it seems like a martial arts academy of some kind is on every corner. When Jamie first had the opportunity to train at Gracie University in Torrance, California, she was surprised by how many jiu-jitsu academies she saw on the short drive from her hotel in Hermosa Beach. Even here, near the "mothership," she thought, so many different styles and perspectives were represented. While the growth of any practice that was once seen as obscure can be positive, there can be a sacrifice in quality when this happens, especially in a capitalist construct. In his book *Fighting Buddha*, Jeff Eisenberg, a jiu-jitsu brown belt and a black belt in several other forms of martial arts, warns of the *McDojo effect* that is all too prevalent in the United States. Being an informed consumer can be tricky under any circumstance, let alone when you are searching for a facility that will honor your personal training journey.

Sometimes trauma survivors can feel overwhelmed by too much choice, especially when they don't know the distinct differences between their choices. In this section of the book, we endeavor to give you some guidance. Because, sure, you may have heard that martial arts training, specifically jiu-jitsu, can be a good adjunct to your recovery process. Yet if you are guided by the wrong instructors in an unhealthy community, you may be putting yourself into harm's way. This section of the book focuses on taking some of the guesswork out of this process based on what we've learned as jiu-jitsu players who also work as trauma therapists.

What, Specifically, Do I Look for in a School?

Our objective of this section is *not* to sell you on one particular style or school of jiu-jitsu. Even though we found our initial home in the Gracie tradition, specifically in the *Women Empowered* program, we recognize that this is not available in every geographic area. Moreover, we recognize that there are more approaches to both Brazilian and more traditional schools of jiu-jitsu out there and that your needs may be met at any variety of schools. We provide you with this list so that you can be an informed consumer who attends to your own needs as a first priority.

As you review these qualities, we recommend that you prioritize what you feel is important to you. A few items may pop out as being critical, or the whole list might speak to your needs. Everyone is very different in terms of what they need to feel safe and ready to train, and it could be that the perfect school doesn't exist for you yet you are able to find pockets of safety within one. Jamie believes that the first school she trained at was not a good fit for her overall, yet she connected with a highly skilled, trauma-informed instructor there (Micah) and identified friends and training mates whom she saw as safe. Moreover, she came into jiu-jitsu training with grounding in the skills that we covered in Chapter 4, and using these was crucial to making her jiu-jitsu journey as fruitful as possible.

If you have many choices in your geographical area, feel free to visit several schools before you commit to a training or lesson package at any one. Most will offer a free trial class or series of classes. You can also let your fingers do the walking to a certain extent, checking out the websites of facilities, and especially the biographies of instructors. How well are they trained in their craft, and what type of lived experience do they present? Does the way they present themselves online match up with what you encounter when you visit the school? Do the values of the instructor and the school seem to align with your own? A one-page checklist is available in the Appendix, in case you want to bring it with you if you visit a school or if you engage in some inventory after visiting a school.

Here are some things to look out for:

IS FRIENDLY AND APPROACHABLE.   Look for gyms at which staff, instructors, and students are approachable. Almost everyone that we interviewed for the book mentioned the need for a positive, supportive vibe in the gym.

PUTS SAFETY FIRST.   You ought to see emphasis during instruction on keeping the attacking partner safe. Technique training should be given from both the defender and the attacker positions and should highlight how to keep your partner and yourself safe as you practice the move.

CURRICULUM SEPARATES SPORT FROM STREET SELF-DEFENSE.
According to Gui Valente, jiu-jitsu as a sport versus jiu-jitsu as self-defense (commonly referred to as "street") in the United States has created a situation in which many of the black belt instructors teaching jiu-jitsu are actually not trained in self-defense. Don't assume that just because a person has a black belt, they are qualified to teach self-defense. In some gyms the focus is on building UFC fighters, not assisting trauma survivors. Refer to the glossary at the beginning of the book for an exact definition of sport versus street. In calling around to inquire about schools, a good question to ask at first can be this, "Is your emphasis on sport or street/self-defense jiu-jitsu?"

CURRICULUM IS STRUCTURED.   A structured curriculum helps you know what to expect. When traumas teach you that the outside world can be untrustworthy and unpredictable, predictability in your own preferred spaces is key to decreasing your stress response. A structured curriculum also allows you to decide in advance if you want to attend a particular class at that time; it empowers you to make choices appropriate for you. Later in this chapter we will discuss how some techniques can be triggering while others are not overtly triggering. Some survivors might find it best to pace when and what they expose themselves to, gaining mastery over less-triggering techniques and getting used to partners and the environment before taking on more triggering techniques. For example, a structured curriculum that is easily available in a printout flyer or online gives you informed choices.

CURRICULUM IS DESIGNED ESPECIALLY FOR A PARTICULAR DEMOGRAPHIC (BEGINNERS, WOMEN, CHILDREN, LGBTQ+).   We recommend looking for programs in which the curriculum is designed especially for a particular target market. Women's needs in surviving abduction and rape, for instance, can be very different from men and women in street fights with and without weapons. While it's true that not all martial arts schools offer LGBTQ+-specific courses, more of this programming has become available in recent years. Although schools in rural communities might not have enough student diversity to offer these demographic-specific classes, trauma-informed schools in large metropolitan cities would be remiss in not creating a safer space for LGBTQ+ students who are more often targets of violence than the general population. We prefer schools that have a clearly outlined curriculum (in writing and/or online) of what techniques will be mastered, when, and why (e.g., sport, women's self-defense, street). If priority is given to techniques for self-defense first and sport later (if at all), this is generally optimal for trauma survivors. This focus can provide a corrective experience to overcome the hopelessness and helplessness that trauma creates. The curriculum lets survivors know that in a real dangerous situation on the street, they will actually be able to apply the techniques they are learning to keeping themselves safe, versus some sport techniques that could leave them open to devastating knock-out punches.

CURRICULUM INCLUDES WEAPONS DEFENSE. Weapons defense is an important topic, as many assaults are committed with weapons. We contend that many programs are sorely lacking in this area, and we hope to see this area expanded upon further as self-defense needs are more fully assessed by jiu-jitsu programs.

CURRICULUM INCLUDES STRIKING AND CHOKE DEFENSES. Many assaults are committed with strikes or chokes, so we recommend preparing to protect yourself in those circumstances.

CURRICULUM INCLUDES A MIX OF STANDING AND GROUND. Gui Valente explained that Helio Gracie's private classes specifically designed for self-defense included 75 percent standing and 25 percent ground techniques. Although jiu-jitsu is powerful on the ground, avoiding the ground altogether is optimal in self-defense situations. Unfortunately, many fights do end up on the ground, and many sexual assaults happen on the ground, so having an understanding of both is key.

CURRICULUM INCLUDES REFLEX DEVELOPMENT (REPETITION). Muscle memory training and fight simulation training are important teaching methods. Gui Valente shares that in order "to prepare for actual self-defense scenarios, you will need to build body memory and reflexes." Another benefit of repetition is it allows you to work with different body shapes and sizes and to make the techniques your own. Instructors often give advice on a particular technique based on the size and weight of bodies. They adjust their advice for those who have, for example, long legs versus shorter legs. In turn, each student needs to try the techniques for their body and with a variety of other bodies to see what works best for them. So there is some experimenting to be done and mastery to be had. Helio Gracie is described as saying that he did not re-invent jiu-jitsu; he just made it better. "It was [as] if I had an oversized kimono and tailored it to fit me perfectly," by emphasizing "leverage, technique, and economy of movement instead of power and speed."[1] In the language of trauma recovery, we call this adaptability.

DELAYS SPARRING. Look for a school where you are not allowed to have open sparring right away. This is a recipe for injury and disempowerment. You need a basic understanding of numerous techniques in order to stay safe and be effective in learning from sparring. Any school that allows sparring on day one is potentially opening you up to injury, both physical and emotional. Typically it takes six months to a year to be ready for sparring. Sparring, according to Gracie University, is also the number one reason why more than 90 percent of people quit training in the first year.[2] Feel you have a basic wisdom of a variety of techniques and muscle memory before you begin sparring.

FACILITY IS CLEAN. Mats should be cleaned regularly. Cleaning them more than once a day if there are many classes on the mats is preferable. Even before our new awareness to hygiene in the COVID-19 era, we would have advised this point. You have every right to ask a potential facility you are seeking out what their protocol is for cleaning and disinfecting.

EMPHASIZES ATTIRE AND HYGIENE. Rules regarding attire can be important. Having a naked sweaty man's chest in your face can be triggering. Rash guards or t-shirts worn under the gi can help to prevent certain flashbacks by having skin covered and perspiration potentially caught in clothing versus dripping onto partners. Please consider asking potential schools about their clothing policies, especially as it relates to hygiene and safety.

OFFERS INDIVIDUALIZED PACING. An individual's personal journey and pace ought to be honored. As noted earlier, a curriculum that allows students to pick and choose classes and take breaks from training when they need to without penalty in finances, enrollment, or otherwise is the most trauma-supportive approach.

MAKES PRIVATE LESSONS AVAILABLE.   Although private training can be significantly more expensive than purchasing a membership to train in a group, having access to private lessons can make all the difference. Even if you cannot afford private lessons regularly, taking a few at the beginning or in regular intervals may allow you more space to learn and to process what may be coming up for you around certain techniques. Jamie attests that she likely wouldn't have stuck with jiu-jitsu if she hadn't begun with private lessons.

HAS FLEXIBLE POLICIES ON STOPPING OR LEAVING.   If a trauma survivor needs to leave the classroom and stop or opt out of practicing a specific technique, this should be honored. Leaving trauma survivors feeling trapped or without a choice is neither optimal nor healing.

HAS SUCCESSFUL STUDENTS OF ALL BACKGROUNDS AND WALKS OF LIFE.   Look for successful students who may be female, persons of color, larger sized, or from any other groups with which you may identify (e.g., LGBTQ+). Seeing faces and bodies like yours can potentially add to your sense of safety. According to the research study we conducted with *Women Empowered* students, seeing a female instructor demonstrated the effectiveness of the move and left other women feeling inspired and hopeful that they could do it as well. Seeing other female students spar had a similar effect. That said, not every school, especially in smaller or more rural areas that are not very diverse, will have this quality. You can still listen to how people and other groups are referenced and discussed. If you sense that those who do not look like the average student at a school would not be welcome, pay attention and honor how that makes you feel.

HAS A HIGH RATE OF STUDENT RETENTION.   Look for schools with high student retention versus high turnover and high new enrollments. Big classes may simply be a sign of excellent marketing, not necessarily training excellence or trauma-informed personnel. One of our interviewee contributors, a purple belt and Marine veteran, describes her experience with this phenomenon at two different schools: "At one school it became a numbers game for the owner. He was not as concerned with students and their well-being and more so concerned with dollar signs. Jiu-Jitsu is [a] cash cow. When it was clear that it had become the school's focal point I decided to move to another school. At the new school the owner would ask 'How's everything going? Do you have any questions?'"

PAIRS ADVANCED STUDENTS WITH NEWER STUDENTS.   Multiple people interviewed pointed out that when advanced students are paired with newer students, beginner classes are generally safer and more productive. Purple belt and assistant instructor Tony White explains that in classes with a fundamental focus, if more advanced students are paired with newer students, it builds camaraderie and effectively gives the newer students private teachers in the middle of group class. Much more to follow in Chapter 8 on how schools can provide extra training or support for advanced students who are helping out newer students.

ENCOURAGES QUESTIONS.   Questions should be encouraged. Helio Gracie himself is quoted as saying that he adjusted the moves by questioning them. "What if the move didn't work? What if the attacker did this or that? So I embarked on a mission to find answers to these questions."[3] Facilities that welcome questions are welcoming exploration and enhancing the students trust in techniques by demonstrating the answers. In addition, instructors who allow questioning of their technique demonstrate humility and, in turn, ensure that everyone has a voice in this space. This alone can be a healing and corrective experience for complex childhood trauma survivors who were not allowed to have a voice or opinion but could have been abused because they spoke up. Even people without trauma backgrounds will often need to ask questions.

PRACTICES *JOY-JITSU*.   Look for training centers that make training fun and enjoyable. Enjoyment is the exact opposite of trauma. Jiu-Jitsu is not always the easiest martial art to learn. Often the techniques are counterintuitive and complicated. If you are going to motivate yourself to stay and get through the training, enjoyment can be key. The longer you spend mastering a technique, the bigger and stronger the opponent it will work on. So, the ability to stay in training as long as possible is a factor in your success. If it is enjoyable, fun, and feels supportive, the more likely you will stay. Katie Gollan, purple belt and jiu-jitsu instructor, describes jiu-jitsu as a never-ending puzzle. She explains that "you never reach a point where you don't learn something new. You never get bored when you are trying to get into or out of positions." When she arrives on the mats "it's playtime."

PROVIDES A SENSE OF COMMUNITY.   Purple belt Staci May explains that a sense of safety and community is established in the messages that she received just walking through the door. We both love the Gracie University front door welcome mat that says "check your ego at the door," sending an important message that this is about cooperation and community. Staci highlights her experience of "amazingly positive people with a positive message that everybody can do it." She describes a sense that the jiu-jitsu community values you. She states that "I enjoy tapping," explaining that when she taps, she has an opportunity to ask to stop and learn something from the person, who is usually excited to share and explain what they did. She shares that she simply asks, "can you do that again? Can you show me what you did?" Our *Women Empowered* research findings echo this concept. Women were often surprised at just how much they felt welcomed into a "tribe of supportive people," a direct quote from one of our research participants.

SHOWS CONCERN FOR PARTNER'S PROGRESS.   Every student should be as concerned about their training partner's progress as their own. Training and sparring should feel cooperative and supportive. This can't be emphasized enough.

DEMONSTRATES APPLICABILITY OF INSTRUCTION AND CONTENT.   Look for instruction that is immediately and entirely applicable. Every street jiu-jitsu technique has the potential to help someone defend themselves at some point, depending on what the attacker is doing. That said, not every instructor does a great job of explaining how and when the specific technique could be used. They need to outline scenarios in which this technique would work and in which it might not. Anna has often heard instructors say that there are no bad students, only the potential for bad instruction. They described that it's not on the student to understand it; it's on the instructor to find a way to explain it. One of the many attributes that could distinguish a good instructor is their ability to describe and show an attacker in a realistic way. If the attack is not real, the student will not be convinced or prepared.

DESCRIBES THE PROBLEM.   Emphasizing the applicability point further, instruction time should be spent explaining and realistically demonstrating specifically what the attacker is trying to accomplish that the technique is attempting to neutralize. This might be referred to as the problem description or the indicators for a specific technique.

AVOIDS THE FIGHT.   Find instruction that teaches how to not fight first. Going home safely is key, and if this means turning over your wallet and keys, do that. If, for some reason, escape is not possible or if someone's life is in danger, that is the time to fight. We are also taught how certain body postures, direct eye contact, awareness, and certain firm verbalizations can send a clear message that you are not going to be an easy target.

EXPLAINS MULTIPLE ATTACKERS FALLACIES.   Trust your inner skeptic when you come across schools that say they have the instant answer for multiple attackers that does not involve running or getting away. Mark Barentine has been training in jiu-jitsu since 2009. Despite his brown belt, he agrees that he could be overwhelmed if he had to take on multiple attackers at the same time. He offers, "One versus the many is a Hollywood myth." He shares that the best guidance he has heard over the years was to try to negotiate to fight the attackers one by one, and if that is not successful, do whatever you can to avoid one of them sneaking up behind your back, which is not always possible. Anna has been told by numerous law enforcement personnel who spend extensive time in hand-to-hand combat training that defense from multiple attackers requires a weapon. We cannot offer instant solutions to this question, yet we suggest proceeding with caution when someone suggests they have solved this problem fully. They may not have left their ego at the door.

DISPELS THE BLACK BELT INSTRUCTOR MYTH.   Many believe that just because you have achieved the rank of black belt you are qualified to become an instructor. On the contrary, just because you are a good athlete does not mean you are a good or qualified instructor. Don't assume that just because a person has a black belt, that they are qualified to teach self-defense. As you can see from so many of the earlier points, there are many facets of being and skills needed to be a successful instructor, some of which we emphasize in Chapter 8. In many of the larger Brazilian Jiu-Jitsu training institutions, prospective instructors must pass expensive and lengthy training programs, continuing education requirements, and have clear background screenings. According to Gracie Jiu-Jitsu, instructors are evaluated on "tolerance, courage, hygiene, punctuality, honesty, manners, intelligence, technique, etc." and the training requires "years of full-time dedication."[4] If those who have trained primarily in sport jiu-jitsu receive no other training, they may only be able to pass on the skills of sport jiu-jitsu to people of similar motivation. Over time this focus can leave the people most in need of self-defense skills overlooked, and it will degrade what many think makes jiu-jitsu special: the small opponent surviving the larger opponent.

KEEPS FACILITY AND PROGRAMS UP TO DATE.   As our world evolves to do a better job of supporting trauma survivors, so should the programs that claim to serve them. If we decide, for example, that the word *victim* has an unhealthy stigma, then we will look to the instructor to evolve to using *survivor*. We are not saying that a program must be perfect in every way at all times; rather, the facility and its instructors must continually work to evolve and keep pace. This commitment can be reflected in facility vocabulary, policy, and techniques. Once they discover that skin-to-skin contact can be a trigger for many, a policy example could be switching from allowing men to have bare chests under their gi to requiring a rash guard under the gi. Technique evolution can be seen as crimes evolve. At Anna's facility, for instance, the t-shirt choke was presented the week after the news reported that a woman was raped in the back of an Uber. The technique was specifically developed and shared as a response to the violence of the week before. Such attentiveness sends a powerful message of caring for students' welfare, reaffirming their ability to trust in the instruction.

SPECIFICALLY TEACHES BREAK FALLING AS A TECHNIQUE.   Find programs that teach how to break fall (a way to protect your body by controlling your fall from standing to the ground, displacing energy away from your trunk, head, and neck and distributing it to your arms and legs). If they are teaching takedowns where one person is brought to the ground from standing, they should address how to fall without hurting yourself.

PROVIDES DIRECT REFERENCES.   You have every right to request to speak with two current students to ask about their experiences at the facility. If you do not trust that who the facility puts you in touch with will give you an honest appraisal, consider going online to check out more objective reviews. Also, check out the school's social media presence and, if possible, the personal accounts of the owner and instructors. If something strikes you as "off" about the vibe you get, respect that visceral information. Alternatively, if you like what you see or what you read, respect that visceral level feedback as well!

Training Agendas and Collaborative Language

Collaborative language can help to set expectations for safety and productivity. Expressing your goals and safety needs directly to your partner or your instructor can be helpful. In turn, you should also ask your partner what they want to work on and if they have any injuries or limitations. The following are some examples of collaborative language and how to start productive discussions in training environments. Listen for whether or not you are hearing similar forms of communication from instructors to students and between students when you check out a school:

- Please go slowly.
- I don't know this technique (e.g., foot locks). Can you show it to me?
- I don't know what I'm doing in the _____.

- Can you show me one _____?
- Is this pressure okay? Is my grip too tight or not tight enough?
- That's a little too tight. Can you loosen your grip?
- Can we start from a takedown?
- Thank you, that's great. Can we start sparring from here?
- My left shoulder is tighter than my right. Can we please practice on my right?
- Wow, cool! Where did I go wrong? Can you help me defend against that?
- Can we start from here? And can you do that again please?
- My foot is injured. Please avoid any foot locks.
- I'm going to go at 50 percent today. Is that okay for you?
- Is it okay for me to put my hand on your neck?
- Please don't put your hand on my neck directly.
- Do you want me to show you how to defend against that or keep rolling?
- Thank you so much for your help. I learned so much from that.

Training Tips and Best Practices for Collaborative Relationships

Okay, let's assume that you've found a facility where you feel a reasonable degree of comfort in beginning your jiu-jitsu journey. We'd now like to transition to offering you some tips for having a good training session during classes or if you end up practicing one-on-one with a training mate. Moreover, all techniques can be practiced as solo drills while you use your imagination to visualize the aggressors' indicators. Some of the specific techniques and approaches referenced in these examples may not have been covered yet in your training. Please try not to get hung up on the specific examples if you do not have a frame of reference for them yet—know they will be coming down the road. Focus, rather, on the encouragement and ideas that we provide.

If you decide to practice techniques with a partner in advance and also in the future, here are some tips for collaborating to create a good training session for everyone:

- *Take turns being the aggressor/attacker.* You learn as both the attacker and a defender in training situations. We often have someone be the defender two to four times and then switch roles. These repetitions allow a little bit of muscle memory to start building. After those two to four repetitions, you may then alternate one repetition each, back and forth.

- *Give positive feedback.* Give praise when something is done well. Point out the small wins, like having the hips in the right spot. Verbalizing praise can elevate the energy and enthusiasm. Verbalizing gratitude for your partner keeps things positive. "That was a great roll. Thank you," or "Thank you for pointing that out."

- *Give constructive feedback.* If you see something your partner might do differently or you would like to help them adjust, ask, "Would you like me to offer some tips?" If they say yes, ask, "Can you pause here?" or "Can you move your hand here? Now try. Does that feel different?" Try to make it collaborative, not condescending. If you are the newer student, notice if the feedback you are receiving or asking for feels collaborative or condescending.

- *Provide specific indicators only.* If you are the attacker, only do exactly what is described. Of course there are other ways the attacker might move to get around the defense of this technique. Once you master this version, you can move on to other variations to address the what-ifs. It is especially important in the early stages of learning jiu-jitsu to cooperate with your training partner. Many times, when you are the "bad guy," you are simply a prop for your partner to use to learn where their body needs to be to execute the technique. Over the course of many lessons, you can begin to resist.

- *Go slowly.* Recall from Chapter 3: *slow is smooth, and smooth is fast.* You may be tempted to go fast in the beginning, especially as a trauma survivor. We want to get out of the uncomfortable position and get out quickly. Not only will this sabotage your training, it is also potentially unsafe. The slower you go, the faster you learn. Going fast in the beginning will inevitably leave your technique sloppy and less effective in the future. Go slow and learn the specifics of where to put your body and why, and the techniques will be much cleaner and more effective in the future. In addition, the faster you move, the greater the chance you have of injuring yourself or your partner, especially with submissions. Sometimes it is only a matter of half an inch in movement that could result in a real injury to your training partner. The majority of injuries we've seen have happened when people were moving too fast. There is a reason that the advanced classes use mouth guards. They are moving fast but have often spent years understanding the possibilities and learning to keep each other safe. Even then, mistakes happen. To ensure the lowest probability of injury, going slowly is always the best choice.

- *Tap early.* Develop a habit of tapping firmly and quickly if you feel any pressure, pain, or discomfort. Not only will this help protect you from injury, it is potentially a significant corrective experience for a trauma survivor. Tapping and having someone quickly retreat from whatever was the causing issue affirms that the trauma survivor is now in control and that their body is respected.

- *Tighten the muscles of the target area.* If, for example, the attacker is attempting to apply a choke, tightening your neck muscles provides support to the neck structure and gives you extra seconds in a real fight if you need them. This doesn't only apply to the neck. Anna has also found it useful in side mount, mount, and double-leg takedown. When she feels pressure or impact to her stomach, it has helped Anna to have counterpressure by tightening her abdominal or core muscles. It is often the difference between feeling crushed by someone and feeling like you are okay and can tolerate the situation.

- *Be aware of triggers, and see triggers as opportunities for growth.* Whether it's with a therapist or not, work to be aware of your triggers so that you can see them coming. Chewy Albin, the third-degree black belt instructor in Louisville we mentioned earlier in the book, believes that "everyone has their hang-ups." He discusses negative self-talk and believes that it's important to be aware that you have a pattern of doing it in a particular circumstance and then be ready for it. He provides an example of one of his recurring negative beliefs: "Visitors from big cities will always beat me." He then works to put himself in positions to gain contrary information. Spar with the people from out of town, and when that thought comes up, squash it and find the contrary information. Look for the evidence that it's not true. Look for the moments in which you held your own and pay attention to them.

- *Have fun.* Like anything else that we want to encourage ourselves to do in the long run, the more fun we have, the more likely we are going to return. Fun is, in many ways, often the opposite of fear. If we are actually smiling and laughing and enjoying "the fight," we are conditioning ourselves not to fear the fight. It doesn't deserve our adrenaline anymore.

TRY THIS Working with the Neck

Tightening your neck muscles can provide support if someone is attempting to choke you. Anna has often heard her instructors joking that in their multigenerational jiu-jitsu training family, if someone even looks at their neck, or if they are going in for a hug, they automatically tighten their neck muscles. Tensing and releasing muscle groups also happens to be a coping skill we outlined for you in Chapter 4. If you have any physical limitations or injuries in your neck, you can instead practice progressive muscle relaxation on a different muscle group that honors your body's needs.

If it works for your body, we invite you to try tensing and releasing your neck muscles. It might be tricky at first for some of you to find those muscles. In order to find and sense those neck muscles we can attempt to

- move the head slightly backward

- look down slightly, and

- pull the chin back in toward the neck

Alternatively, some people can find and tighten those muscles if they make a look of disgust or repulsion on their face. This might instinctively recoil our head and chin away from whatever is in front of us. Once you have found those muscles, see if you can now hold them tightened for a count of ten and then completely relax them for a count of twenty seconds. If it feels appropriate and available in your body, consider lying down to rest the neck completely, if possible, when focusing in on relaxing those neck muscles.

Six

For Trauma Survivors: What to Expect

The sangha is a community where there should be harmony and peace and understanding. That is something created by our daily life together. If love is there in the community, if we've been nourished by harmony in the community, then we will never move away from love.

—THICH NHAT HAHN

In order to find a healthy, supportive training community, we recommend you look for content that lets you know they have considered your safety and communication that demonstrates that they are trauma informed. Here we will build on what we discussed in the previous chapter and demonstrate specific techniques and ways of communicating that we believe are ideal for assisting the trauma healing journey and why they are best taught by a trauma-informed instructor.

We do not include techniques in this section to promote a do-it-yourself or read-from-the-book-and-master-it jiu-jitsu. Jiu-Jitsu can be a physically rigorous activity, and we recommend that you practice it only with a qualified instructor or when guided by a training partner who has ample experience with their own training. Although the following techniques may seem noncomplicated and easy to master, having an instructor to help you make minor adjustments to the placement of hands and feet and the positioning of your body is crucial. We include these techniques here, with our personal commentary, so that you have examples of strategies that are important for you to learn as a survivor of trauma. In seeking out an optimal training environment for yourself, we recommend making sure that these are covered as part of the curriculum. If you have already begun your training journey guided by someone qualified, you can work with what we are presenting here as refinements.

> *NOTE* **Trigger Warning.** The following sections may be triggering for some readers. Compared to other sections of the book, these include more visceral descriptions of assault and violence. In order to clarify our recommendations, we needed to get more specific about typical acts of violence and how they relate to the curriculum. We suggest that each reader consider if they need time to prepare for reading this chapter. You can do this with the support of a therapist if you need to.

The Need

We chose to emphasize the techniques in this section based on our own lived experience with assault, the lived experiences that clients have shared with us, and data from the National Violence Against Women Survey.[1] Jamie and Anna found it notable that this study is now twenty years old and has not been updated. Anna knew that researching the history of jiu-jitsu would be difficult, but she did not expect to have tremendous difficulty finding facts on how specific acts of violence are committed. After searching online and contacting numerous police and FBI personnel, she was left with the discovery that although police might collect the exact nature of violence in their reports, it is not then collected into a database for further analysis. There are neither the resources nor the funding to do so, and that is unfortunate on many levels. These omissions suggest that violence against women is not a priority for society at large, and the lack of good information also makes it harder to verify that you are in a realistic self-defense program.

We present some basic data here to underscore the need for realistic self-defense programs. You can read the full report from the National Violence Against Women Survey via a PDF made available on their website,[2] yet we feel it's important to note some of the highlights to underscore the seriousness of the matter at hand for all genders. Of people surveyed, 51.9 percent of women and 66.4 percent of men report being physically assaulted. These forms of assault include being slapped, pushed, grabbed, and shoved, being hit with an object, having hair pulled, having something thrown at them, being kicked, being choked, and being threatened with a knife or with a gun. Of those surveyed, 14.8 percent of women and 2.1 percent of men report having experienced completed rapes, with many more having endured attempted rape. According to the Bureau of Justice Statistics, "From 2015 to 2018, the portion of U.S. residents age 12 or older who were victims of violent crime rose from 0.98% to 1.18% (up 20%)."[3] The Bureau broke out specific demographics for persons age 12 or older:

- Male victims up 29 percent to 1.21 percent

- Female victims up 13 percent to 1.16 percent

- Rape or sexual assault up to 2.7 per 1,000 in 2018 (1.4 in 2017)

- Unreported violent victimizations up to 12.9 per 1,000 (2015–2018)

When you look more closely, and specifically at how members of the LGBTQ+ community describe their experience with violence, another grim picture emerges. According to a 2015 survey of transgender individuals, 47 percent are sexually assaulted at some point in their lifetime, with numbers being higher for those who identify as Black, Indigenous, or as a person of color (BIPOC).[4] Some incidences of violence are underreported, especially among BIPOC individuals, and often these incidences are at the hands of law enforcement.

According to the National Intimate Partner Violence and Sexual Violence Survey conducted by the Centers for Disease Control

- Forty-four percent of lesbians and 61 percent of bisexual women experience rape, physical violence, or stalking by an intimate partner, compared to 35 percent of straight women.

- Twenty-six percent of gay men and 37 percent of bisexual men experience rape, physical violence, or stalking by an intimate partner, compared to 29 percent of straight men.

- Forty-six percent of bisexual women have been raped, compared to 17 percent of straight women and 13 percent of lesbians.

- Twenty-two percent of bisexual women have been raped by an intimate partner, compared to 9 percent of straight women.

- Forty percent of gay men and 47 percent of bisexual men have experienced sexual violence other than rape, compared to 21 percent of straight men.[5]

While we work to change the societal conditions that permit such violence toward vulnerable individuals, we can also equip those who are more vulnerable with the skills to keep themselves as safe as possible. For many of us, learning such skills can be a reparative and healing experience in and of itself.

According to Helio Gracie, "there are a finite number of basic techniques. But there are an infinite number of variations."[6] He shares over 133 basic moves in his classic book on self-defense. So how do we choose which moves to share in this book, let alone recommend that you learn? We compiled the following collection inspired by the above statistics and recommendations from those we interviewed. Our overall goal in choosing techniques from the thousands that exist is eight-fold:

1. To give you a sampling of basic techniques and make the broad range of options more usable. Options are essential for trauma survivors, especially if our traumatic experiences have left us feeling like we are trapped or have no choices.

2. To relay information on street techniques that can be used in self-defense.

3. To showcase techniques that give you some initial ideas on how leverage, not strength, is used in jiu-jitsu, making these available to anyone.

4. To begin getting students accustomed to the kind of physical contact experienced in jiu-jitsu.

5. To demonstrate a variety of techniques from standing and ground, to high and low contact, to basic and more in-depth. We want to demonstrate jiu-jitsu's comprehensiveness. We also want students to be aware of the variety of potential triggering physical interactions they may encounter.

6. To highlight what to look for in quality instruction.

7. To describe the valuable lived experience of those we've interviewed. Clearly they have a great deal to share, as we've already cited their wisdom at various points in the book. We asked them which five to ten techniques they believe would be important for trauma survivors to learn, and we've integrated their feedback into this collection.

8. To reinforce participants' ability to communicate with their partners, especially if something feels too far past their edge of comfort. If a technique makes you feel as if you are traveling too far past your edge and that you need to slow down, you can always consider saying things like this or something similar:

   • "I'd like to watch this and sit out for now."

   • "I'd like to solo drill this one."

   • "Can you leave the _____ (punch, kick) out for now?"

   • "Can you move in slow motion for me?"

   • "Can you coach me on where to put my arms?"

In the sections that follow, we cover selected techniques with as much detail as seems appropriate for this book: healthy awareness/vigilance vs. hypervigilance, base (push and pull), tactical stand up, managing distance/situational awareness, trap and roll (*Upa*), the clinch, and the punch block series.

Healthy Awareness and Vigilance vs. Hypervigilance

A common theme across all the self-defense courses we have taken is that the bad guys or aggressors are looking for an easy target. They would like to find someone who is distracted, on their phone, unaware, shy, avoiding eye contact, and visually small. They don't want a big fight or to call attention to themselves. So, if they get the impression that you are more trouble than they want, they will move on to finding someone else. However, many women have been socialized to make themselves small, to keep their legs closed, to speak quietly and not to be loud or rude unless they want to be labeled a bitch. How you carry yourself through the world sends a message. In jiu-jitsu we begin to learn that we have choices in our tone of voice, eye contact, posture, and more.

Since we started training, we have learned to do the opposite of cowering, especially in situations in which we feel even the slightest bit threatened. If we're standing alone somewhere at night and someone approaches us, we now instinctively make ourselves a little bigger, standing with our legs hip-width apart or slightly more. We make eye contact, look the person directly in the eyes, while giving them a nod hello. We might even go so far as to position our bodies so that a would-be aggressor doesn't have a chance to sneak up from behind. Prior to jiu-jitsu, some unnecessary adrenaline may have been pumping by this point, causing us to feel more hypervigilant than vigilant. *Vigilance* is generally defined as a degree of awareness that is within normal limits that are appropriate to the situation and context. *Hypervigilance* as a phenomenon, which can show up as a symptom of PTSD and other stressor-related disorders, suggests a higher degree of fear or reactivity. This heightened sense of reactivity can actually make the person experiencing it less safe because their cortisol levels are too high or the amount of stress they are experiencing impacts their ability to respond appropriately. Because of jiu-jitsu, we've learned how to stay simultaneously vigilant and at ease.

Jamie's primary coach, black belt Micah Bender, believes that situational awareness is one of the two most important strategies for survivors of trauma to learn (the other being breath, covered in Chapter 2). The founder and director of Combat Athlete Performance Academy in Warren, Ohio, the gym where Jamie trains off and on, Brian Needham (also a Marine veteran and former MMA fighter), is a jiu-jitsu purple belt and master of tactical self-defense. Brian also worked as a weapons trainer for the state of Ohio for over twenty years and has studied several other forms of martial arts. He shares that situational awareness is the first of five major principles that he teaches his students. Similar to what Sun Tzu emphasized in *The Art of War* millennia ago, the best defense in a conflict is to avoid the fight in the first place. For more on honing situational awareness as a protection skill, visit the "Try This" practice at the end of the chapter.

Trauma survivors have several potential things to consider when using techniques for developing healthy situational awareness. Hypervigilance is a common symptom among many survivors. One key consideration is making sure that we are learning when, where, and what we need to pay attention to. Instructors should, for example, discuss the circumstances in which we can have our head in our phones and circumstance in which we should not. A second consideration that needs to be discussed is the difference between hyper- and healthy vigilance. We need to learn to what degree we need to be aware. The more training you have on what this situational awareness should look like, the better you will be able to tell when you are in a hyper state versus having healthy levels of vigilance. If you and your jiu-jitsu instructor determine that you continue to stay in a hyper state after acquiring all the necessary knowledge, it might be helpful to work on strengthening your emotion regulation skills with a mental health clinician.

Base

As we established in Chapter 1, base is the first technique you will typically learn in the study of jiu-jitsu. Not only is base foundational, it is key to and required for many standing techniques. One time Jamie attended an advanced seminar with Master Pedro Sauer, and they spent an hour playing with base alone!

Please consider revisiting the "Try This" exercise that we include in Chapter 1 on base. This is a technique that most people can begin to work on safely whether or not they are under the direction of an instructor. For the purposes of this chapter, let's get a little more specific.

The primary objective of achieving and maintaining a strong base is to be able to stop an aggressor from controlling your location. The aggressor wants to move you from one place to another, perhaps from the street into their vehicle. In building skills to defend against pushing, you learn how to stay grounded in one spot despite them pushing. For survivors of trauma, this is an excellent way to work on grounding and assertiveness as you literally learn to sink in and hold your position. The jiu-jitsu strategies of working with base teach us to position our bodies in such a way as to make it extremely difficult for an aggressor to stop us from standing up or for them to move us where they want us to go.

Look for instructors who make the scenario that we are fighting against as real as possible. Aggressors are not going to simply push you in one direction, for example. You should be taught in a way that portrays a realistic physical struggle with a person who really intends on moving you. That said, it is also important for instructors and partners to respect the intensity the student is ready for. Like many jiu-jitsu techniques, base can be practiced at varying degrees of intensity. There can be a significant difference between practicing this with a 100-pound person versus a 200-pound person and/ or a person pushing with all their strength versus a person only applying 10 percent. You have complete permission to speak up about the intensity that you prefer: "Can we go slow as I try to find my footing?" or "Can you challenge me and really try to make me move?" Given that this is one of the first moves many students tend to learn, it is a first experience with jiu-jitsu. If a really aggressive partner, who is not coaching you or helping you with where to put your feet or how to angle your body, pushes you away or knocks you down, this is probably not going to be a corrective experience. If this is happening, you can ask, "Can we slow down?" You can also ask to switch partners. "I think I need to try this with a different body type, I'd like to switch partners." You might also get the attention of the instructor: "Can you help me? I'm not sure how to keep from getting pushed."

Tactical Stand Up: Getting Up in Base

Consider that the aggressor might want to prevent you from getting up from the ground. Jiu-Jitsu teaches you how to get up despite their efforts, in a primary skill that is often called *base get-up*, *getting up in base*, or *tactical stand up*. Tactical stand up is a key extension of the base concept. We've established that aggressors want an easy target. They want to quickly and quietly subdue and isolate their target from any potential assistance. Let's say, for example, that you are alone at the park and on the ground when you notice a stranger is walking toward you. Depending on the time of day, your whereabouts, and whether or not there are any potential bystanders to assist you, it may be best to simply get to your feet as soon as possible. Walking or running away is always a potentially good option, and sometimes it is the best option available. If, however, you have not gotten to your feet and this aggressor is now in close proximity, you could consider many defensive tactics depending on what they are doing or saying. Instructors should clarify a variety of scenarios and solutions, such as whether the aggressor is trying to punch or kick you and the ways to stay safe. If the aggressor is simply trying to keep you on the ground, then a strong option is to get up in base. Look for instructors who provide key details such as keeping eye contact with the attacker and standing up without turning your back on them. If you can't see the aggressor, you don't know what they are doing. It is key to keep your eyes on them at all times.

Some of the specifics of this technique are covered in the "Try This" exercise in Chapter 1. We've learned that the more you practice getting up in base during your training, the more naturally it will translate into life. As a yoga teacher and meditator, Jamie spends a great deal of time down on the floor; sometimes she even does therapy down there with her clients if they believe it helps them stay more grounded. Jamie jokes that it is impossible for her *not* to get up in base at this point in her life—she always plants both hands firmly beside her to support the getting up. She even teaches this simple strategy to her yoga and dance students.

This technique is best practiced solo numerous times before it is challenged by a partner. Simply learning to establish the triad is a necessary skill, and then the next step is having someone attempting to stop you from getting up. Over time, when the student is ready, the partner can increase the intensity. Students can use language similar to what we used earlier: "I would like to solo drill some more before I have you try to stop me." Then "Okay, I'm ready now. Can we go slow, while I'm still finding my footing?" Then "Please challenge me and don't let me get up." Speaking up for yourself is crucial in these situations because having an overly aggressive partner pushing on you when you first begin can be problematic.

Defending against Pushing

We cannot stress enough how extremely important this move is to avoid being taken to a secondary location. You might feel like Anna did, that defending against someone pushing seems like a very simple concept. On the contrary, and like many concepts in jiu-jitsu, it is all in the fine details. The movement and positioning of your body will create the leverage you need to make the techniques work. You want to seek instructors who are skilled in conveying the specifics. Remember our example from Chapter 1 of the wind or the aggressor pushing from the left to the right after we walk out the door? Here are some steps you need to defend against someone pushing you and the types of details you would expect to see from good instructors.

You want to have your feet firmly planted on the ground, wide enough apart to create stability against the pressure from the aggressor. Lean your body in the opposite direction from which an aggressor would want you to go. Again, this can be counterintuitive, as it puts your upper body closer to the bad guy. Some trauma survivors may find it difficult at first to move their upper body closer to the attacker. Partnering with a person who is similar to a prior attacker in that they are the same size, gender, or share other similar attributes could make this exercise more challenging. In addition, practice and repetition help you get used to the idea of close proximity.

Keeping a straight line from your head down to your toes is key. If you are leaning your legs but your upper body is vertical, then you are push-able. Try it both ways and see the difference. The better your angle, the less muscle and energy is required to defend against the pushing. The better you get, the more exhausted the bad guy or your training partner will be. You are also more pushable if you are facing them with your upper body. Instead, orient your chest perpendicular to theirs. This limits what they have available to push against; you're only giving them your shoulder. You may need to make minor adjustments by shuffling your feet in the direction the bad guy wants you to go in order to obtain the base factors just described. When we are pushed, the goal is not to move the bad guy, but instead to move our own body to obtain this optimal base position. If we are not going to move them, then we have to move ourselves. This may mean shuffling our feet toward the right, especially the right foot, while keeping the upper body as stationary as possible (see Figure 6.1). In the scuffle, the bad guy may actually move you a couple feet, but it is better to lose a couple feet and obtain a good base than it is to lose base altogether and be pushed where they want you to go.

Figure 6.1: Defending against pushing.

Trap and Roll/Upa

The *trap and roll* (also known as *Upa)* is a very standard move across many different jiu-jitsu schools. Although a ground technique, it is a first move that an instructor may show a new student to teach them about leverage and the power of jiu-jitsu. The probable scenario or indicators for this move are that the good guy is now on the ground and the aggressor is on top. This scenario could play out after you fall to the ground and the aggressor then climbed on top. This could also happen if you are pushed onto a couch or bed with the aggressor then positioned on top. In a real-life scenario, the aggressor might actually be sitting on the opponent's belly, legs straddled on either side in mount. The aggressors' hands could be doing a variety of things from punching to choking to pinning the opponent's hands down. Of course, there are a variety of responses to each of those scenarios. For the purpose of simply getting familiar with the basic movement, we will assume that the aggressor simply has their hands on the ground on either side of the opponent's shoulders.

The first skill in learning this move is the *trap*. In order to roll the aggressor off of you, you must trap the aggressor's leg and arm on one side of their body so that they cannot post them out to stop the move. For the sake of simplicity, from the good guy's/defender's perspective, let's choose to trap the aggressor's right arm and leg in this scenario—the left side of the bad guy's body when they are facing you. Grab their right wrist or forearm using a monkey grip with your right hand (see Figure 6.2), and secure it to just above the general vicinity of your armpit.

Instructors might not give details, as specific as *monkey grip*, when they explain this type of move the first time. Although instructors need to download a great deal of information to you on how to be effective, in the beginning, they also don't want to overwhelm you. These kinds of details do, however, make a difference in the effectiveness of a technique. When you apply the appropriate grip, it often reduces the amount of strength you need to succeed in using a technique. Look for these kinds of details to be shared over time

Figure 6.2: The monkey grip.

in a school providing quality instruction. Talented instructors put a great deal of thought into the effectiveness of their teaching. They will work to give you just enough detail to get you started and then help you refine from there and over time. There is a small window in instruction between overwhelming your students with too much detail and not giving them enough, rendering them ineffective. Seek instructors who leave you feeling like you have learned something, are somewhat effective, and are not overwhelmed. As you work with bigger or stronger partners, the nuance of your grip will become more and more important so that you are using leverage instead of strength.

Also seek an instructor who will highlight common mistakes students make when learning. A key mistake for this technique is for the good guy not to have their own right arm and elbow pinned down to their body. When you glue your arm to your body, the aggressor is no longer dealing with just your arm muscles but also your back muscles. This motion prevents the bad guy from posting out their right hand to stop you from rolling them. These are the kinds of details that you might not get by watching any old YouTube video.

Although you have now prevented the effective hand post, the bad guy can still pull their hand back and potentially punch you with it. Good instruction will let you know how to stay as safe as possible from knock-out punches. In order to prevent that and secure your body weight to their right arm, you will need to C-grip (see Figure 6.3) the back of their right arm with your left arm.

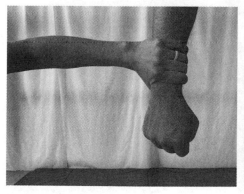

Figure 6.3: The C-grip.

Again, your instructor may not discuss the type of grip in a first lesson, but it will eventually become important. Now with the C-grip on the back of the aggressor's triceps, they should not be able to simply pull their arm back and away from the good guy's left arm's grip. The partner pretending to be a bad guy should ask if they can test pulling their arm out and away and, with approval, do so. Good communication between partners should be encouraged and described in quality schools. Instructors will often explicitly say, "ask your partner if you can test their grip." If you have both arms secured as just described, then the aggressor shouldn't be able to pull their arm back without picking you up off the floor.

Now that the aggressor's right arm is securely trapped, you can work to trap their same side leg (aggressor's right leg). This means that the good guy's left knee should lean over to the left (see Figure 6.4). The positioning of the knee is another nuanced detail that good instructors will emphasize more over time. The aggressor should now be unable to use their right knee to post out to the side. Quality instruction always works to provide safety precautions. As a caution, the practice partner who is taking on the role of the aggressor should tuck their right shoulder, keeping it as low to the ground as possible to avoid injury.

Figure 6.4: The trap.

Now that the right side of the aggressor's body is trapped, the roll is possible. The good guy needs to place their right foot in between the bad guy's legs and position their knee so it is facing up and is as close to the bad guy's bottom as possible. The positioning of the foot is another fine detail to be shared over time. The good guy will now use that foot (both if they need to) to press into the floor in order to lift their hips as high and as fast as possible. If you have any familiarity with yoga practice, this motion is like coming into bridge pose. The higher the hips, the better the leverage. Gravity will then take effect and the aggressor will roll to their right off of the good guy. If the good guy has done this with enough momentum, then they will also roll toward the bad guy's trapped side (roll-out side) and land on top of them (see Figures 6.5–6.7).

Figure 6.5: Hip up.

Figure 6.6: Roll.

Figure 6.7: Stay safe.

Surf boarding up can be done by putting your hands on the aggressors' hips while jumping to your feet (see Figure 6.8), landing with one foot forward and one back in a strong base just like one you would use if you were moving to a standing position on a surf board on a wave at the beach. From this standing position, the good guy can begin to shuffle back and away, while keeping an eye at all times on their bad guy and maintaining good base (see Figure 6.9). Then, you can make an escape when it is safe to do so. Instructors will likely show you many variations on how to get up or what to do next.

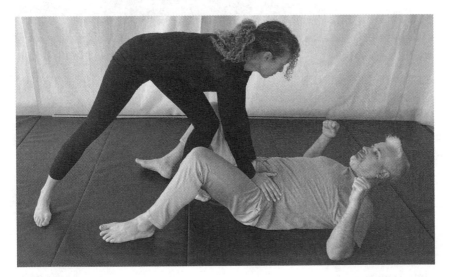

Figure 6.8: Surf board up.

Figure 6.9: Shuffle backward.

This move can be particularly difficult for some survivors as they are now on the ground with someone on top of them. However, some survivors are not bothered by this at all. We don't want you to assume that something will be tricky for you just because it has happened to others. We do want you to know that you have options if you have reached your limit. You can always ask to sit out and watch. You might say, "I'm going to sit this one out for now. I'll let you know when I'm up for trying it." You can also again work to choose partners who will make you feel the safest when you are first starting. Some of Anna's clients needed to simply work to get comfortable being on the bottom and did not focus on attempting the rest of the move. They simply worked to regulate their feelings as they lay on the ground with their partner in mount. You can simply ask, "Can we stay here for a moment, I want to catch my breath."

Like the others, trap and roll (and all its variations and options) should be practiced numerous times in order to build muscle memory. As a review, at a minimum, each practicing partner should practice being the good guy at least four times and then partners should alternate thereafter. The more repetitions the better.

Managing Distance and Situational Awareness

Manage the distance, manage the damage is something we've both heard many times and in many gyms. Distance management and situational awareness are the first lines of defense. In beginning to explain this larger concept, we must state explicitly that we do not ever suggest that a trauma survivor should have done something differently to make their assailant not come after them. We do not condone victim blaming in any way, shape, or form. In the United States, our judicial system works to discredit any accusing person's testimony. This can leave the trauma survivor further traumatized and attacked. Women in particular are often told that they shouldn't have worn certain clothing or shouldn't have been by themselves, or in a particular location, or out after dark. This practice is deplorable. We stand firm in our conviction that victim blaming has no truth to it and can cause further trauma to those whom have already suffered so much. We want and should have a world in which everyone feels safe and respected. We would expect nothing less from the instructors who teach jiu-jitsu. If instructors engage in any kind of victim blaming, that is a red flag.

Unfortunately, that *safe world* is not the one in which we presently live. Although we are both doing our part to create that better world, until it is here, jiu-jitsu provides many solutions for self-preservation and protection. We cannot go back into the past and undo what has already been done. We can, however, learn new tools and thinking so that we can work to prevent further traumas.

As we discussed earlier, there is a difference between healthy vigilance and hypervigilance. Managing the distance between you and a potential attacker begins with healthy vigilance by developing situational awareness. Attackers don't usually like crowds in which someone might come to a person's aid and potentially witness and videotape their attack. As a result, attacks are more likely to happen when a target is alone, out of earshot and eyesight of anyone who could help. How vigilant we need to remain often depends on where we are. If you are, for example, on a crowded beach on a sunny day and many people and lifeguards are in sight and earshot, it's theoretically safer to sit back and read a book. If, however, you are sitting in a park alone and sunset is near, it might not be the best time to read a book.

Quality instruction ought to provide realistic scenarios and physical demonstrations of the simplest concepts. Rener and Eve Gracie often demonstrate what they mean by asking a group of their students to indicate when Rener is too close to Eve in this hypothetical park scenario. He starts all the way across a very large room from her, and then he turns toward her and starts walking. New students often wait until he is ten to fifteen feet away before they say he is too close. Then he returns to his corner and states that he was too close when he turned in her direction. Even the shift of his body toward hers has indicated something, especially when he starts walking toward her. They teach that it would have been best if Eve had stood up *before* he got too close.

If the fight is on, managing the distance is vital. The principle at play is that you either want to be too far away (in which case the strikes and kicks are unavailable to the attacker), or you want to be so close that these strikes become ineffective. If you have ever watched a professional boxing match, you have likely seen the *clinch*. Anna remembers the first time she watched the clinch happening and wondered why one boxer seemed to move in so close into an embrace that looked like a hug. What Anna learned many years later in jiu-jitsu was that if you are "hugging" your attacker, pulling them in close, their punches won't be any stronger than they can punch their own chest. Don't get us wrong—these punches will hurt, but they are not knockout punches. So being in the clinch is "all the way in" versus being out of reach "all the way out."

The Clinch

The clinch is so important that it warrants a separate section. With some techniques, being in the clinch helps you not get knocked out. Psychologically the clinch can feel like one of the harder techniques to master because it is counterintuitive. You are hugging up against the punches, *embracing the suck* as we mentioned in Chapter 1. In the children's classes, Instructor

Alex Ueda says "helmet, hit, hug." Look for instructors who provide a few key words that sum up a technique. If you were learning to ride a bike, the first challenge would be glide, brake. In the clinch this is "helmet, hit, hug," a technique we describe next. An expanded version that includes "walk and bow" will be covered in Chapter 7.

The first step is to make a helmet with your arms. Depending on which side the next punch is coming from, you want to use your arm on that same side. (You bend your arm and place your wrist by your ear, holding the arm close to your head to protect that side of your head.) The other arm that is not on the side of the incoming punch will also be bent with your hand on top of your head and your elbow in front of your face. You can practice this reflex just by switching which arm is positioned to block a punch and which is ready for the hit (see Figure 6.10). Keeping your eyes on the attacker the entire time is crucial. Many newcomers find this challenging; they find it difficult to both not hold their breath and close their eyes as they move in.

Figure 6.10: The helmet.

The next step is the hit. After you have made your helmet, you will shuffle forward, while maintaining your base, in order to hit the attacker in their chest with your helmet. The key to success here is placing your elbows forward so that your arms/elbows take the brunt of any impact and not your head and neck (see Figure 6.11). Look for instructors who demonstrate details on how to stay safe and protect your body.

The hug normally happens as soon as the helmet makes contact. Your body is positioned slightly to one side or another. On the side to which you are more connected, wrap that arm around the aggressor's back, making a fist. Reach your other hand around the other side and monkey grip your other arm just past your wrist if possible. Then the challenge is to stay glued to the aggressor. Imagine a small child wrapping themselves around the leg of an adult that they are trying to prevent from going anywhere. You are glued to the attacker's body in that same way. Your hips should be close into them and hugging tight (see Figure 6.12).

Figure 6.11: The hit.

Figure 6.12: The hug.

The clinch (helmet, hit, hug) can be particularly difficult for the reasons just highlighted but also simply because of the punching. For obvious reasons, it is possible that trauma survivors who were punched during real attacks might find the motion of a fake punch coming at them during training triggering. If your adrenaline starts pumping and you've gone past your edge, it's okay to take a step back and consider your options in approaching a technique. Solo drilling is almost always an option. If you need help understanding how to solo drill a particular technique, you can always ask your instructor. Using clinch as an example, you might try imagining the punches coming from either direction and switching your arms. You could then practice slowly and gently making contact with a wall while keeping your eyes open. This will give you some ideas of how to use your arms to protect your head from any impact. Again, it can be helpful to ask instructors for clarifications on how to keep yourself safe while practicing. Another option for most techniques is to ask your partner to omit or adjust their arms and hands. Using clinch as an example, you could ask your partner to omit the punch. A third option is asking your partner to go slow or even in super slow motion. (Think *The Matrix* movie.) In this technique you might ask, "Can you give me a slow-motion punch?" Ask your partner if they would be willing to coach you through: "Can you tell me when to go in?"

Because of the counterintuitive nature of this technique, it can take time and patience to master in a trauma-supportive way. Even people without trauma impact can find this strategy challenging. Anna explains her process of working to overcome her stress response:

> My body knows what a real punch from a big guy or multiple people at once feels like. As a result, I did everything you are not supposed to do in attempting this technique. I held my breath, closed my eyes, and hesitated, not wanting to go in at the right time. I thought I had finally mastered it when I was called up to the front of the class. Before I could even decipher what technique I was being asked to demonstrate, a fist was coming toward me . . . . and so I ran. I ran away from his punch, while I let out a scream. Everyone, many of whom knew and supported me, laughed, and they all yelled out, "Anna clinch!" Bright red, and laughing at myself, I walked back toward the instructor and he told everyone, "Now, running is a great option too. As a matter of fact, it should be our first option, if we are able to run." From that day forward, I asked everyone for their help. I asked them to always greet me with a very slow punch, so that I might clinch my way into the hug that I ultimately wanted. Slowly over time, two years later, I stopped hesitating. Still to this day, I will occasionally catch myself holding my breath or closing my eyes.

Jamie also found the idea of clinching to be odd at first, yet when Micah pulled out his *embrace the suck* teaching, it started to make loads of sense based on mindfulness practice. Genuine mindfulness practice encourages us to embrace it all—whatever the moment or the day might bring. By leaning into something we might ordinarily resist, we can allow it to pass through our experience more efficiently, and it can go on to affect us less, if at all. As is often said in recovery, what we resist can persist. The clinch is a prime example of how a jiu-jitsu technique brings these powerful mindfulness and recovery lessons to embodied life.

Punch Block Series

The punch block series covers staying safe on the ground from an attacker who is throwing strikes. This technique does a great job demonstrating the power of jiu-jitsu while you are on the ground on your back and the attacker is at a variety of distances from right on top to standing nearby. The series demonstrates important jiu-jitsu principles such as *all the way in or all the way out, or if they make space, fill it*. We will break down these five different attacker distances in this section.

- *Stay facing them.* One difference between the clinch and the punch block series is that the good guy is on the ground while the attacker might still be standing. If you have not managed to get to your feet, the first step is to stay safe on the ground while facing them. While keeping your back to the ground, you can keep one leg bent with your foot on the floor and the other bent and ready to kick if the attacker comes close enough (see Figure 6.13). The direction of the attacker's movement determines which foot is on the ground. The grounded foot should be the foot in the direction of your attacker's movement, helping to "pull" your body into place. If they move to the right, then you use your right foot on the ground to move your body so that you continue to face them as they circle right, with your other leg bent and ready to strike if they come closer. You would then switch legs if they changed direction. Your ability to see the attacker clearly and have your feet between them and you is your first line of defense.

- *Stop their momentum.* If they suddenly rush toward you trying to get on top of you or to punch you, you can stop their forward momentum, prevent them from getting on top of you, and create space from punches by putting your legs up, placing your feet on their hips,

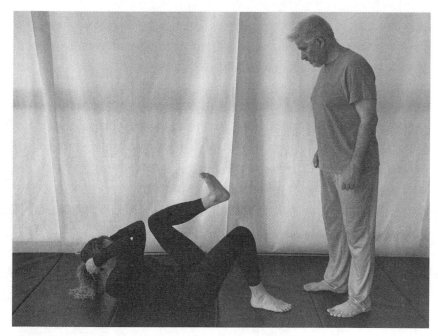

Figure 6.13: Stay facing them.

with strong, slightly bent legs. The aggressor might then work to remove your legs. These are details you will learn during in-person instruction. In addition to using your feet to block their body from advancing, you also need to block punches with the same helmet position you took in clinch (see Figure 6.14).

- *Pull them into guard.* One of the keys to making this technique work is making the timing of your moves unexpected by shifting your position when they least expect it. We are taught to not keep the bad guy standing against our feet for long. So after you block their initial approach, and if they are still leaning in toward you, you then pull them into your guard. Retract your legs and lower them toward you, all the while maintaining your helmet to block for any punches. As soon as they are close enough, you need to wrap your legs around their body, lock your ankles together, and use your arms to hold their neck and arm in guard if you can (see Figure 6.15). There are other

Figure 6.14: Stop their momentum.

Figure 6.15: Guard.

details you can learn during instruction to keep them close to you, to prevent punches, and to stop them from sitting up by forcing them to keep their hands on the ground.

- *Fill the space with your legs to prevent punches.* Even though you have them in guard, they may try to punch you in your ribs. You can use the principle of *if they make space fill it.* If you have your legs wrapped up high on their body, you will feel when they retract their arm to make the punch, and in that moment, you can also retract that leg, fill the space in front of their arm with your bent knee and, using your hand, grab their triceps and then slide your grip down to their wrist, securing it against your leg (see Figure 6.16). Further detailed instruction are often provided on the nuances of placing your legs to fill the space and how to bring the aggressor back into guard.

- *Push knees into their chest.* If they push back against your chest to make space to punch you, fill the space by bending your knees and

Figure 6.16: Filling the space with your legs to prevent punches.

pushing them up into the attacker's chest (Figure 6.17). This is often best practiced with someone the same size, so they can easily push back against your knees. Instructors are there to help if you and your partner are struggling to make it work. Sometimes they ask to have you switch partners or help the aggressor make adjustments to support the technique in the beginning.

- *Place feet on their hips.* If they go from in your guard to trying to push away and stand, you will make them work for it, by hanging on to them as long as you can with your arms and legs and while working to stay safe from punches. This drains their energy and lets them know you will not be an easy target. Then when you cannot safely hold on longer, you can give a push to their shoulders as you return to putting your feet on their hips and using your legs to push them away (see Figure 6.18). Look for instruction that discusses the safety issues of being picked up off the floor and when to pull them back in.

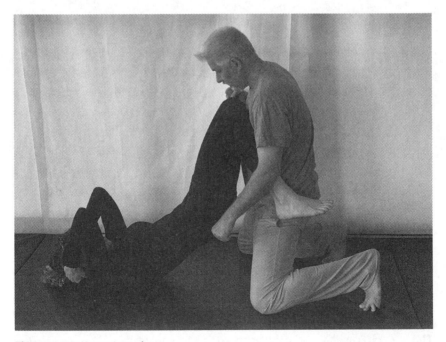

Figure 6.17: Knees into chest.

Figure 6.18: Feet on their hips.

- *Manage distance and timing to keep them confused.* A key principle being used here once again is *manage the distance, manage the damage.* If you can manage to keep them away all together by standing and retreating, this is often the preferred situation. If, however, they are committed to having a physical encounter, then you can either keep them far enough away or pull them in so close that their strikes are ineffective. If they work to make space, you make it difficult on them, exhausting their energy, while conserving yours. If they are finally able to make space in order to strike, fill the space with your legs.

In most systems this strategy is taught in stages. Working with a qualified instructor will help you to understand the various parts of the breakdown. Given the complexity of this move and its different stages, you can see how it could hold a wide variety of triggers for a trauma survivor. This technique is a great example of how the right partner might really help a survivor meet the challenge. If this is the first time a survivor is using guard, it can be difficult for them to have someone in-between their legs. Some students benefit from having a same-sex partner or someone they feel most comfortable with when they are first learning this move. If you are feeling you need a different partner you might simply state, "Thank you for partnering, I would like to try this with a different body type, so I need to switch partners." You might also consider communicating with your instructor that you are triggered and see if there is someone in the room that you both think could help you through the move.

Why Do Jiu-Jitsu Techniques Work?

As we covered in Chapter 1, there is something very unique about jiu-jitsu that can make it well suited for practice by trauma survivors. In this chapter we've explained some of the specific components of why this is the case, equipping trauma survivors so they know what to look for as they seek training. Other martial arts that rely on strikes for effectiveness are counting on years of training in order to know how to land a correct punch to the correct spot on a potentially moving and aggressive target. They also rely on strength and power to make the punch effective. Depending on the size and strength of the attacker, this might require a considerable force. In addition, striking martial arts are depending on the strikes to inflict pain and therefore win a fight by causing pain. If the attacker is high on drugs, they may have an extremely high pain tolerance, causing striking to be ineffective. If this is the case, the attacker may not even feel the pain of a broken arm delivered by a jiu-jitsu technique. However, that arm is now out of the battle and rendered ineffective in assaulting someone. Once more, jiu-jitsu is specifically designed to help a person, regardless of strength or size, defend against a larger, stronger opponent.

The techniques and approaches that we covered in this chapter will come alive for you once you can begin putting them into practice, especially with a safe partner and preferably under the guidance of a high-quality, trauma-responsive instructor. Like many helpful practices, just reading about them in a book will have limited benefits—you must get into the arena and practice them. We continue to wish you success on that journey and hope that some of the ideas in the book, specifically in this chapter, are proving helpful to you in starting, rebooting, or continuing your journey.

TRY THIS Situational Awareness Drills

Situational awareness is an important phrase in self-defense, and it is a skill that can be built without ever once stepping inside a jiu-jitsu school. When Jamie asked Brian Needham, a tactical self-defense specialist and the owner of Combat Performance Academy in Warren, Ohio, how she can better practice the attunement required for situational awareness, what he shared with her sounded just like a mindfulness exercise. He threw in a little psychodrama for good measure by suggesting that you can also learn a great deal by stepping into the mental role of an attacker, even if just for a few moments.

Here are two specific practices that you can try. Like we say in many forms of mindfulness training, and in trauma-focused therapy in general, notice whatever it is you may notice. This is a learning experience above anything else. Use the feedback that your body-mind complex gives you, and perhaps document what you discover in your journal, or consider engaging in conversation with your therapist, your jiu-jitsu instructor, or a trusted friend.

Practice #1

- Go to a public place like a park or a festival. Set an intention to scan your environment and notice anything that is a certain color (e.g., red).

- Then scan the same environment with an extra attention to detail. Let's say specifically look for people who are wearing red.

- Pay attention to both the mental devices (e.g., what you see or hear) and what you feel at a body or visceral level.

- As you continue to work with this practice, especially listening to the mental and verbal cues in your body, notice if anything seems out of the ordinary. Does your body especially give you any information that might suggest something is off or doesn't quite seem safe?

Practice #2

- Take five minutes in the parking lot of a place like a large department store or a shopping mall, a place where you feel safe enough to be in your vehicle and won't draw too much attention to yourself.

- As you are willing, step into the role of a predator and think how they might think. Who looks like easy prey? In this people-watching and attunement exercise, pay attention to who might be most susceptible.

- Remember that aggressors or predators generally observe first, even before they move into posturing or positioning. This applies to violence of all kinds. What can you learn about situational awareness through the practice of observing? How can taking on the role of aggressor, if only for a few moments, help you learn what you may need to know in order to keep yourself safe?

Seven

For Clinicians, Therapists, and Educators

There are an infinite number of ways in which people suffer. Therefore, there must be an infinite number of ways in which Dharma is available to people.

—A 98-YEAR-OLD CHAN BUDDHIST MASTER,
AS SHARED WITH JON KABAT-ZINN

Non-clinicians (for example, trauma survivors and jiu-jitsu instructors/ practitioners) are invited to read this chapter in an effort to familiarize themselves with the options therapists may consider in assisting survivors and instructors on their jiu-jitsu trauma-recovery journey. We hope that this information will help the survivors among you communicate your expectations and help you find a good fit with the right therapist for your own individual work. For the instructors, the information presented here may assist you in choosing clinical partners with whom to build collaborative relationships in your community. Therapists vary greatly in terms of the therapeutic approaches that they use and their philosophical orientation. Many therapists can still be oriented in a Western-dominated mindset of orientation in the head and heart, as cultural somatics expert Tada Hozumi observes in his writing.[1] While there is an increasing shift toward understanding more body-oriented approaches to healing than are necessary for effectively working with trauma at all levels, including healing our own connections to racial and intergenerational trauma, many therapists still lack this vital somatic education and reorientation.

Good therapists are on the constant lookout for new tools, skills, or approaches that can help their clients. Sadly, the top-down approach of modern graduate schooling in the West leaves many of us unprepared or underprepared for dealing with the realities of trauma. Although both Anna and Jamie have experience in training other therapists, offering trauma-focused therapy training is Jamie's primary vocational mission. She regularly meets therapists who come for training because they recognize that what they have in their skillset is simply inadequate for fully treating trauma. Because conventionally cognitive or verbal approaches to therapy only work outside-in, leaving the body and often the emotions out of the equation, even very naturally skilled people find themselves stuck. Educators often face the same problem—they may have a deep desire to really reach students, regardless of the age group with which they practice. Yet unhealed trauma can cause great activation in the body, making cognitive connections difficult, if not impossible. In therapy, all human services, and education we must not neglect the wisdom of the body. The body provides us with a treasure trove of information about our own stressors and responses, and the way to full and total healing runs through the entire body-mind complex.

All of the martial arts, especially jiu-jitsu, may be an option for your clients in their healing journey. We are not suggesting that you have to learn physical jiu-jitsu to teach it to them, yet having a grounding in some of the philosophy (at minimum) can be helpful. Working with the "Try This" practices throughout the book may also seem doable for you. And you may be inspired to work collaboratively with jiu-jitsu instructors in the community in a variety of ways.

This chapter highlights many of the benefits that a healthy exposure to jiu-jitsu can provide and orients clinicians to how these qualities can enrich a therapeutic experience. These qualities include improved self-awareness, increased emotional regulation skills, improved communication skills, practicing the art of choosing, building connections to a community, and learning the power of altruism through being a good partner and passing on lessons learned. Although our language in this chapter is largely therapeutic, other human services professionals (e.g., nonclinical social workers, probation officers) and educators can apply what feels relevant and useful for them. We give further insights into how clinicians can assist clients in finding the best possible training environments for the people that they serve. Additionally, elements of jiu-jitsu philosophy are presented that clinicians may consider weaving into their work, whether or not they ever personally step on a mat. Who knows? You may discover that there is something in the practice for you, too!

We write this chapter recognizing that your interest in this area may simply be at the level of finding an appropriate facility or trainer for your client or student. If that is the case, we hope that you will be able to integrate what the client or student is learning from their jiu-jitsu training into your work together. Some of you may be just as enthusiastic about jiu-jitsu or other martial arts yourselves, so there may be more dynamic opportunities for collaboration. And others of you may fall somewhere in the middle. We hope that this chapter gives you some ideas that will serve your clients and students while working within the parameters of your practice.

Vetting Your Jiu-Jitsu Facilities and Instructors for Partnership

If you are going to assist your clients in having a healthy and healing jiu-jitsu experience, the first challenge is to find jiu-jitsu facilities and instructors for collaboration. As we emphasize throughout this book, some facilities, instructors, and students have the potential to cause trauma and would be contraindicated at best, retraumatizing and damaging at worst. Optimally, you want your clients attending a program that is truly invested in being trauma-informed. More and more teachers and facilities are desiring to make this commitment, and we've written Chapter 7 to assist and guide instructors and facilities in the ongoing process of being and staying trauma informed.

Please consider that one school may work well for certain clients or students and their ideas, and another school in the same town may be more appropriate for someone else. For instance, for female survivors of sexual trauma, finding a school with a good women's program, like Gracie University or others in that system, may be imperative. For a veteran or a person working in public safety, a facility like Brian Needham's Combat Performance Academy may be a better fit. Brian explains that a primary mission of his school is to create community for veterans and public servants, describing that on some days, people just show up to hang out, and connecting at this level is welcome.

At a minimum, we recommend that you visit multiple facilities in the same way that we ask our clients to do, perhaps taking it a step further. If you personally train, then get onto the mats and experience the vibe for yourself. Put yourself in the shoes of a severe trauma survivor and observe what is helpful and potentially unhelpful at this particular facility. In Chapter 5, we gave an in-depth explanation for trauma survivors of what to look for at a facility and why such qualities are important. Please make sure you've read that chapter yourself, and remember that the checklist we've prepared for evaluating a facility appears in the Appendix. Keep in mind that finding gym owners and a staff who are willing to learn and to collaborate might be more important than getting a perfect score on this checklist.

Ask Questions

You will want to interview the facility owner and instructors to understand if they have any knowledge of trauma, are claiming to be trauma informed, and are willing to partner and learn. Asking them some questions about how they handle people being triggered can help you know how they might treat clients if they are struggling. Notice how you feel in your own body when you listen to their responses to get a read of both their vibe and the quality of their approach to working with survivors.

The following are some questions that you may consider asking:

1. Have you ever experienced a student who experienced panic, a flashback, or other distress in class?

2. If so, how did you handle that situation?

3. Did you do any follow-up with that student that night or the following day?

4. What do you know about how trauma affects our thinking and behaviors?

5. Are students allowed to come and go from class as needed?

6. What is your approach for working with larger-bodied students?

7. How do you handle students (or instructors) who may show disrespect to other students?

8. Do you have any vetted psychology professional resources on file to provide to students who are struggling with mental health issues?

9. What is the overall focus and mission of your school?

This list is not exhaustive but does offer a good start. If there are questions you may need to add based on knowledge of your client base or the dynamics in your region, go ahead and ask.

Recommending Jiu-Jitsu to Clients

Like all therapeutic modalities, jiu-jitsu might be indicated or contraindicated for a particular client. Some clients might come to you who are already training in jiu-jitsu and have been triggered or who have gone through a negative experience. Some have already chosen to try jiu-jitsu but haven't picked a school yet. Many clients won't even know what jiu-jitsu is, let alone that practicing it may be helpful.

Research of specific clinical treatment protocols for jiu-jitsu is only just beginning, even though an emerging body of research covered in Chapter 1 speaks to the healing and therapeutic properties of jiu-jitsu. In Chapter 9 we will share our thoughts on research that we hope to see in the future. Until then, you should carefully consider the question of when it is appropriate to offer jiu-jitsu to a client as a therapeutic tool. Long before we found jiu-jitsu for ourselves, we often examined the option of self-defense with our client population, knowing that there were protective benefits and perhaps opportunities for reparative experiences. Now, after having several years of jiu-jitsu experience and research in hand, we sometimes specifically recommend jiu-jitsu to trauma survivors, or people experiencing anxiety, depression, self-esteem issues, and a variety of other problems caused by adverse life experiences.

At various points in therapy based on what the client is presenting with, we will offer jiu-jitsu as a potential option for the client to explore. We will summarize the preliminary research that shows the benefits of trauma-informed jiu-jitsu on improved sense of self-efficacy, self-esteem, and empowerment as well as providing a new way to process and recover from trauma. Based on our clinical training and legal advisement, our therapeutic implementation of client treatment incorporating jiu-jitsu can generally be described as follows:

1. If anxiety and fear are prominent in the client presentation, psychoeducation on the option of self-defense training and referrals to three different trauma-informed resources can be considered in treatment planning.

2. If a seasoned client to your practice is stable enough, has exhausted all other therapeutic options, has built emotion regulation, awareness, and communication skills, and feels stuck or ready to try something new, jiu-jitsu can be considered in treatment planning.

3. If you feel that the risk of engaging in jiu-jitsu might outweigh the benefits for a client, consider consulting with colleagues on that particular case prior to bringing the idea of jiu-jitsu into session with the client.

4. If the clinical decision has been made to share the idea of jiu-jitsu, assess the client's knowledge of it, asking if they are aware of jiu-jitsu and any thoughts they have about it.

5. If your client does not have knowledge of jiu-jitsu, explain jiu-jitsu's core concept of using leverage as a defensive advantage against a bigger, stronger person. We often show the client a very abbreviated version of the wrist release, explaining that the weakest point lies between the thumb and the fingers. This technique demonstrates that leverage is often counterintuitive, because in order to release the wrist, you need to get closer to the attacker. Moving closer to

someone with bad intent is often the opposite of our instincts. It is not uncommon for workshops filled with newcomers to jiu-jitsu to exclaim "wow" throughout their first training, as easily executed wrist releases are shockingly effective. For trauma survivors, Anna might also share how a person being held down can use points of leverage to quickly reverse the roles and get to safety. These types of experiences, in turn, help to rewrite our brain's and body's experiences of not having any control over our own safety and can, over time, instill in us a sense of confidence. Preliminary research suggests that this can not only work to heal trauma but also empower survivors to take this newfound courage into many other aspects of their daily lives with work, family, and more.

6. The pros and cons of jiu-jitsu in the client's eyes and based on clinician's knowledge of both client triggers and the jiu-jitsu experience are examined. Because we have both trained in jiu-jitsu, it is easier for us to answer the many questions that clients might have if they don't know anything about it. If you as a clinician are not a jiu-jitsu practitioner, you can bring jiu-jitsu instructors into the process at this point to answer questions.

7. We believe that client choice is imperative in healing and always accentuate that the clinician will support whatever decision a client makes. Clinicians must never pressure a client and ought to make it clear that they gain nothing personally if the client decides to try jiu-jitsu.

Treatment protocols and best practices will continue to evolve and develop as research and experience is gained. We simply share this outline as a point of discussion that will surely become outdated as we discover clinically indicated changes. We recommend that you keep up to date with any research available to support your clinical approach.

Work with Your Clients to Explore a Variety of Schools

When your client is ready to begin the process of exploring schools, there is much you can do to assist them. Exploring schools can be an important part of the trauma healing process. Empowering clients to research their options reaffirms that they have choice. Again, trauma is done without choice, and therefore every point at which choice can be emphasized is important to the healing process. Help them review the list of considerations and value their individual impressions and experiences of each facility and the instructors that they encounter. Such review accentuates the power of their choices and validates their experiences. An interesting note that speaks to the varieties of individuals' experience: some people we interviewed for this project had wonderful experiences at a school that they shared with us, and other interviewees offered negative feedback about the same school! No one school is perfect, and even that is in the eye of the beholder. The better challenge may be to help people find the school that is the best possible fit for them.

Validating choice at any moment is also key. Some trauma survivors have been shamed and blamed by saying that they "led their perpetrator on." A great deal of work is being done in many communities to educate people of all genders that it is okay, at any point in time, to express that you don't want a physical interaction with someone. Just because an intimate experience has started does not mean that both partners are mandated to continue. This is also true of our attachment to instructors and facilities. In many sports and martial arts communities, there can be an unspoken rule on the need to be "loyal" to your gym or instructor. In many ways, such implied pressure can mimic abuse, or at very least, toxic family dynamics, for clients. Let them know that they have absolutely no obligation to stay at one facility or with one instructor. They have a choice at all times to stop, switch, or move to different facilities or instructors.

The Politics and Culture of Jiu-Jitsu Schools

So let's say that your client or student has been inspired to at least try out jiu-jitsu, or maybe even to join a school. As the process unfolds for the student, we encourage clinicians to make sure that students know that they are allowed to switch gyms at any time. That said, we must acknowledge that the belt or ranking system at most schools can feel complicated, and this may prove to be another point of discussion for your client's healing process. Some clients may not even be interested in belt rankings at all; they just want to learn a bit of self-defense to help them recover from their traumatic stress issues. This can make all this talk about belts, rankings, and tests that they hear about at schools even more overwhelming. In the sections that follow, we give you a brief orientation to some dynamics that may come up at schools and how you can help clients address them.

Many schools of jiu-jitsu have a belt ranking system as follows; stripes indicate gradient levels of progress within a particularly belt category:

1. White (1–4 stripes)
2. Blue (1–4 stripes)
3. Purple (1–4 stripes)
4. Brown (1–4 stripes)
5. Black (1–6 degrees)
6. Seventh-degree black belt = coral belt is awarded (also known as Master).
7. Ninth-degree black belt = red belt is awarded (Grandmaster of which there are very few in the world).

Some programs have differentiated belts for children under 18 (yellow stripe, solid yellow, orange stripe, solid orange, green stripe, solid green), women (pink), and self-defense street fighting "combative belt" (blue stripe).

Clinicians might want to open a discussion with the client on the process of switching between schools. New instructors and training partners provide an important opportunity for students to practice proactive communication to advocate for themselves and share their goals and needs. Role-play practice in session with the clinician can be useful for some clients. Some trauma histories leave survivors fearful of asking for what they need or expressing their feelings. There is a potential therapeutic opportunity to have a corrective experience in which the client's voice is welcomed, heard, and honored. Some examples follow.

If you are a purple belt at one facility, you may not be given that status immediately at the next facility. You may or may not even want that. This is because a purple belt in the new facility may be expected to have knowledge in certain techniques that you do not. If your training partners believe you have that type of experience, this could cause issues in sparring and even potential injury. On the other hand, you might know more than you realize and have a potential advantage over other partners in the new facility, which means you could be sand bagging. *Sand bagging* is deliberately underperforming in a race or competition to gain an unfair advantage.

Anna remembers when she first heard of sand bagging as it relates to jiu-jitsu. She spent a great deal of time treating clients who train in jiu-jitsu because of a connection between the sober living community where she worked and its connections to a jiu-jitsu school. Anna was shaped by the pain and frustration that her clients expressed for the lengthy periods of time between belt promotions in jiu-jitsu. Other clients with professional sports careers also left their impression on her. There was a win-at-all-costs mentality that, over time, gradually grew like a cancer in clients young and old, and in their families, too. Physical pain, emotional pain, extensive amounts of time, and significant financial investments were made for winning at the sport at the expense of everything else. No time or energy was left for resting, connecting with friends, or enjoying hobbies. Despite all the desperate efforts to win, clients were often left with nothing significant but injuries to show for it. The main takeaway for Anna from this was that she should never lose sight of why she chose to engage in any sport in the first place. Her clients had lost sight of the fun. Their focus on the next belt or the next medal dried up every last bit of enjoyment and replaced it with intense emotional suffering.

As Anna started her jiu-jitsu journey, she was very satisfied with her white belt. She had no desire whatsoever for the next belt or even the stripes that began to accumulate. That thinking was only magnified one day when she was starting a roll with a new partner whom she had never sparred with before. She shared that she didn't know any foot locks and to please not use them because she wouldn't even know when to tap. The gentleman said in response, "Don't worry, I won't really go for them until you're a blue belt." He had a cat-like predator smile as he said it. Anna was definitely not on the mats to become someone else's prey. She sincerely believed that he didn't mean any harm, and yet it sent a clear message. Anna's immediate conclusion in that moment was that she never wanted to have a blue belt. In her head, blue belt now equated to "my ankles and feet are now at risk." Since then, she has had many corrective experiences with other partners who supported her and thanked her for asking them not to use foot locks. Regardless, this experience still informs her that the higher-ranking belts hold a type of responsibility. They hold responsibility, to not only protect and not hurt their partners, but also be ready to defend their bodies from a vast variety of potential injury.

When instructors started to ask Anna when she would test for her pink belt (the special belt awarded in the *Women Empowered* curriculum that is not a part of the mainstream ranking system), it was a sign that they felt she was ready and knew the *Women Empowered* curriculum. She contemplated the meaning of the belt testing for herself:

> I came to the conclusion that yet again, I didn't want the next belt, but I did indeed want to assess my skills. So I decided to belt test. As soon as Rener explained that I had passed, my next question was, "Do I have to wear the pink belt, because I would rather not. I'd like to keep my white belt." I explained why. Rener stated simply, you must wear the new belt, "if not you are sand bagging." It struck me that people could definitely see it that way. Even though that was not my goal or intent to have any hidden advantages in any way shape or form. So I wore the belt and the next two after that, as communication tools, even though I still don't really want them in my heart of hearts.

In addition to preventing sand bagging, the belts help to identify who has what to offer to newer students. In an effort to provide a positive experience for new students, many facilities ask the higher-ranking belts to train with lower-ranking belts. This helps both partners. Most schools have belt rankings from novice to expert as follows: white, blue, purple, brown, black. At some schools they designate special belts for women's self-defense programs (pink) and also for street fight skills (blue stripe). The white belt can gain insight on the techniques and is often safer training with a higher belt who knows how to move bodies so that people don't get hurt. In turn, the higher belt gets to practice explaining and showing, reinforcing their knowledge and even making them think through questions they might not have considered before.

Even within a gym, there are expectations of what a student knows and is able to defend against based on their belt. Switching across gyms complicates this further, as the curriculum to achieve a specific belt can vary greatly. If a new gym insists that new students come in with their prior gym belt status, they can work to stay safe by simply telling partners to go slow, until they discover what they know and don't know in their new jiu-jitsu house. Students may require some time and adjustment to get to know their new community of training partners and instructor(s), and you as clinicians may be valuable in supporting them through this transition. The goal for them is to be patient and communicate well on what they know, what they are trying to learn, and how the roll energy is for them. Numerous tips for communicating with training partners are discussed in Chapter 5.

Identifying Goals and Intentions

All clients will make up their own mind as to the significance of the belt promotions. You can help them examine what healthy goals are for them in a way that optimally serves their recovery. Some clients may have corrective experiences in having the promotions or competitive events, which is not bad either. The main consideration is that you keep an eye out for any unhealthy shifts from enjoyment, growth, community, and acquiring safety skills to obsession with the next promotion, unhealthy levels of training, and/or any mental health symptoms that are caused or exacerbated by the color of their belt. Discuss the clients' goals in advance of training and come up with a value statement that it can help to refer back to in case the client drifts into difficulties. However, this is not to say that changing goals and working to become a black belt, instructor, or gym owner is something negative. On the contrary, if these activities are supporting mental health for this client, then they can be healthy goals too. As you already know, it's an individual journey. Respect and support a healthy journey for your client.

Jamie, for instance, continues to train in jiu-jitsu without any clear-cut goals. Her initial goal was to learn how to more effectively be in her body and then to better defend herself. Once she realized that there was a specific belt in the Gracie University system for women's self-defense (the *Women*

Empowered pink belt), she pursued that with gusto. Shortly after earning her belt, she was able to leave her toxic marriage, which felt like the real reward of engaging in this work. After that, training to earn more belts, or even learning how to spar, never really appealed to her. She recently had a conversation with her coach (Micah Bender) on her continued goals for jiu-jitsu. Jamie honestly answered, "I don't have any goals, but my intention is to keep reviewing and to keep training so that my body feels as good as it does after a session . . . with greater regularity. I missed that when I stopped my regular training."

Jamie's emphasis on intention brings an important concept from yoga, Buddhist meditation, the martial arts, and many non-Western approaches to healing. An intention is a seed that you plant, not an outcome that you force. With intention, you are setting a clear aim, yet the overwhelm of striving to meet goals is not an issue. As one of Jamie's yoga teachers, Dr. Kamini Desai, taught her, intentions are more reality-friendly; they are malleable. They come with a dimension of letting go of the outcome even though you are setting a definite course of the journey. Jamie also teaches in other areas of her work that for trauma survivors, intentions may feel more doable than goals at first. Or it could be, as in Jamie's case, that the language of intention will always work better than the language of goals.

We also recognize that the language and meaning of goals may work better for other clients. Consider the potential healing opportunity in helping your clients to avoid any unhealthy shifts in goals. Many start out in their particular sport because they enjoyed it and wanted to learn more or grow stronger. As time goes on, goals can shift to focus on winning and promotions. Gui Valente believes that unhealthy shifts in judo and jiu-jitsu can occur when they become purely competitive sports. He explained how there are two key elements to both judo and jiu-jitsu, one of which gets lost in the switch to competitive sport. These elements are the principle of maximum efficiency/minimum effort, and mutual welfare and benefit (*jita-kyoei* 自他共榮). Gui explains that you can only do well if everyone else around you is doing well. Gui shared with us that before grandmaster Helio passed away, he was upset at what was happening to judo because of the competitive sporting element. According to Valente, Helio never kept any of the money from fights for that exact reason. Gui points out how this happens across many sports, not just judo or jiu-jitsu. This win-at-any-cost mentality can be seen in the NCAA and in professional sports of all kinds. Valente highlights that this aspect of the sports world can cause people to lose sight of the original fun and growth that they were seeking.

Such a mentality is not just a problem in collegiate and professional sports. Western society, with its historical focus on head and/or heart orientations without paying attention to the fullness of the body, has become increasingly driven by success and performance-based metrics. This influence has sadly permeated into so many societies and cultures globally. In our experience, many people end up abandoning physical activities like jiu-jitsu and other sports or enjoyable activities such as yoga, dance, or the arts because they believe they are not good at it. What if we took this performance-based language out of our vocabularies? What more could we learn about ourselves and the process? This mentality does not negate the pursuit of excellence by any means. We are simply suggesting that there might be more to gain by trusting the process instead of obsessing over the outcomes. As therapists, other helpers, and educators, we are in prime positions to help people consider these shifts in approach.

The Therapeutic Approach

We now transition into some best practices in the realm of the therapeutic approach for working with clients who want to add jiu-jitsu to their healing journey. Like with any other trauma client, you will want to establish a good working alliance with these clients and do thorough, trauma-informed assessments. It is also essential that you help them build an emotion regulation toolbox and ways to communicate and name escalation of any symptoms and/or emotional flooding they experience. These practices will allow your clients to share or otherwise process their stories with you at a healthy pace. While specific recovery goals may vary from client to client, our hope is that clients who engage in therapy will be able to live a more healthful and adaptive life.

A major part of Jamie's teaching is that gone are the days of sending our clients to a *specialist* to work on trauma. Unhealed trauma is so ubiquitous that all helpers are trauma therapists whether they realize it or not. All human services professionals and educators are working in the world of wound care. If you need a review on these realities, please revisit Chapter 2. While specialty training in trauma is optimal, preferably in advanced modalities like EMDR therapy, trauma-focused CBT, Somatic Experiencing, or Sensorimotor Psychotherapy, we hope that you are at least inspired to get some more training on universal best practices for working with trauma as highlighted in Chapter 2, especially if you don't have it already. One of these strategies, as identified by the Substance Abuse and Mental Health Services Administration (SAMSHA), is to create collaborative opportunities with all available resources in the community. We've emphasized how you can do this already by suggesting jiu-jitsu or working with clients who already use their practice in concert with what therapy can afford. What follows are some more specific ideas for therapeutic engagement that will help you further unite the possibilities.

Building the Tool Box: Extended Grounding

Many basic tools for emotion regulation were outlined in Chapters 4 and 5. If your client has already read those chapters, some of the psychoeducational work has been taken care of for you. Confirm their understanding of the tools and that they have practiced and mastered. In session, work to answer any client questions and also practice raising their scaling number (Chapter 4) by talking about things that cause them agitation. As a reminder, 1, 2, 3 is at ease, 4, 5, 6 is uncomfortable but where the work and growth is happening, and 8, 9, 10 is often too much. We can then have them practice using the tools they developed such as progressive muscle relaxation or grounding, for example (also covered in Chapter 4), to see if they are able to move the needle in the right direction. We always remind our clients that they have complete control over the objectives of the session and whether or not they want to work on tool building and that they can always stop or pause working on a tool at any point in time or change subjects if they need the grounding or assurance.

Jamie likes to share with her trainees that she has been practicing EMDR therapy for over fifteen years, is a yoga teacher, a meditation teacher, an expressive arts therapist, and a jiu-jitsu player . . . *and* she is still always on the lookout for new grounding tools to show to her clients. Anna feels similarly—you cannot have too many. For those reasons, we have placed a lengthier grounding process in the following "Try This" exercise that clinicians can use to assist their clients in the extended grounding process that goes past simply finding your toes.

TRY THIS Noticing the Surface Below You

Lift and place each foot on the ground with the intention of noticing, without your eyes, what you think the surface is made of.

Anna's office is on a second floor with carpeted floors. She asks her clients to put aside their visual channel or their memory to describe what the surface below them is made of. Is it concrete, wood, sand, dirt, or something else? She has them guess all the way to the ground. Here is an example:

Client: There is a carpet under my feet.

Therapist: And under that?

Client: Wood flooring.

Therapist: And under that?

The answers are usually carpeting, plywood, beams, drywall ceiling, the room below, the floor under than and finally the earth underneath. Then ask two more questions:

- Will this surface hold you?

- Are you safe? Or at least safe enough?

From there, notice how your clothes start touching your legs. If you are wearing jeans or pants, you may already notice a sensation at your ankle. If you're in shorts or a skirt, the sensation may be higher up your leg. Describe the sensation. Are they tight, loose, soft, or scratchy? Is the sensation comfortable or uncomfortable? Then move up and notice your bottom connecting to the surface below it. Next, work to find the spot where most of your weight is being held. Connect to that spot and how it feels to sit on that surface. If you are sitting on a wooden chair, that would be different than sitting on a couch, a sandy beach, or in the grass. Describe the sensation. For instance, a couch wraps around you a little, but the wood of a chair is firm. Notice if it's comfortable or uncomfortable. Is there anything you can do to make it more comfortable? Again, ask the two questions:

- Will this surface hold you?

- Are you safe? Or at least safe enough?

Now see if you can allow your back and head to lean or rest against a surface behind you, if possible. We both keep a variety of couch pillows in our offices and ask people to try having pillows under their arms and to notice if they feel more secure with the pillows or without the pillows. Many clients say that having support underneath is better. People with tension in their necks will often feel some relief there when they relax their heads back. The goal here is to relax or ease your body as much as possible, sinking into the surface below you and allowing it to hold you.

Body Scan

Body scan techniques are also very useful in clinical work. Unhealed trauma can leave clients feeling very disconnected from their bodies, as we discussed in Chapter 2, so while on the surface body scanning techniques can seem very elementary, they may play as radical and new interventions for your clients. There are many ways to guide clients through body scans, from the very simple approaches used in EMDR therapy (e.g., "Scan your body from head to toe . . . what are you noticing now?"), to more intricate, part-by-part awareness strategies from the mindfulness traditions. In this section, we go through a few more approaches to body scanning. You are also welcome to check out Jamie's video resources site at www.traumamadesimple.com/videos for more ideas and experiential instruction.

BASIC BODY SCAN.   To set up a basic body scan, we generally invite clients to follow our direction as they scan the body, part by part, from the top of the head down to the base of the feet. In the spirit of variation and offering modifications, you may suggest that clients may feel better about starting at the base of the feet and working their way up. You can start by asking them to notice any muscles, for example, in their face, that are doing any work. Eyelids can be particularly difficult to let go of. Then, invite them to be curious, to notice if they can let those muscles go. See if they can allow those muscles to get heavy and be supported by the surface below them.

Then, move slowly on to the jaw, neck, shoulders, triceps, biceps, forearms, wrists, fingers, chest, back, belly, bottom, gluts, quads, knees, calves, ankles, feet, and toes. See if they can let those muscles go. For each body part, ask them to notice and investigate if they can allow those muscles to get heavy and be supported by the surface below them. At the end of any style of body scan, it is generally advised to have your client or student scan their body as a whole—from the top of the head down to the feet, and/or from the feet up to the crown of the head.

PICK YOUR FAVORITE PART AND MAKE IT YOURS.   This is a somewhat lengthy process, but it can be interesting to ask the following:

- What was your favorite part of this experience?
- Where did you notice the biggest shift?
- Did you like or dislike the exercise or parts of the exercise?

All opinions are valid.

Although it can be time-consuming to do this whole grounding exercise, clients can eventually pare it down by first practicing the whole thing but then later selecting a part that resonates the most with them.

Sometimes that's simply noticing the toes. Giving yourself permission to allow your muscles to get heavy and feel supported by the surface beneath is often a favorite part of this experience for many clients. They may also customize this activity and put whatever language they relate to in the exercise. If they want a recording or your voice on their phone guiding them through the process, consider providing it—that can make it easier for them to practice and recall it when they need to.

Helping Clients Orient and Examine Their Choices

Preparation is a collaborative process between client and clinician. After the client has properly prepared a full toolbox of awareness and emotion regulation strategies, the process of building a desensitization plan can begin. Clinician and client can work together to prevent or at least manage flooding with the practice of scaling (see Chapter 4). If using scaling, please be advised that how people experience the various numbers may vary—a 7 for Jamie may feel like a 4 for Anna. So please avoid making assumptions and use scaling as a helpful guide if the clients find it helpful, not an absolute measure. Clients may need to engage in the process of *titration*, or alternating between discomfort and putting down the proverbial weight and transitioning to something more restful. They can then "lift the weight" again and then rest, just as they would with repetitions in a gym. Plan to have the client de-escalate and rest before the end of the session to help them leave the session in as calm a state as possible. Clients should be forewarned that this type of work can leave them with some intrusive recollections and vivid dreams. Remind clients to use their tools and/or call for assistance if they need it. You know your clients best; sometimes they have difficulty naming their number or don't want to use this approach, in which case, you have to keep your eye out for signs of distress and collaboratively determine the best plan of action. Remember that protecting your clients from all experiences of distress is neither realistic nor helpful. Rather, how can you help them manage the distress and work from their plan of action when it does arise?

When we work to create a desensitization plan, some clients will be able to move more quickly through the process than others. In clients for whom flooding happens quickly and the trauma was severe, it is a good idea to go slowly and proceed with care. Remember the jiu-jitsu teaching that *slow is smooth, and smooth is fast*? Much of that same logic can apply here as well. Although the skill of desensitization has many applications in therapy, in the sections that follow, we will be offering you examples specific to jiu-jitsu. As a note, depending on what type of training your client may choose to pursue and at what level of intensity, some of these strategies may not apply. Use what feels relevant and leave the rest.

Hearing the List and Descriptions of Techniques

Every client is different and every treatment plan will vary as a result. How trauma affects one person can be extremely different from the way it affects another, as we outlined in Chapter 2. There are clients who will not need or want to read a list of techniques in advance and who are ready to dive in right away. Others will want to know more about what to expect, and in severe cases, private lessons (if available) with an adjustable curriculum might be best. The following is a description of one way to approach the most severe cases; you can scale back this approach as needed. We acknowledge that not all clients will be able to afford private lessons and not all schools will be comfortable with curriculum changes. In those cases, clients can develop a plan to either (a) not attend a specific class, or (b) simply sit out of certain moves in the beginning and observe. The key is to accentuate that the client has a choice.

Many clinicians reinforce that clients choose how to use their therapy session time. Specifically, they can choose how much planning they feel they need to do in advance of jiu-jitsu training; they can choose how much control they need over what they are exposed to when. To understand where your client is, we suggest simply asking them what they know about the training, what they are expecting it to be like, what they think they might like about it, and if they foresee any challenges. You might simply explore options in exposure therapy: ask clients if they think it's useful to review the curriculum together, to gather more information via videos, to break down the possibilities in instruction, or whether they are excited to simply jump right in.

In the most conservative approach, the first step is simply working to read the list of training techniques (see Chapter 6) and then starting to describe what the specific techniques involve. Clinicians who train will be able to share some guidance. Clinicians who do not will need an instructor's assistance and might simply invite the client to discuss the techniques with their instructor. Anna likes to check in with her clients, asking them, "What is it like to hear the names of the techniques?" Typically she gets a range of responses, from excitement to learn more and get started, to anxiety simply from hearing the names. If a client expresses concern or fear, Anna invites them to explore the worry. "Would you like to discuss more specifically where the concern is coming up for you?"

Client responses vary. Sometimes a specific technique that concerns them will come up or a sense of being overwhelmed by the number of moves or even general questions about how the class begins and how partners are chosen. This discussion can bring up a wealth of information on what the client is thinking and what they might find difficult. If you have watched the classes or attended yourself, you will be able to speak to their concerns and/or offer them the possibility of talking directly with the instructor. Not only can such a discussion provide further client assessment, it can also work to desensitize them to what to expect. For those clients who find it necessary, work to prioritize the list from least triggering to most triggering, or simply have them identify any techniques that seem triggering.

If, for example, a client has been assaulted from behind, any techniques that start from or involving an attack from the rear might be moved down to the end of the list if this feels appropriate to the client. In this way, the client might gain some momentum and self-efficacy with less-triggering techniques first. Starting with least intimidating moves can allow clients to get used to jiu-jitsu in general. This also allows survivors to acclimate to a new environment, with new types of physical contact with strangers. The hope is that once they have gained confidence and strength in some basic skills, and with the support of familiar partners and a trauma-informed environment, the triggering techniques won't be so intimidating. When the scaling numbers are moving in the right direction and staying low, your client could potentially be ready to move onto the next step. The hope is that we can help clients tolerate discomfort and avoid flooding, or at the very least, manage it well if it happens. As a therapist, you could check in with the client to ask again, "What is it like for you to hear the descriptions of each technique?" Sometimes clients need to take breaks or even retreat to prior steps. If they have other current difficulties outside of overcoming the trauma, they may not have the capacity at this time to continue the work. Timing is important.

For all of the following topics of consideration, it is an individual decision whether a clinician's assistance is needed for the process of not. Some of these topics are things that can be discussed in the clinician's office in advance. Discussions concerning what order techniques are learned, who the client would like to bring with them, whether the client needs to watch a technique before trying it, and so on can be discussed and planned in advance. Similar to exposure therapy, in these situations clinicians work with clients to make plans to build tolerance to the challenging experience and carefully consider an individual client's potential triggers. In more severe cases, it can be useful to examine all these topics up front in-office and then plan to have the clinician present to assist in assessment (scaling) and de-escalation if it is needed while at the school. In less severe cases, clients may not need any planning in advance or any in-person support from a clinician. However, even without a trauma history, many people feel safer doing something new when they have friends along.

There are choices to make regarding which of the techniques your client wants to explore and in what order. For example, a client could choose to

1. Only do certain techniques they deem important.

2. Do all the techniques that are less triggering across the steps and then circle back to take on a single triggering technique. This could be done by potentially skipping specific group classes until the client is ready or by taking private lessons.

3. Do all techniques in whatever predesigned order they want in order to master them all in each step before they move to the next. This would most likely require private lessons.

Therapists can work with their clients to examine what is needed and to make a potential plan. Anna often simply lays out the potential options and then lets the client examine what they feel would work best for them.

Every survivor is different, and some will not require all of the suggestions in the following sections. Another potential consideration is to ask what they plan to do after they leave every training. Having a post-training ritual, which can include listening to certain music, taking a bath or shower, getting something to eat, or checking in with a friend, may be useful. They may want to journal about their experiences, take notes on the techniques, or shift gears away from the experience. We highly recommend that you discuss these post-training plans with the client, just as you may discuss what they do in between intense trauma therapy sessions. Some survivors have no problems on the mat, but later they can recall new memories or have vivid dreams as their body and mind begin to reprocess prior traumas. In severe cases, it can be a good idea to plan to check in a day or two after exposure as part of the process.

Seeing Pictures or Watching Videos

A next optional step can be to simply find pictures of and/or watch videos depicting the move in action. Many programs are offering more and more online and through video training, especially in the COVID-19 era. Although a variety of free videos abound on YouTube, quality can vary. Advise your client to check in with their own instructors about what sources are best for good content. As a therapist, you could check in with the client and ask, "What is it like for you to see the moves in action?" You can then work with them to process anything difficult that might have come up.

Jamie can personally attest to the power of watching videos, having completed her pink belt in the online forum. Before she went for her private training with Coach Micah, she'd watched the video of a specific move several times. This helped her to be less afraid of the move, and it gave her a good working idea of what to expect.

Watch In-Person at the Gym

Watching others do the move in person might also prove to be helpful in the process of desensitization. Clinicians can discuss options for the client to watch a larger class in progress, or a private lesson. The choice should be based on what helps the survivor feel safest. If the private lessons are held in a smaller room, it can be helpful to offer the student a choice of the door being open or closed. Clinicians can discuss this option with a client in advance and advocate on their behalf if they need to by sharing the client preference with the instructor in advance or while they are with the client in person at the training. When a person is flooded, it becomes difficult for them to remember to ask for things like having a door open that can actually have a significant impact on their sense of safety.

Recall that in Chapter 2 we discussed how Jamie and many of the women we interviewed for the book project were first inspired to train by watching their own children. There can be great power in observation. Jamie also recalls that during certain group training sessions when she became overwhelmed and needed to opt out, she would still remain on the edge of the match and watch. Yes, it was helpful for her continued learning, but it was even more valuable for her continued desensitization.

The clinician's role can be discussed with the client in advance. On the most conservative end, the clinician could be present on-site to help the client take space and de-escalate if they need to. Having a clinician ask their client what their number is in the middle of a class could identify the client to any fellow students and instructors as a person in therapy and could also reveal vulnerable details as to how they are doing to anyone present. An option for keeping communications confidential could be predetermined hand gestures that are chosen by the client. For example, the clinician can have a gesture, such as crossed arms, that signals that the clinician is checking in. The client could then indicate back that they are doing well with a smile, or if they need to take space, they could cross their arms as well. Plans could be made in advance to meet in the hallway or outside the building in the case that the client did need help from the clinician in de-escalating (which they indicated by crossing their arms). Clinicians could also simply arrange to be on call (available via phone) while the client is at the gym. Communication can happen via phone, videoconferencing, or text while the client is on-site without the clinician being there in person. This also helps to protect confidentiality. In Anna's experience, clients have not typically needed on-site assistance to watch a class in person.

You may want to give some thought to whether you want to offer this kind of on-site or on-call assistance and if it is appropriate for a particular case. What we do not want to do is provide or suggest more than necessary. This could send a message to the client that they cannot handle this experience without us. Instead, we want to empower them to stretch into the discomfort zone in a healthy way. Spend time with them exploring their thoughts, expectations, and any concerns; this can help shed light on what is appropriate therapeutically. Clients often need to process what they have watched. Anna uses her open-ended questions to start the conversation. "What was it like for you to see instruction in person?" Clinicians can then process anything that has come up and also offer to facilitate a direct conversation between the client and the instructor if needed. If, for example, the student has concerns about how the students are paired with partners, this could be a good opportunity to have your client connect directly with the instructor and begin to build rapport.

Do It by Yourself—Solo Drilling (at the gym or at home with videos)

The COVID-19 pandemic has offered instructors and students new, creative options for solo practice and preparation. Clinicians can discuss these possibilities with their clients. This solo drilling can be done in group or private lessons or at home via video, with and/or without clinical support or friends and family. Where Anna trains, the instructors specifically demonstrate what a solo drill would look like at the end of every technique demonstration. They simply state "and by yourself, this is what it looks like." With the clinch, for example, Alex Ueda's five-word sequence (helmet, hit, hug, walk, bow) can be walked through without a training partner. It's similar to the concept of shadow boxing, in which you spar with an imaginary opponent. In the case of the clinch, the client can take Alex's "helmet, hit, hug, walk, and bow" (extended version of "helmet, hit, hug" described in Chapter 6) and make all the motions, as if someone was in front of them to do it with. Anna would often say it out loud as she did it:

"Helmet," she'd say as she covered her head to block imaginary punches.

"Hit," she'd say as she shuffled forward connecting her helmet to her imaginary opponent.

"Hug," she'd say as she wrapped her arms around their imaginary waist and grabbed her own wrist.

"Walk," she'd say as she walked forward, keeping the hug.

"Bow," she'd say as she leaned forward while she pulled her arms in closer.

Solo drilling was particularly helpful to Anna when she was learning a move called *rear takedown*. She found it incredibly difficult to tuck her elbow, even after six months of practice. Unfortunately, tucking your elbow in this move is a safety issue and needs to be mastered in order to avoid injury if you use it off the mats and on the streets. Only through numerous sessions of solo drilling was she finally able to consistently tuck her elbow.

Full Contact In-Person Training

When clients move to full-contact training, several things can be considered. Moving from the least amount of pressure and aggressiveness to gradually increasing pressure and aggressiveness over time is an important consideration. For example, when to shift from hands on the shoulders for choke defenses, to hands actually on the throat, to hands actually applying pressure, should be carefully considered. Scaling can help guide clients as to when to shift. The clinician's role in this particular example is one of helping the client discuss how to communicate their training needs with their partner. The aim is to instill that it is not only appropriate to make requests, but also imperative if clients are going to last in the long run and have a corrective experience. In addition, one of the many trainings of jiu-jitsu is to empower the student's voice as a part of growing stronger in their abilities to hold boundaries. One of the hardest classes, according to Eve Gracie, is the STOP! Block. Frame. class because of this aspect. Jamie and Anna have both spent extensive time assisting clients through the challenges of having a voice and holding boundaries.

Some clients will benefit from being the bad guy or aggressor first. If you are in private lessons, or if you are at a school that groups partners in threes, it can be easier to step back from either role without impacting your training partner's work. Getting an idea of what will be happening by being the bad guy first can help the survivor's body start to explore and grow tolerance as to what physical contact can be like. The experience also puts them in the helping role of being a "good" bad guy. In order to be a good bad guy, many techniques require that you put some pressure or resistance on your partner. In Chapter 6, we shared the punch block series technique. In the stage where we put knees into chest, for example, if the bad guy isn't leaning forward aggressively, putting their weight against you, then you don't have anything to push your legs against in order to lift your hips. In order to be a good bad guy, you need to put energy and effort into it to help your partner train effectively. Altruism can be a healing factor for many trauma survivors. It can also give them a better idea regarding when they are ready to switch to practicing the good guy role. Some clients might be ready to try both good guy and bad guy right away. The clinician's role at any given time is to continually reinforce that the client always has choices in how they train—when the client wants to do more, and when they want to do less. Clinicians can ask, "Are you looking forward to trying both roles?" This will give the clinician information on any client concerns that need to be discussed further. If they are indecisive, scaling is one option you can use to help clients decide if they are ready to do both roles. If you have both determined that it is appropriate to have you there in person, you might ask how they are doing in a predetermined way (either directly or by using a signal/hand gesture) during training, and then you can assist in de-escalating if needed.

Some communication or collaboration with instructors may be needed, especially if the client is not taking private lessons. The client might want to discuss their ability to sit out of any particular technique, good guy or bad guy role, with either their training partner or the instructor. The clinician could be part of this conversation as an advocate if there is a therapeutic reason for this kind of support.

While the client is working to physically tolerate and master techniques as the good guy, simply allowing themselves to pause in difficult positions, can be something to aspire to. For example, having hands on your throat can be triggering to many people. Spending a few extra moments learning to breathe and stay calm with someone's hands on your neck (not applying pressure) can be a useful exercise to build up to. A clinician can discuss these things in advance with a client in the office and/or also be there in at the gym to ask if the client feels it is helpful to pause in an uncomfortable spot. Again, clinicians can assess via scaling if the pause is building tolerance for the difficulty (4,5,6) or if they are flooded (8,9,10). Other survivors have reported that staying in a moment, for example, while being mounted on the floor, can be a difficult challenge to overcome. As always, discomfort is okay; unhealthy extreme pressure is not. As discussed in Chapter 2, clinicians can assist their clients in discussing and working to notice their edge—when they can push further and when they need to slow down or stop. These types of discussions could take place in the office before or after, or during actual training if that is needed.

If clients are requesting a clinician in-person at training and are wanting to maintain confidentiality, communication protocols can be agreed upon in advance. Anna, for example, has simply folded her hands together while looking at the client and the client has responded by putting between one to ten of her fingers on the mat to indicate their stress level (1–10). They made agreements in advance that if the client's number reached 7, they would walk off the mats and take breathing space in the hallway. There, in the hallway, Anna would join them to assist in de-escalation with preselected emotion regulation tools. Other clients have been in less need of confidentiality and were happy to have Anna ask about their number verbally while they were on the mats. Anna has had a variety of clients on the mats from children to adults. She often offers clients the option to create a plan for each potential scenario A, B, and C:

1. When training is going really well the client needs less presence and help from the clinician on the mat.

2. When things get more intense, the client discusses what they believe they will need from the clinician to stay in a stress level of 4 to 6 on the mats.

3. Discuss what the plan is if things get more intense than expected (7, 8, 9).

Anna finds that simply making the plans often puts clients at ease. She tells them it's like car insurance. You buy the policy so that you won't have to use it. A client's preference on confidentiality is of paramount importance, and if a client wants to stay anonymous, meaning they do not want others at the dojo knowing they see a counselor, the clinician will need to do everything they can to respect and protect that relationship on the mats.

Building Reflexes

Some schools provide reflex development classes in which seasoned students can work to gain muscle memory. These classes offer an opportunity to experience random attacks based on the techniques they know. Developing reflexes in this way is a good method to evaluate if they can remember how to defend themselves with little to no reminders. An optional final challenge can be having their eyes closed during reflex development. This challenge, as well as future belt testing, can be a true test of a person's skills to stay calm and retain effectiveness. By the time some clients get to this stage, they might actually feel it is simply a fun game to test their skills. For others, this could potentially be another trying stage. Sometimes Anna will ask a question such as, "Are you looking forward to trying reflex development?" Their answer will help her understand if they need to prepare in session and examine any negative self-talk or negative experiences to date in jiu-jitsu. Don't assume that every client will need help with this process. When Anna went through reflex development training, she remembers it being scary for a minute and then rapidly turning into fun and laughter.

Belt Testing

Earning her pink belt was a particular moment of healing for Anna. She vividly recalls the hour after she passed her test:

> I found myself looking at the online photo of my attacker. I instinctively said out loud, "I forgive you." I could finally let it go. I felt more powerful and safer than I had ever felt in my life.

In Jamie's office, her pink belt certificate hangs right below her PhD certificate. Jamie says:

> I knew that the PhD was something I could do going in. With the pink belt, I was flooded with doubt, especially at the thought of taking a timed test. Passing that test and watching myself take it on video was one of the most special achievements of my life. I sense into my warrior energy every time I think about it.

As noted earlier, we should *not* assume that this is scary to our clients. We need to ask, "Are you looking forward to belt testing?" Depending on their response, you may need to examine further. Again, don't assume they will need to work on it in session with you.

If your clients are nervous about an upcoming belt test, it can be helpful to normalize that with or without trauma; many people feel a little nervous about testing. Part of the mental test *is* working through the nerves and discomfort. Anna recalls:

> I was super nervous about my test. Many of my partners knew I might test soon, as they had witnessed instructors asking me when I was going to test. A few others knew because I had asked their advice on testing with Rener, who triggered my old trauma memories. Everyone I asked advised me that it was a personal decision that only I should make. Regardless of how they knew I was testing, everyone was extremely supportive. Many people asked me if I needed any pointers or if I wanted to practice with them before. Everyone encouraged me and said that I would pass, no problem. Unlike my trauma experience of the past, in which the community at large was anything but supportive, this was a new and corrective experience. I had a sense that everyone "had my back."

Although there are many success stories to share when it comes to belt testing, there are, of course, inevitably occasions in which clients do not pass the belt test and need to revisit their training. This is yet another potential opportunity for processing the "failure" or "mistakes." It can be particularly useful for clients struggling with perfection tendencies to examine their self-talk and beliefs around the process or learning. If a client is training at a trauma-informed, supportive gym, the instructor will also likely work to be encouraging and supportive and normalize the client's next steps in retesting. Some clients whose trauma story includes childhood punishment connected to performance can prepare in advance of testing. An example of performance punishment could be that they were disciplined for poor grades or sports ability as a child. Jamie and Anna recommend discussing both outcomes—what it will be like if they pass and if they don't—with these clients in advance of testing. In this way, clinicians can work to help prepare these clients for either outcome. The goal or intention is to identify and correct any negative self-talk around the learning process and mistakes.

Clinician Involvement

Clients will have a wide variety of preferences regarding a clinician's direct involvement in their jiu-jitsu training experience. In this section, we highlight some best practices. If you as a clinician are also an active participant in jiu-jitsu, you will have more to offer clients in terms of being present during training and having an intimate understanding of what they will be taking on. This is not 100 percent necessary for you to be of assistance, however. If they need you on-site, you might simply be available from the sidelines. If you have relationships with several training facilities, this can also leave clients with more options should they choose to want your presence. Again, please consider making the effort to research facilities for yourself. Your favorite internet search engine, social media connections, and good old-fashioned word of mouth are invaluable parts of this process.

State Licensing Board Ethics and Legal Considerations

We are early in our journey of establishing jiu-jitsu as a therapeutic benefit. In addition, not every facility, instructor, or partnering student will provide a positive experience for your clients. We highly recommend that you seek guidance from both your licensing board and the company that issues your malpractice insurance as to what is within your scope of practice. They may also be in a position to offer you other valuable insight on a state-by-state basis. Scheduling a consultation with your attorney about informed consent language is optimal, particularly on the matter of physical contact. What is written in this book is not definitive legal, ethical, or physical guidance. Unfortunately, we live in a litigious world, and you will need to cover yourself, and also in the process, protect your client and set very clear expectations about your role and involvement.

If you are training in jiu-jitsu, you are aware that it can involve extremely close contact, in ways that might make some students feel uncomfortable, even without trauma. Every clinician has to carefully consider their role and its implications for the client. Anna generally prefers to avoid direct physical contact. She has, on occasion, directly assisted in the very first moments on the least invasive techniques, such as base and wrist releases, which involve very little physical contact. She also takes a sense of relief in the fact that the facility in which she trains has video cameras taping for the protection of students and instructors alike. If you are choosing to have any physical contact with a client, you might want to know if cameras are recording interactions for both your and your client's protection. We cannot stress enough that there are numerous reasons in which a clinician's direct physical contact could be considered not helpful, unethical, or unprofessional.

Anna has experienced clients who wanted to design private lessons accompanied by both their clinician and friends. They wanted to simply watch first and then, with the support of the clinician, make a decision about whether they were ready to participate without any external pressure. Other clients of Anna's have simply needed help getting started. These clients practiced emotion regulation tools, just outside the building or in a vehicle, until the client was ready to go in. This can also be done via phone with the client sitting in their own car and the clinician in theirs or both in the same car (discussed further in a moment). They also worked on a few signs and signals in which the clinician could, from a distance, check in with the client on their scaling without asking the question verbally. These steps were taken to maintain confidentiality.

Clinicians need to carefully consider and define good boundaries around client contact. The structure clinicians put around the therapeutic space (office, gym, walk-n-talk, and even the car) can have an impact on a client's sense of safety. Anna's training has been that above all other considerations, the therapy has to be humane. For example, although touch is prohibited at central juvenile hall in East LA where Anna has worked, she did not shove a client away when they gave her an unexpected hug. And although sitting in a car in a parking lot may seem odd, it may also be the only option that helps provide a private therapeutic space so the client can regain their footing while preserving their confidentiality. Like almost everything presented in this chapter, clinicians are going to have to make decisions on a case-by-case basis and have sound clinical reasons documented for the decisions they make.

Jamie sticks to showing people getting up in base (and leaning into some of the pushes), wrist releases, situational awareness, assertiveness techniques, and some basic striking. She uses crash pads for training and teaches her clients the general technique of moving from the tip to strike toward the ear. This also works wonders as a *somatic bilateral proactive measure* (or *interweave*) when clients are stuck in EMDR sessions. Similarly, such striking techniques are also not uncommon in Gestalt psychotherapy work and newer somatic therapies where physical release of energy is essential. In her service notes, Jamie always documents that the client gave verbal consent for such physical work during any given session and the clinical rationale for working this somatic instruction into a therapy session.

Anna often discusses the concept of base and specifically the "stop" aspect of STOP! Block. Frame. Clients who are working on self-esteem and boundary issues often benefit greatly from learning to stand in base with their shoulders back and their head up. They often struggle with their ability to project a firm confident voice in telling someone to stop. When they are finally capable of asserting themselves with a firm voice, there usually has been a significant shift in their therapeutic work overall.

That said, a case could be made for circumstances in which a clinician might actually be partnering with their client during jiu-jitsu training. Neither Jamie nor Anna recommends any isolated physical contact in which

client and clinician are alone in a room, however. An argument can, however, be made for reasons to partner. People who train in rural and remote
areas may not have as many people to select from to run training drills. If
there are only five people, for example, in a particular class, and the instructors indicate that they want people to continue to switch partners throughout training, not switching to pair with the client could indicate something
to the class. This is an area in which complicated details should be both
considered and brought to consultation. Please consider documenting your
therapeutic rationale either way.

Laws and ethics will continue to change on a day-to-day basis. You have
the responsibility to verify what the current laws and ethical codes are at
the time you consider partnering with a client on the mats. Not knowing is
not a defense in court. Moreover, asking and obtaining the knowledge you
need may help you to feel more empowered about introducing jiu-jitsu or
any other physical practice into clinical work. Please do not let your fear or
uncertainty stop you, especially when ample guidance is available in this
process. We hope that someday, trauma-informed jiu-jitsu training will be
more widespread, understood, and supported. Until then, your time spent
thoroughly contemplating the ethical and legal use of jiu-jitsu as a mental
health treatment benefits you, your client, and the greater jiu-jitsu community. We are grateful for your effort!

Telehealth

Thanks to technology and the changes to telehealth accessibility during
the COVID-19 pandemic, many have gotten used to having a clinician
available via an online platform. This is yet another option that you could
consider to support clients as they approach, enter facilities, or participate
on the mats. They could simply arrange to have a half session before they
enter, perhaps from their phone in their car in the parking lot of the facility.
Anna has also helped clients simply work to de-escalate as they approached
the facility. She explains that getting in the front door is often the hardest
part. They might also want the clinician on-call for the next hour, should
they need help de-escalating from a trigger during training.

Stepping Down Involvement

The ultimate goal is to get clients self-reliant so they no longer need a clinician's presence in any form. This process can happen relatively quickly for many. Often the worst hurdle is simply walking through the door of a gym. Anna has also worked to educate instructors and advocates on behalf of the client with the client's written permission. Vetting, knowing, and educating instructors will help clinicians trust that their clients are in good hands. A clinician's comfort and confidence with facilities and instructors can translate into nonverbal behaviors on their part as they encourage their clients, at the right time, to take the next step without them. So again, doing your homework and building that relationship with facilities and instructors can be invaluable. You will want to trust your words if you indicate that they are in good hands (literally).

Find the Right Schools

To emphasize the importance of facility and instructor research, we will end this chapter with inspiration from Gui Valente. Gui described his family's journey in the jiu-jitsu world. He explained that his family (he, his brother, and his father) were fortunate enough to have spent more training time with grandmaster Helio Gracie than anyone else. In addition to that experience, he has spent years researching the roots, history, and philosophy of jiu-jitsu on a global scale. His reputation for wisdom on the topic is well earned.

When we asked him at the end of our interview for a final thought on what he would want trauma survivors to know, he said what creates the right atmosphere for healing in a school is critical. Once more, having a black belt does not qualify someone to teach. Gui shares that at one point, jiu-jitsu in Brazil was perceived as "thug activity" done by "pit boys" with shaved heads, cauliflower ears, and body-builder physiques. His family has worked to correct that perception. They have worked to create a balance between a fighting spirit and therapeutic benefit. He specifically shares that his school has worked hard to de-emphasize unhealthy bravado and competition and instead emphasize cooperation and community. He makes the analogy to the MVP basketball player who is positioned as a role model, a superman for his performance, and who, meanwhile, mistreats women and uses drugs. He references how champions are doing bad things and getting away with them. Gui describes how this behavior reflects badly on MMA coaching today. Such behavior can be so prevalent that the Valente brothers have been criticized by colleagues who say they are not qualified to teach because they have not fought professionally in MMA; they are "soft."

On the contrary, it takes strength to do what the Valentes have done and bring about what they've created. Gui admits that it has taken courage to go against this MMA mentality, and he believes it is one of the reasons that his school is so successful. Gui stresses his message to survivors: to ultimately *find a good school.* We hope that this chapter—in fusion with some of the others—has given you, as clinicians, some guidance for steering your clients in the appropriate direction.

Eight

For Jiu-Jitsu Instructors

The water's formation avoids the high and rushes to the low.
So an army's formation avoids the strong and rushes to the weak.
Water's formation adapts to the ground when flowing.

—SUN TZU, THE ART OF WAR

Jamie remembers being terrified during her first public women's self-defense class at the gym where she would go to train and then overwhelmed months later when she decided to try out a class with her family. Even her teenage son Brendan said, "Take a class with Micah before you decide either way. Trust me." Jamie immediately felt that Micah had something special about how he worked with people, and she knew that if she could learn jiu-jitsu, it would be from him. After deciding to begin her training journey with Micah through private lessons, she spent half of the first lesson orienting him to how her brain can very easily melt down due to the extent of her trauma and dissociative tendencies. Micah first listened then helped her to develop practical solutions for addressing these tendencies, both in private training and then eventually in group classes. Jamie went on to do things in jiu-jitsu she never thought possible, including earning her pink belt and running a trauma-informed women's self-defense seminar with Micah. She is delighted that he remains in her life as a healing presence.

> When I think of the healers that I really credit in saving my life and helping me to thrive, Micah is in that group . . . along with my recovery sponsors and trauma therapists who have worked with me over the years.

A jiu-jitsu instructor can be a powerful presence in an individual's life. You are facilitators of transformation, and we sincerely thank you if you embrace your vocation to teach as such! To be clear, we do not expect you to be trauma experts or therapists for your students. The real goal is to become trauma informed. For you, being trauma informed means being aware of how trauma may impact your students and how your teaching approach can help or hinder their healing process. For severe cases, jiu-jitsu may be optimized as a healing tool when partnered with the professional support of a licensed clinician if you are willing and commit to work in collaboration.

In this chapter, we give you as many ideas as possible to enhance your effectiveness working with trauma survivors. Even if you think that your school doesn't attract many trauma survivors—think again—and consider reviewing Chapter 2 about the broad impact of unhealed trauma. We discuss the importance of presence, language, attunement, and environment in helping you to facilitate transformative experiences for your students. We give practical solutions for how to respond to survivors who are triggered or otherwise activated during training experiences, and we present a series of best practices for creating and maintaining trauma-informed training environments. Throughout this chapter, we encourage you to look within and conduct some manner of self-inquiry. Perhaps you will even discover that further training or reading in trauma will benefit you both personally and professionally.

Your Potential Impact

Purple belt and assistant instructor Tony White understands that the impact of unhealed trauma is everywhere. He cautions that we need to keep in mind that all students could be coming in with some pretty serious troubles. He asks the following questions: How do we connect? How do we get to know students before they are thrown in with others? How do we teach students how to be good partners? How do we and our facilities become trauma informed?

As you read in prior chapters, many people walking in the doors of your training center have a history of trauma, which can show up in a variety of triggers. In addition, your students could have suffered head injuries (concussions) that can impact their ability to think clearly and perceive situations accurately. Challenges could arise from childhood experiences. How people are raised and if they felt securely attached to their caretakers can impact how they interact with people later on in life. So many things have shaped the perceptions of people as they arrive on the mats. People who potentially need this training opportunity the most might never get it because of triggers created by all of these factors and more. As instructors, you have an enormous impact on the accessibility of jiu-jitsu. Even the smallest of interactions with survivors can make all of the difference. We don't say this to overwhelm you; rather, we say it to encourage you to carefully consider your approach and seek ongoing information as you grow. Much like jiu-jitsu, best practices in welcoming the wounded and helping them heal will continue to evolve indefinitely. You can choose to be part of the solution.

Cultivating a Supportive Culture

If we created our own school, we would have a video that explicitly conveys the inclusive and supportive culture that we would want our students to watch as part of joining our gym. In that video, we would clarify language that we want to promote. We might include things like the important differences between the expressions *survivor* and *victim*, pronoun clarification for inclusion of LGBTQ+ individuals, and extensive examples of how to communicate on the mats with your training partner. We would also consider having instructors and students who are advancing in the belt system view this video and pass a test to demonstrate their understanding. Another option could be offering students, at any level, the opportunity to be identified as partners who work to welcome any newcomers. They could be given a patch for their gi or belt once they had watched the video and passed the test. These are more direct and explicit approaches to communicating cultural expectations. There are currently programs in which these types of things are expected from the instructors, but it is rarer to see these types of things being asked of students. Many programs have more of an oral tradition of setting culture and weaving their messages into the training of everyday class.

Regardless of culture videos and testing, creating an emotionally safe training environment starts with you, the instructors and leadership at each school. Nick "Chewy" Albin states that healthy training starts from the top down. An underlying ethos of his gym is *as we build ourselves up, we build up everyone else around us. As I move up, I reach down and pull someone up with me. Be a builder.* Chewy shares that he uses his online videos to communicate and explain the unwritten rules. He refers to them as being *unwritten* because he has no formal process of requiring viewing or testing but has a strong oral tradition of sharing his gym's culture goals in everyday class. He sometimes points out a particular video if it applies to a particular student concern. We see great power in having both the oral tradition in everyday class and the tradition amplified in writing, video, and testing to send a very strong message about what it is that you are working to create.

One of our contributors, purple belt Staci May, explains that she has had very different experiences in different jiu-jitsu schools. She is disappointed that jiu-jitsu has become a "cash cow." She feels that students will inevitably notice when money is the owner's focus. While we both understand that in tough economies bringing in new students can be vital to survival, as a trauma-informed value, it concerns us when your students can pick up on this as being what drives you and the school.

Staci reflects that at her current school, the owner regularly texts his students: "How are things going? Do you have any questions? Do you have any concerns?" As schools started to reopen after the initial COVID-19 shutdown, he explicitly stated, "I'm not interested in onboarding new students right now. I'm more interested that you are all comfortable. I don't care about class size or dollar signs." These interactions and more left Staci feeling that he is legitimately concerned about his students. We believe that the focus on students first and money second will actually financially benefit businesses long term in lower rates of student turnover.

Incorporating Principles in Your Training

In a review of João Alberto Barreto's book titled *Do Valetudo Brasileiro ao "Mixed Martial Arts,"* Robert Drysdale gives praise to João's sport psychology knowledge and highlights the following passage:

> He aptly describes what he calls the "path to sports excellency" (*O caminho da excelência esportiva*) as: talent, aspiration, discipline, commitment, perseverance, non-conformity (with current status), motivation, courage, extreme training, confidence, joy (in what you practice), overcoming limits, humbleness, affirmation (of individuality), responsibility, un-comfort zone (by creating these in practice), be aware of "traps of success" (that can sway you from your target) and control of performance (to always seek excellency).[1]

Clearly, there are many points of philosophy in training in jiu-jitsu, and choosing which ones you emphasize can shape your students' experiences. In a trauma-informed gym, it will be critical to work to eliminate the bravado or the *win at all costs* attitudes that are often associated with jiu-jitsu. Lessons on the principles of jiu-jitsu, such as benevolence, are something to consider in creating a curriculum that fosters a supportive culture.

For example, consider that discipline, commitment, perseverance, motivation, and courage could be affected by traumatic experiences. Yet students may have deep desires to cultivate these qualities in their lives. Students should be given great leeway as they tackle not just the physical, but the mental aspects of overcoming trauma triggers on the mats. Humbleness, affirmation, and responsibility can be potentially important parts of creating a welcoming and safe-enough space for a trauma survivor.

Helping Students Grasp Complicated Concepts

Black belt instructor Alex Ueda explains that being concise can be difficult but is especially important in teaching jiu-jitsu. He shares that you can always get into the details, but "if you don't have the broad strokes," dwelling on detail isn't going to be helpful. The last thing most trauma survivors need is extra unnecessary frustration and self-doubt. Alex explains that "you can get lost in the weeds talking about techniques too much." Jiu-Jitsu will present plenty of frustration for survivors to tackle without additional complexity due to overwhelming or difficult-to-understand instruction. For example, Alex describes the clinch and body fold by saying: "If you can't stay away to protect yourself, then just get in there and hug them" (clinch). Then "walk at them and bow" (body fold). Alex sometimes explains the science behind why it works. "When the bad guy's back breaks a certain plane, their legs can't keep up with someone who is walking forward while they are walking backward and they will just topple over." Alex's emphasis is always on being concise first and foremost. "When I teach, I like to speak as if every next word will have less value."

Share Your Vulnerabilities as an Instructor

Sharing your own personal stories can set the norm for sharing vulnerability and to what depth doing so is appropriate in your gym, school, or class setting. Sharing your own stories of trials and challenges in your training and in life off and on the mats will let students know that survivors are welcome. We are not trying to turn training on the mats into a survivor's therapeutic support group in which people reveal their darkest traumas. Normalizing, however, that it's okay to share when we have been triggered by something on the mats is appropriate. The ability to share has the potential to be a significant corrective experience for many trauma survivors if it is handled appropriately.

We've both heard instructors tell stories of times when they experienced panic-like emotions on the mats. They briefly describe the trigger that caused the emotion flood, what happened next, and how they moved past it. Stories like these can inspire hope and give survivors a path to follow in their own recovery. Many survivors can feel shame around being triggered or activated, and these stories can help them show appropriate compassion to themselves. Showing such vulnerability can also encourage them to see you as a person who might understand what they are encountering, making you a trusted other. Some facilities go so far as to provide an official time and space, before and/or after class, to process experiences and provide support in how to communicate with partners on the mats. Some programs provide direct messaging and training on how to create a trauma-sensitive and welcoming gym culture to more advanced students and assistant instructors.

Chewy shares his personal story with his students on how his introduction to jiu-jitsu was via high-school wrestling, and that he almost didn't attend at all. He explains that he had signed up, but when they called over the intercom for students to come for the meeting, his negative thoughts that told him that he couldn't do it took over. Later, he had yet another opportunity, as he was recruited first for the football team and then by fellow football players to try wrestling. He replays the pit in his stomach as he walked in to a wrestling training, overwhelmed by fears. He managed to look around and say to himself, "If they can do it, I can do it." Speaking directly to the readers of this book, he wants you to know: "You are not the things that happened to you. The circumstances you experienced . . . that's not who you are. Even if you're scared, it's a place to take back some power. Jiu-Jitsu can be your anchor in getting past these things."

Shaping Student Interactions and Language Supporting Survivors

In addition to sharing jiu-jitsu principles and your own stories of challenges on and off the mats, your everyday training language is key to supporting trauma survivors. Tony White described a situation in which he was concerned that he might have inadvertently caused a fellow female classmate to leave jiu-jitsu:

> I thought everyone should be doing review at beginning of class. I was assertive about it. I asked a girl next to me if she would like to do a review. She said yes. I asked, "What do you know?" She said trap and roll. I said, let's go. I was assertive. Yes, that's where we need to be, I thought. I tried to do the right thing and I didn't know how. The girl never came back after that class.

Tony has learned since then that questions often work better than commands. In trauma-informed instruction of any kind, we call this the language of invitation instead of the language of command.

Staci May highlights the difference between language that might trigger and language that is supportive. She gives the example of directing someone to "spread your legs" versus "I will be in-between your legs" to practice this technique. "Spread your legs" can come across as a demand (which also comes with a sexual connotation for many) versus "I will be in-between your legs," which is more just stating specific information. This second statement offers the sparring partner a pathway forward and a choice in whether or not to participate.

So much of effective trauma-informed instruction comes down to language. A subtle way that we have tried to model that throughout this book is to use the language of *survivor* instead of *victim* in referring to people who have experienced trauma. The language of invitation instead of command is another example, as is being deliberately conscious about how you say things in class and when you're working with a person one on one. If you get feedback that how you are explaining a technique isn't helpful, are you willing to reevaluate your approach? Do you have a commitment to being more inclusive in your language, opting for general words like *folks*, *friends*, or *teammates*, instead of *you guys*? Such inclusion can be very important to women and to members of the LGBTQ+ community.

Jamie, for instance, struggles with the jiu-jitsu slang of *good guy/bad guy* and prefers more neutral language wherever possible like *aggressor*. Micah's willingness to use this language with her, especially in private lessons, made her feel safe enough to proceed. If you, as an instructor, do end up collaborating with a clinical therapist, other human services professional, or educator in your community, they may be able to give you further insight on language choices. Please review Chapter 2 on the fundamentals of trauma competency if you need to review these principles at any time, or consider taking a closer look at the language we use to write up the "Try This" and other specific approaches throughout the book.

Cultural Adaptations

Knowing your likely audience in a given area can inform how you talk to and work with your students. However, be advised that we are living in an increasingly changing world, and you can do a great deal of good for the health of your students, and grow your community, by being inclusive. Ayesha Kamal, whose story we highlighted in Chapter 2, believes that jiu-jitsu, by its nature, is globally applicable. She began her training in Kuwait, where she still teaches, and also spent a great deal of time training in the United Kingdom. She notes that in some more conservative cultures, mixed dynamics in training, especially sparring, can be even more sensitive. Instructors must be attuned to these dynamics and address them accordingly. She recalls her father's initial reaction when he learned that she was training jiu-jitsu; it was something in the vein of "Why are you rolling around on the floor with boys?" She was eventually able to explain to him that she was learning to protect herself, not just rolling around on the floor with men. Ayesha emphasized, and we heartily agree, that intentionality and how you word certain explanations makes a great deal of difference in introducing jiu-jitsu and adapting it to meet the needs of certain populations.

Language and Instructional Approaches for Communicating on the Mats

Chewy Albin explains that an ability to communicate where you are *at* on any given day is important for everyone. He explains that as you get older, there might be a time when you need to say, "Hey, my neck is a little jacked up." We believe that it's appropriate, as students, to say, "Let's go slowly," or "Don't hold onto my neck." Adapting to this feedback is also good for the training partner, as they have to figure out how to spar without grabbing the neck or other injured spot. So whether you are affected by a physical or mental injury, being able to communicate this to your partner is critical to the journey, and instructors can model how to do this for students. Teaching your students how to speak to each other in a supportive and respectful manner and how to ask for what they need is important. Such an approach not only protects all students on the mats from unnecessary physical injury, but provides a corrective experience for trauma survivors in giving them a voice and influence over how their body is touched. We explore ideas on enhancing your instructional approaches in the service of adaptability in the sections that follow.

New Students Matched with Instructors and/or More Advanced Students

Being a new student can be a very scary prospect for a trauma survivor. How they are approached and what they experience in their first training weeks can determine whether or not a student stays or flees the proverbial scene. Numerous facilities report that they work to take good care of the newcomers by specifically matching them with their instructors and/or students that they know will help the newcomer feel safe and productive in their technique training and first sparring. They also make it clear that it is permissible to take breaks if they need to or sit out of a particular technique.

Gui Valente shared that his father's vision was to preserve the therapeutic aspects of Japanese jiu-jitsu, which had diminished over the years due to the impact of competitive sport. As a family, the Valentes believe in a balance between the fighting spirit and the spiritual aspects of the tradition. They work to transfer those beliefs into everyday instruction on the mats. One example Gui shares is making sure not to over-praise the tough guys. By cultivating a climate in which there is room for everybody to learn, you ensure that no one gets the idea that they are more deserving of focus and attention than anyone else. Another example of this commitment is in the Valentes' Montessori-like approach to instruction. They often explain that *the best way to help yourself is to help others.* A third example of this commitment is their approach to hand-selecting who is paired up with whom during training. In this way, they work to ensure that all the newcomers have a good experience by being with a higher belt who will work to help them. Gui explained that his beginner-level classes often have more higher rank belts than white belts, which makes it easy to provide newcomers with an experienced partner. As an instructor, you have a tremendous influence to shape the culture of your facility. You do this in how you structure your curriculum, in how you deliver your instruction, and in how you treat all of your students, especially those who are new to the mats.

If you are looking for inspiration in how to set a supportive culture in your language, structure, and curriculum, consider reading up on the *Bushido code* or the system that the Valentes developed called the *753 Code* (see Chapter 3). Gui Valente explained that his father emphasized the importance of academic study to counterbalance the animal instincts that we are entertaining by practicing jiu-jitsu. A key concept in the Bushido code, Gui explains, is benevolence. He shares that in the codes of ancient Japanese and Chinese warfare, honor is very important. The way you behave in victory or defeat is important. Showboating is discouraged. How you treat your training partners, and approach the training itself, is paramount to your growth. You can set the tone for honoring these values either as a school or as an instructor.

Start Simple

Programs should start simple and move to more complicated maneuvers. Learning a flying triangle day one would be an enormous deal breaker for most of us. Mark Barentine describes this skill:

> The flying triangle requires closing the distance quickly, leaping up, landing one of your legs so it wraps around the bad guy's neck on one side, while the other leg sweeps under the opposite side arm of your opponent in order to cross your ankles behind their back. Complex techniques such as this one are not practical for someone starting out. They involve very specific circumstances to perform and do not translate well to self-defense.

Simple techniques for real scenarios are the best place to start. We recommend a curriculum that emphasizes safety and population-specific self-defense first. The reasoning behind this is described in depth in Chapter 6. Many schools do have a specific class dedicated to a self-defense curriculum that is specifically designed to start easy and build up to most challenging and lethal of moves. Despite that, they still have to solve the problem of when new students join and where the class is within that school's curriculum. Many schools will also work to design the self-defense class with very basic and accessible moves and avoid the flying triangles with which most people would have difficulty. Some schools work to solve this problem by doing biannual free workshops on self-defense. At those workshops they might work to get people started with moves that are easy to comprehend and execute, but they might also share techniques that demonstrate the unique effectiveness of jiu-jitsu.

Another way schools are addressing the challenge of students who join mid-curriculum is by always starting the current students in 15 to 20 minutes of practice of prior moves, while they take new students to the side of the class to provide a brief introduction. The instructors might give a very topline introduction to a couple techniques. They might also hand-select a partner for each new student, working to ensure that their time is spent in a productive and safe manner by matching them with a student trained for that purpose. Another supportive option for students entering mid-curriculum is grouping students in triads instead of pairs. Not only does this more easily allow a student to sit out of a technique if they want to, it allows the observing student more time to see the move in action before they attempt it. Anna often finds herself doing solo drilling alongside the pair in preparation. If one of the three students wants to sit out and watch, it does not inconvenience their partner and can take the pressure off of a newer student. A side benefit of the triad is also a third set of eyes to help stay safe and overcome any struggles in executing the move. We highly encourage gyms to consider triads in entry-level classes.

Be Encouraging

Because jiu-jitsu is so complicated, getting 30 percent of a basic move during the first attempt is a significant accomplishment. Anna often hears instructors explicitly explain this in class and encourage students to try to grasp 50 percent the first time they are trying something new. They explain that with each repeated class, you often get 10 to 20 percent more of the details and nuance of exactly where to put your hands, feet, and body to execute the move most efficiently. Because we all live in different-shaped and -sized bodies, it also takes some time and experimentation to find the best way to, for example, use shorter or longer legs to execute a sweep. Encouragement in pointing out what the student is doing right, even if it's just a good energy, can be helpful. You can set an example while walking around the class and commenting and by specifically encouraging students to notice when their partners are remembering parts of the move correctly. They might say, "Great, yes, that's exactly where you want your hand." "Awesome." "Thank you for training with me." Many survivors of complex trauma spent their childhoods being chronically criticized and punished for performance. This is an opportunity to provide a corrective experience. Whether or not there are trauma-survivor students in the class, this type of language has the potential to set a tone for a supportive culture in your school.

Meaningful Mistakes

Some jiu-jitsu techniques can be relatively simple, but many are indeed complex. If students are not encouraged to "fail forward" and try again, then they will likely leave. When instructors share stories of their own jiu-jitsu challenges, they make it safe to explore, learn, and ultimately mess it up over and over. Anna has heard examples of how they "failed" at a technique for long periods before they got it, and it helped to both normalize the process of learning and acknowledge the effort it takes. Anna often shares her example of how she ran away when clinch was the appropriate response in front of a large class. She shares it because she wants to set a tone of embracing our mistakes, finding meaning in them, and owning our humanity. Small moments of communication like these can potentially be a significant corrective and healing experience for complex trauma survivors. If any of the abuse they endured centered around performance and mistakes, humanizing mistakes and promoting a healthy learning process may be a first-time profound healing experience for many. Gui Valente confirmed the story that Helio Gracie gave his own son $10 for winning and $20 for losing a fight in order to take the pressure off. Consider setting a culture tone in your gym that takes the pressure off and creates a space where mistakes are welcomed as gifts from which we can learn.

Individualized Pacing

Programs should be created so that students can go at their own pace without being reprimanded or scorned for inconsistency. Students will vary considerably in their ability to grasp techniques and in the potential trauma histories that may impact their learning process. Respect that every student is bringing their best effort to the mats. We understand that instructors value both consistent and frequent attendance in class. Unfortunately, many students might be not only recovering from but still in harmful circumstances physically, emotionally, spiritually, and/or financially.

If a gym has a one-size-fits-all-policy of signing a year-long contract membership with a monthly fee, it might be eliminating a large pool of potential students. Students who are not ready to commit to a year or students who are having their financial resources restricted in domestic violence situations are just two examples of people whom this membership policy could discourage. Options for single drop-in classes at reasonable fees opens up options for clients to take it at their own pace.

Program pricing options are not the only way to welcome these students. Language is powerful, and so are behaviors. Condescending, scornful comments about lack of attendance by instructors and co-students alike may not only discourage trauma survivors, but potentially trigger feelings of being trapped and/or abused again, causing retraumatization. If the instructor is paying more attention to the most frequent students and not checking in on everyone, they are sending a message. Anna notes her experience of instructors who shake each student's hand at the beginning of class while they are lined up on the wall. Even though it is a very brief interaction, it is a moment of connection, looking at each student in the eye and connecting with them physically. These instructors circulate the class often, checking in to keep everyone safe and progressing. Anna says that, if anything, the less-consistent students might get a little more attention than the others in order to keep them safe and progressing.

Choice in Pacing

As we've said repeatedly, choice is imperative to trauma recovery because trauma is inflicted without choice. Giving people a choice of speed at which they train is a small, actionable way to promote choice. Chewy Albin feels that trauma survivors have to be able to build up incrementally. They should build things up at their own speed and not be thrown to the wolves.

Chewy has had students tell him they are having problems related to trauma, and he recommends that such students don't roll (spar) in the beginning.

"Just do the technique and become comfortable being really close to people," he advises.

He specifically notes that with mixed-gender sparring, some women may need time to get used to it. Ultimately he wants them to feel that they are in a safe environment and to feel comfortable. Much like the scaling outlined in Chapter 4 or the concept of distress tolerance discussed in Chapter 2, it's important for instructors to challenge their students outside of comfort zones to build a tolerance to discomfort. Chewy also highlights that the environment is there to create a stimulus and a stress, but it's not there to destroy. It's there to build people up.

He has seen trauma survivors unlock or wake up a warrior-like energy inside themselves that was dormant. He has watched firsthand how these students find out that they are stronger than they thought they were. Chewy described the importance of having a variety of classes at varying degrees of jiu-jitsu mastery and intensity so that a student can grow comfortable with their instructors and fellow students as they take it to the next level with an instructor's encouragement. He explains (and we agree) that there will come a point at which you need to face something uncomfortable in jiu-jitsu, and it should be done when you have established a comfort level, good communication, and trust in the people you are training with to successfully overcome it. Chewy described his experience of once needing to tap out regularly because he felt like he couldn't breathe. We find this phenomenon to be a common experience on the training mats. Chewy goes on to share that after three months of training, and with the encouragement of his coach, he was able to pause, breathe, and work to relax in this uncomfortable position.

Full-Speed Demonstrations

As you begin to demonstrate a technique, doing a first run-through without a detailed explanation is key. Simply showing what the whole move would look like in real life timing can inspire hope and comfort in survivors. This demonstration lets the viewer see the defending person quickly escape to safety and allows them to have an extremely brief exposure to the potential triggers on the first viewing. If, for example, a person has been traumatized by being held down on the floor, seeing someone else in that position can be triggering. Their adrenaline levels may raise and flooding can occur. If you do this quick demonstration, they are ever-so-briefly exposed to the adrenaline pump, and then it is shut down again as they see the solution come quickly and safety. Before the brain can start spiraling into detailed memories or really get the adrenaline flooding the body, the solution is already in front of their eyes. In more severe trauma cases, seeing the move executed a few times quickly might reinforce that solution and ensure that safety can be accessed. Once the brain acknowledges that this is a corrective and safer experience, moving into the slower details and seeing the person stuck underneath for three to ten minutes of explanation is not as upsetting.

Independent Drilling

For those students who are not ready to be touched, giving instruction on how to practice a move by yourself is helpful. Any opportunities for a student to practice how to move their own body first without anyone touching them can work to assure them of their own agency and strength. It also allows them time to visualize and desensitize themselves to the idea of eventually being touched when they are ready. Where Anna trains, the instructor specifically demonstrates what a solo drill would look like at the end of every technique demonstration. The instructor simply states, "and by yourself, this is what it looks like."

Slow + Mindful

If a client is triggered or otherwise activated, it can be difficult for them to execute the moves slowly and mindfully. They may need to execute the moves with speed at first. Even if the moves are sloppy in technique, important new learning about their abilities and a newfound sense of safety are being absorbed. This is another reason why partnering new students with more advanced students can be helpful. More advanced students can help the new student stay safe, even if they are technically sloppy and moving fast. The advanced student will be more prepared for potential mistakes and be able to avoid injury better than two new students paired together.

Over time, students can be encouraged to work to slow down. Emphasize that when you are able to move slower, you can work to reconnect to your body. This reconnection helps to stop the dissociation that so many survivors experience. This will become a key skill in their jiu-jitsu journey, as they will need to sense their body to make the best jiu-jitsu choices. These embodied experiences are also significant factors in healing the trauma. Learning that it is safe (or safe enough) to be present in our bodies after trauma is critical to healing. Any work that can be done by the student, at their own pace, to learn to slow down is vital.

We have both been triggered to the point of activation during our jiu-jitsu training. Anna specifically remembers that she became extremely quick in her movements when paired with a certain instructor. She remembers feeling spastic and frantic. She couldn't get away quickly enough as soon as he was nearby, let alone, with him touching her. This activation became super apparent as she was called on to assist in demonstrating a technique for the class. The instructor told her over and over to slow down and listen to his voice. Anna felt her heart pounding, and she struggled to stay still throughout, especially in compromising positions beneath him. Despite all of her positive experiences with this instructor over many months, her mind had declared that he was not safe. Searching the mind for answers, she eventually realized that he looked extremely similar to someone who assaulted her. Even as a clinician, Anna was somewhat surprised at how this childhood memory, a moment in time, was affecting her, especially with someone who was there to help her. Anna's mind was transported back to that day, and all the years of therapy and work she had done to address it had not erased it from her body's memory. Luckily for Anna, the work that she did in therapy prepared her for the continued healing she was about to do.

Jamie experienced (and continues to experience) more triggers in her jiu-jitsu training than she can automatically recall. She's now learned to see them all as opportunities for growth. One specific example touches on an issue that we have not yet directly covered in this book—how training in a full gi can be stifling, overheating, and uncomfortable, especially for large-chested women. Jamie prefers training no gi (only a rash guard and pants), which is an option for her private lessons, yet may not work for group classes at schools where a gi is required. She decided to rise to the challenge of learning to train in the gi, embracing it like the carpet in which Rickson Gracie rolled himself in to deal with his claustrophobia. During one group class she became so dysregulated due to being overheated that she asked the instructor if she could sit out for a while and watch. She did, taking the jacket of the gi off as she watched. After a while, Jamie had sufficiently grounded, breathed, and hydrated herself. When the instructor came to check on her, Jamie then decided to advocate for herself: "I can continue with the class," she said, "But only if I can leave the jacket off." She was surprised that the instructor she didn't know well granted her permission for that class and was grateful for it. Although she was able to train in full gi again, being able to speak up for her needs in that moment following a major activation was a turning point in her healing.

Breathing

Being able to breathe in jiu-jitsu can be a challenge with or without a trauma history. Jamie's coach Micah Bender believes that learning how to breathe properly during jiu-jitsu training is the most important skill that anyone, especially a trauma survivor, can learn. A variety of videos and blogs are available that discuss everything from therapeutic breathing to practitioner breathing while practicing jiu-jitsu. Many people hold their breath when they are exerting themselves or when scared. Numerous videos can be found on Jamie's website www.traumamadesimple.com. There, she discusses seven breath strategies and offers even more variations on how to use yogic breathing in your daily life.

Marty Josey, a board-certified psychiatric nurse and brown belt in jiu-jitsu, has created a breath training protocol specifically for enhancing your jiu-jitsu performance. Unlike breathing for emotion regulation, this protocol works to enhance your biomechanical breathing muscles. Emotion regulation can of course be a side benefit, but the overall goal is to enhance your ability to breathe in uncomfortable positions. Marty would suggest that breathing is so important to jiu-jitsu performance and health in general that five minutes could be spent in every jiu-jitsu class simply to work on tips for breathing. He would also like to see schools offer more advanced, ongoing, breath-only focused training and biannual workshops with experts to deepen everyone's knowledge. For those readers who have sparred, you know that this isn't just about cardio; this is about your ability to breathe when you are on the bottom of side mount, or knee on belly, and so on. To learn more, you can go to www.breathingforbjj.com.

In other circumstances in jiu-jitsu, you can feel crushed by an attacker's weight. It is not uncommon in the more advanced levels to find people tapping from feeling uncomfortable in relation to their ability to breathe. Yet this reality of training can also provide people with an opportunity to learn how to adjust their breath. Jamie's teenage son Brendan reports that learning how to breathe by engaging his diaphragm when he trained is one of the most valuable ways that jiu-jitsu helped him. Although he is no longer actively training, he shared that the deep breathing he is still able to engage in when he is stressed out or when he has difficulty falling asleep is a practice that he learned through his jiu-jitsu training.

Whether we are experiencing a trauma or being triggered, one of the first things to change is our breathing. We constantly emphasize the importance of breath to our clients. Many mental health clinicians help clients work with breathing, using everything from diaphragmatic breathing to various styles of yogic breathing. Some clients are happy to learn that by simply controlling their breath (see Chapter 4 for more ideas), they can actually begin to slow the amount of adrenaline being released by their body. We highly encourage you to incorporate the breathing techniques of your choice into your training curriculums and to keep emphasizing the importance of breath as you drill techniques. Feel free to borrow this favorite line from Jamie that she uses when teaching yoga and dance: *Holding your breath does not make it easier.*

Teaching Children

Unfortunately, many children also fall into the category of trauma survivor. Teaching children in general is a special skill. Experts like black belt Alex Ueda take the task of teaching children very seriously. Alex believes that many people would approach the task from a place of "How can I transfer this knowledge into their heads?" He believes that is only 15 to 20 percent of the job. Of prime importance is connecting and having fun. Alex explains that you have to "convince them through your behaviors that you're there to have fun and that you care." He wants you to respect them as you would anyone else and show them you come from a place of caring first. Once you have earned their trust and made a connection, then they'll listen.

As soon as children start arriving, Alex shares that he is there to share stories and tricks from his elementary school years. If he runs out of ideas, he'll ask questions.

"Too often the whole world passes them by and people talk over their heads," he shares, "It leaves them in a place of 'I guess I'll belong someday.'"

Alex explains that if you are interested, you don't have to worry so much about being interesting, so the goal is to interact in a way that sets a tone that this is all a game, we are family, and it's cool just to be back together again. Then you can move into the structured warm-up, the stretch and talk, jiu-jitsu techniques, and then end with a dodgeball game, commonly seen in jiu-jitsu schools that teach children.

Alex explains that if you formulate your questions properly, you can stimulate thinking about meaningful and even adult topics. Alex likes to start the talk with questions that are then broken down with an example that plays into the jiu-jitsu techniques of the day. Talking about privilege is one example. Alex shares one of his exercises: While standing off center of the circle of students, Alex raises his hand and says, "The first kid to touch my hand gets an extra life in dodgeball." The kids are almost too stunned to move, and he says, "Did you hear what I said?" Before he has finished saying it again, some kid has touched his hand, and everyone has gotten up.

Then they all sit down and process what just happened. And here is a place where Alex inserts a valuable life lesson in his teaching:

> Why didn't you guys move? What made you guys so eager? Was this a fair game? And of course it's not, as it favors the tall kids and the ones closest to me inside the circle. What would make this more

fair? Eventually we get to the fact that real fairness would be when you would have no problem switching places with someone else. When you're not willing to trade places, then you know something is wrong.

Alex's lesson works to inspire cooperation, which is key in jiu-jitsu training. He wants the kids to realize that you can hoard your power in the arenas where you find yourself privileged and powerful and only get so far, or you can decide to share, set a trend for sharing, and get further together. That might lead into a jiu-jitsu lesson where we discuss when to use our jiu-jitsu skills. What happens when you see someone else being bullied? They discuss the spectrum of responses. If, for example, there are multiple bullies and one kid, you have to play it smart and get help. The underlying lesson is that injustice anywhere is injustice everywhere.

Teaching Adults

Alex shares that teaching adults presents its own special challenges, as adults tend to self-sabotage. He has found that it's not so much the words that help to combat this, as it is a growth mindset vibe. For example, when adults challenge his knowledge, he doesn't treat it as a challenge to him in a personal sense but as an interesting riddle that he might figure out because if there is a novel solution to it, he would be excited to know.

Alex described how one of his students shared that she was a perfectionist and needed a couple more months so she could get a 100 percent on the belt test. He advised her to pass now and worry about "perfection" later.

"If you need things to be perfect before you do them, then you are missing the point," he teaches.

"It's not about perfection; it's about progress, it's about rolling with the punches. It's not about asking for a world where punches don't even happen," he continues. "To be fair, I would like to live in that world too, but we know better."

His guidance to this student is that perfectionism is a name we give to our fear, not our ambition.

What do you think, in your experience as an instructor or in working with adults in any capacity, makes accepting this teaching more difficult for the adult mind? More importantly, how can jiu-jitsu serve as a vehicle to teach your students the power of process over perfection?

Rising Above the Violence: A Choice Available After Safety Is Established

One of the beautiful facets of jiu-jitsu is the huge range of techniques available and the potential application of submissions at varying degrees. Jiu-Jitsu offers many choices, a quality that can make the practice especially helpful for trauma survivors. Allow students to have choices about the degree of damage they inflict. If they don't need to inflict harm, they can choose not to. Anna personally finds this to be one of the most powerful aspects of jiu-jitsu. There are many self-defense tools that someone can learn. Krav Maga, for instance, is another powerful form of martial arts self-defense. However, in interviews and based on personal experience, we find that in many of the other forms of self-defense, such as Krav Maga, serious injury to your assailant is more likely while you are defending yourself.

In Anna's work with men in sober living, she spent countless hours assisting them in their personal struggles to regulate their anger in response to others. They described a culture of dog-eat-dog where violence was the only option available to determine who was safe and who was not. After years of working with this population, seeing her clients not take in an attacker's anger or mental sickness was the true point of success. Defending against an assailant by becoming an assailant doesn't feel that much better for long. There is an undercurrent of stress; you know that you will most likely have to defend against this person who might later look for revenge. So true winning is protecting yourself without needing to physically hurt the aggressor. Anna also believes this is in line with how many women feel about violence. Jamie attests that as a person who is quite the pacifist, the potential for violence of any kind unsettles her, even though she is optimistic about what martial arts training can do for her trauma recovery. When female clients and students learn that you can defend without eye gouging and striking, they are often happily surprised. And many women, like Jamie, learn that violence and empowerment are two very different things. Jiu-Jitsu is about helping people tap into their inner source of power.

There are many stories of people's experience about the level of violence and choice. Terry Crews is a celebrity weightlifter, and he shares his experience in an online video about witnessing domestic violence as a child.[2] He explains that he watched his mother being attacked as a small child, and he wanted to protect her but he couldn't. At age thirteen he found weightlifting. He grew strong and committed to never allowing that to happen again. Then the day came that he responded to his father's violence with violence. He describes the rage he was left with, after assaulting his father, and that it didn't help anything. So he learned to rise above the violence, in his own words. These words stuck Anna as powerful and inspiring. His weightlifting felt similar to her experience with jiu-jitsu.

Anna felt grateful for his courage in sharing his story and hopes that it inspires others. Although Terry's message and experiences resonated with her, she was left feeling uncomfortable with the message to "rise above the violence." There is a great deal of pressure on survivors of domestic violence to forgive, heal, and "rise above violence." Anna was left with questions. She thought, "Now that he is large and strong and not easily physically threatened anymore is it easy for him to tell the rest of us to rise above violence?" Anna fully supports work to inspire healing and forgiveness; however, she feels a key step is missing that not everyone can reach through weightlifting. "I had to feel safe before I could forgive, and having this moment of forgiveness and letting go of the hurt was one of the most powerful experiences I have ever had in my life."

Prior to jiu-jitsu, Anna felt she had two options in response to violence. One option was to simply endure it. She learned to smile regardless of what was happening and to ignore her body. As a small child, it was her only option. There was nowhere to run, and what can you do as a child when the adults in your world are abusive? The second option arrived when she had grown big enough to fight back, which is exactly what she did many years later. Anna didn't have jiu-jitsu as a teenager. She was so enraged when she finally fought back that she blacked out. She has no memory of the seconds in which she actually struck her attacker. She only knew that when she came to, that person was screaming out in pain and far away from her. She felt a release of the pressure that had been building for over a decade. The rage simply exploded out and all over. Unfortunately for other innocent bystanders, she found herself unconsciously letting that rage leak onto others as well. Her rage found outlets in alcohol, extreme sports, mosh pits, and one-hundred-hour work weeks. These outlets served her well enough for many years, until her body put on the brakes.

Decades later she discovered jiu-jitsu. It was a powerful tool in which she could keep herself safe regardless of the size of her attacker. With numerous corrective experiences, and surrounded by caring, supportive training partners, she grew strong and began to feel safe for the first time in her life. Things she didn't even know she felt threatened by started to be corrected. So although Anna sincerely appreciates Terry Crews's message to rise above the violence, she adds to it with the following:

> In order to not respond to violence with violence, I had to feel safe first. In order to rise above the violence, you have to feel like there is no real threat. To even see that there is no threat accurately, prior traumas need to be healed. You have to lower the body's protective adrenaline defense system via corrective experiences. With jiu-jitsu, my body has learned to trust that I am safer than ever before and can now "rise above the violence." If I could go back in a time machine to my childhood self with my knowledge of jiu-jitsu, I would block the strikes, take my abuser to the ground, and hold them there keeping us both safe. Maybe it could have been a corrective experience for us both. Maybe it could have provided the love and safety we both desperately needed—my attacker in their childhood trauma and me in mine. Maybe we could have begun to heal the pain that left *so* many triggers for us both, like mines in a field.

In the rest of this section, we give you and your students ideas for how you can use training techniques to help people feel safe first, and then, ultimately, rise above the violence.

Supportive Sparring

There is variability to the intensity at which students should be sparring, and you, as the instructor, can set the tone. One way to set that tone is by asking the students to go at 50 percent of their capacity (speed, strength) or less. Anna reports that where she trains, the instructors will ask for 10 percent if they are introducing a new technique or if there is a big difference in belt status or weight between partners. Chewy Albin shares that he doesn't directly teach students to be trauma informed, yet he sends many messages that work to make his gym a safe environment for everyone. He described how he specifically talks in class about different weight classes and how to spar. If you are sparring with a person who is 120 pounds and you are 200, you wouldn't necessarily put all your weight on them. He goes on to explain that you get different things out of rolling with a 250-pound person versus a 120-pound person. You might, for example, find that you get a good technical lesson from rolling with a smaller person. If you are now sparring with a person who is heavier than you, this gives you a feel for how to stay safe despite that weight difference, and you might not hesitate to put your full weight into the spar.

The same is true of sparring with different belt classes. Chewy states that "you wouldn't spar with a white belt the same way you would spar with a blue belt or black belt." If you were teaching a friend to ride a bike for the first time, you would not bring them to the top of a steep hill with lots of car traffic, sand, and other technical hazards they had to navigate. You would most likely find flat ground and simply show them how to operate the brakes and slowly glide forward before they even put their feet on the pedals. Jiu-Jitsu is no different.

White belts are just beginning the journey, and slow and steady is the way to pair with them if you are more advanced. Anna has often heard the description that white belts are learning the ABCs of jiu-jitsu. Blue belts are putting the letters together to make words, and purple belts are stringing whole sentences together. So, if a purple belt is pairing with a white belt, they will have to go slower and possibly spend some time teaching if it's wanted, and they will definitely have to pay attention to safety precautions for both people. This might leave you feeling that there is a burden on the higher belt in this situation. Anna and many of the other higher belts we've talked to firmly believe that helping lower belts helps those with higher belts sharpen their technique. This is the practice of beginner's mind in action.

Triggers: Emotional Flooding and Flashbacks

Anything in the realm of human experience can be a trigger for intense expression (affect), emotional output, or shutdown. When human beings encounter sights, smells, sounds, tastes, touch sensations, body positions, or pressure that feels in any way similar to or reminiscent of what they experienced at some point in the past, problems can ensue. Especially if the source injury of that experience was never fully healed or processed. Triggers can originate from any source—heck, if you play a TV in your waiting area or lobby and a certain program or song comes on, someone could feel triggered, or at very least annoyed, if the content elicits some kind of response. Jamie, for instance, is easily activated by any loud background noise and does not like it when schools or gyms use loud music, especially as a training device. And loud waiting rooms, while not necessarily a trigger anymore, are certainly irritating. On the other side of the coin, some people are triggered by intense silence, so having some background music on can be useful for training.

There is no such thing as creating a completely trigger-free environment for a trauma survivor, especially when you are working with so many people in one space. Avoiding triggers altogether is not the goal. However, we can use our common sense to put some best practices into place, many of which we've covered in this chapter and throughout the book. Moreover, building up a healthy capacity to be in the presence of triggering sensations can take time, patience, and slowly increasing exposure. For this to happen, the least amount of triggering aspects at first is best. In more severe cases, a student's therapist can help to develop a desensitization (exposure therapy) plan that may start by simply exposing a survivor to the training environment. For Jamie, this happened when she first walked into the school to watch her sons train. Once an initial step is mastered, increasing levels of stress, potentially in private and then group lessons, can be introduced.

At the very least, and to benefit all students, some useful steps can be taken with good common sense to make your school as safe as possible for the greatest number of people:

- Keep extra training equipment (fake practice weapons like rubber guns and knives) out of sight until they will be directly used.

- Keep the space empty of potential clutter and unnecessary objects of any kind.

- Encourage students to come to class free of perfumes, perfumed deodorants, cologne, essential oils, and so on. Scents can be powerful reminders. If possible, recommend scent-free fabrics softeners to your student body for washing gi. Emphasizing student hygiene is important. Require that students come to class showered with a clean gi. These steps not only benefit trauma survivors, but take into consideration the needs of students with allergies or other sensitivities.

- Set up training rooms and spaces that are visible and wide open.

- Smaller private lesson training rooms can often be triggering and need some getting used to. Keeping the door propped wide open can sometimes help. Asking what a particular person prefers can prove useful.

What It Can Look Like When Someone Is Triggered

Any behavior that is unusual for a particular student could potentially indicate a moment in which they have been triggered. How one person is affected by a trauma can be very different from another. Getting to know your students will help you understand if they are in distress. Many symptoms of triggering can also happen to people who do not actively identify as trauma survivors, such as sweating and fast breathing. So again, knowing your students well will help you spot someone who is struggling. The good news is that you don't have to be a mind reader. If you see someone, especially someone who looks like they are experiencing multiple triggering characteristics, you can simply check in with them in the least intrusive way possible. We will discuss ways to ask without being intrusive later in this chapter.

The first step is learning to identify the potential signs. The following is a list of just a few to look out for. Although it looks similar to a list we offered you in Chapter 4, we've taken care in this chapter to list some jiu-jitsu-specific examples:

- *Dissociation* can often look like someone simply zoning or spacing out. It might seem like they are not present, or that their body is here but their mind is somewhere else. When you are teaching, you may notice that students have a faraway look. When you approach them individually, there may be a hesitancy to make eye contact with you. Some students' voices get really soft when they are shutting down in this manner. If students ordinarily make good eye contact and speak directly, and suddenly they are not, this could be a sign of dissociation. Review Chapter 2 content on dissociation if necessary.

- A *flashback* is a memory of the traumatizing event popping back into the mind, often incomplete, unexpected, and unwelcomed. Diagnostically speaking, it can be considered a dissociative response. Sometimes it can even feel as if the trauma is happening in the current moment, right there on the mat. In severe cases it can be hard for the survivor to know what's real and current and what's not. Getting them reattuned to the present is key and can sometimes require the help of a mental health professional.

- *Freezing* is as it sounds. If their body stops moving, even for short periods of time, they might be just thinking and defending or they might not. Checking in and asking how they are doing or how the technique is going for them may give them an opportunity to express if they need to take a breath. You, as the instructor, modeling a deep and healthy breath can also make a world of difference.

- *Overt startle responses* are when you, for example, come around the corner and scare someone who jumps. You haven't done anything to scare them, and they might have even known you were coming. However, if your appearing from around a corner makes them jumpy, then they could be experiencing a trigger. When we are startled, we often cannot feel our feet connecting to the ground. Simply having them sense into their feet, perhaps in practicing good base, can be a way to calm the nervous system once it has been triggered in this way. You might offer to practice push base ("Defending against Pushing" in Chapter 1) if that feels appropriate for them.

- *Changes in body posture or defensive postures* can be seen in many different ways. The body curling inward like a ball, shoulders high, chest caved in, head down are a few examples. Think of how a child or dog might curl up if they felt threatened. Jiu-Jitsu exercises and stretching are offered during class in some schools. The option to work to stretch the body is one of many possibilities in a moment like this.

- *Accelerated breathing or heart rate* is especially hard to spot, as jiu-jitsu can sometimes be strenuous and rapid breathing would be understandable. If it is excessive, that might mean the student is simply not in good cardiovascular shape, or they could be triggered to the point of activation. It might also mean that they are holding their breath for periods of time, leaving them breathless after. Holding the breath is another very common behavior for people with and without trauma backgrounds. If your school has a particular breathing technique, this might be a good time to teach and/or practice it with the whole class without putting a student on the spot.

- *Excessive sweating* can also be seen in people with and without trauma histories. This, in conjunction with other symptoms noted here, might be indicative of a person being triggered. As suggested earlier, simply checking in during or after class to see how their learning is going is an option. Taking a breather to get some water might also be a helpful option to explore.

- *Wide eyes or lack of eye contact.* Scared, wide eyes are not uncommon to many people new to the mats. If the eyes are not improving as time goes on in class, this could indicate triggering. Inability to make eye contact is another potential sign of trauma memories happening in a moment. Alternatively, many people who suffer from social phobias and anxiety disorders may have trouble making consistent eye contact. Wide eyes, like many of the already mentioned potential indicators, do not necessarily mean that we need to come to the rescue. Many times, simply checking in after class to see how everything is going is a good option.

- *Fidgeting/difficulty staying still.* Sometimes students with attention deficit hyperactivity disorder (ADHD) or even an autism spectrum presentation will arrive on the mats and have the wiggles. Other times, it could be the flight behavior of the fight, flight, or freeze reactions in trauma survivors that is presenting itself. Either way, these students can find it very difficult to sit still and may be better able to listen if they are pacing the floor or wiggling their legs. Attempting to restrict their movements should be avoided if it's not disturbing the class. If it is, making arrangements for private classes or other opportunities to train might be an option.

- *Leaving the room.* A need to leave the room could again be the flight of the fight, flight, or freeze reactions in trauma survivors that is presenting itself. Allowing students to leave the room to decompress and return can be helpful for their ability to graduate their exposure to triggers. As in the previous point, restricting people's movement can make them feel trapped and retraumatized, so if someone needs to leave the room, it is best to allow them to do so. Checking in and asking how things are going is a potential option. Following up after class or the next day is another option.

- *Hypervigilance* is a key symptom for many trauma survivors. Scanning the environment for anyone or anything that poses a threat is a key survival skill, for example, in those who grew up in traumatic environments and/or who are have served in the military or law enforcement.

- *Hypervigilant hearing* is a more specific manifestation of hypervigilance. This vigilance can impact a person's hearing and understanding. If, for example, a child has grown up in a violent or unpredictable household, they can come to learn that words are less important than the tone in indicating their safety. As a result, they don't hear the distinct words, instead focusing in on the tone or speed of speech.

This in turn slows down their ability to decipher and to process the words. In addition, if this same child in sitting in a classroom and a person in the back of the room shuffles or makes some noise, the child will have to scan to assess any danger related to the noise. They may even have a boost in adrenaline preparing them to move their body if they need to in order to avoid the threat. By the time they have assessed the threat as neutral, the adrenaline is already pumping and can take time to stop, further affecting their ability to focus on the words said. It is not uncommon for trauma survivors to be mistakenly diagnosed with learning disorders or ADHD for these reasons. This is not only true of children. Adult survivors can suffer from the same hypervigilance and hypervigilant hearing as child survivors do. As the instructor in the room, it can be a good idea for you to repeat the instructions several times in several different ways in order to give them an opportunity to hear it in different ways that reach different learning styles.

- *Difficulty concentrating* is common in trauma survivors, making it difficult for them to focus or concentrate, especially when something highly detailed is being communicated. We both remember times when we were being told to notice something about our body in order to facilitate a move. When you are triggered to the point of activation, you can start to lose touch with sensations in your body. So although we might have heard and even interpreted the words correctly, there was a disconnect to our body's ability to make the connection. You can see this happen often with students. As in the previous point, work to repeat instructions and/or circulate around the room and make sure there aren't any questions.

- *Self-destructive behavior.* Anna has had a long history of participating in adrenaline-stimulating sports. She explains that when you are focused on keeping your bike on top of a spine with drop-offs on either side, there is no room for anything else in your head. Your focus has to be laser-sharp in order to stay safe, so all the other stressors disappear. Although this might seem like healthy coping,

Anna's physical injuries have been significant and numerous over the years. For many, the daily adrenaline shot is something they have grown accustomed to while growing up in traumatic environments. It's not something you necessarily grow out of either. In jiu-jitsu, Anna has found herself inclined to walk straight up to the biggest, most-aggressive-looking person in the room. Instructors are encouraged to consider being on the look-out for students who might be pushing themselves too far. Encourage new students to pair with same-sized students when they are trying a technique for the first time. Talk about staying within healthy limits for yourself at any particular stage in your training, and share examples of mistakes you have made in pushing too far.

These are just a few examples of what can happen to people who are being triggered and how it might show up in jiu-jitsu training. The actual experiences of being triggered will vary greatly from person to person. Overly aggressive or displaced anger, nausea, stomach aches, headaches, body aches, and avoidance are just a few additional examples. Ultimately, behavior that seems unusual for a particular student is sometimes a giveaway that they are being triggered.

What to Do if Someone Appears Triggered

Above all else, keep a calm, grounded presence. We share a chemical and electrical space as humans, and our heart rate will affect another's. In many cases, if you are calm, your body and voice will send messages to others, assuring safety and security. If you get nervous or escalate along with your student, it will make it worse for them. Keeping the calming presence is the number one skill that all trauma-focused therapists must have, and you can practice it as instructors as well. Make sure that you are grounded, breathing, and calm. Use any item from the toolbox or your own personal practice to remain grounded. You can even model it for them and then invite them to join you: "I'm going to take some slow breaths. Join me if you would like."

None of us are perfect at handling triggers, so please be assured once more that we are not expecting you as instructors to become experts in this process. Anna and Jamie are still both prone to making mistakes even though they are trauma therapists who have been teaching embodied practices for quite some time. These are best practices. If, as you read them, you are convicting yourself for doing harm in the past, please show yourself some compassion, especially if you did not know any better at the time. The key here is how you can learn and do better the next time.

- *Avoid touch.* Many people, with the best of intentions, will offer to give a hug or wrap their arm around someone else's shoulder or touch their knee. This is dangerous territory for a survivor who has not requested it. Even if they have asked for a hug, I would recommend that you play it as safely as possible. A side hug is a reasonable option if someone requests one. This is a hug in which you stand to their side and wrap your arm around their shoulder. Be careful to let go when you sense that they want you to. Many training facilities have installed video cameras for the protection of both the students and instructors. Misunderstandings concerning touch are not uncommon, and it's wise to proceed with caution with any touch. While hugs may feel innocuous to you, they may feel invasive to others. Jamie routinely shares that when she is in high distress, the last thing she wants is a hug; it feels like she's being trapped more, and her emotional expression is being restricted. After the intensity passes, if she feels safe enough with the person, a hug may be appropriate.

- *Check in* with your student being triggered in the least intrusive way. It's important to not put someone on the spot in front of the class. If the students are actively engaged in practicing a technique and you are circulating the class, this is a good time to check in on someone. You might simply ask, "How are things going? How are you feeling?" And pitch the question to the student and their training partner together. Again, the goal is to not put the person on the spot. You might also, or instead, check in with the person after class.

- *Have an assistant take over the class.* If someone is actively crying, visibly shaken, and/or is leaving the training room, consider having an assistant take over the class, or perhaps send the assistant to attend to that person if that feels more appropriate. Doing this with the least amount of class disruption is key, as you want to avoid putting too much of a spotlight on the affected student. Once the assistant has taken over, you might ask the person if they would like to take space and/or get some air (just outside the classroom, or just outside the front door). Simply offering if they would like to take some space outside the room could be helpful. Asking if they would like to get some water is another option. The idea is to give them some space from other people's sight and judgment if that's helpful. It can be a good idea to have identified potential spots inside or outside of your facility to bring someone, if they need to catch their breath. They may not want to get some air and may just need to sit down and take a break from the lesson. Simply normalizing that taking a break is not only permitted but supported can potentially be helpful. Don't press them to talk if they don't want to.

- *Avoid dictating; ask and listen* for what a person most needs when they are upset. We cannot emphasize this enough. Even as therapists with master's and doctoral degrees in mental health, we cannot assume that we know what is best for our clients in any given moment. We need to gently ask what they need, attempt to provide options, and affirm the client's request. Follow the student's lead in what they feel they need. They may, for example, not want to leave the class and just want to be left alone. Ask how you can best support them. Following their lead is critical. For many survivors, they have often been told "how to" or that they "have to" do something during abuse. Offering options and respecting their choices and requests could be a significant corrective experience for them. Often they may not know, so having some options to share from your personal toolbox is helpful. If someone shares their experience of being triggered or of a traumatic experience, the best thing we can offer is a confidential, listening ear. It's a privilege to have someone share private information. They are letting you know they trust you to hold space for their confidence. Refrain from interrupting them, telling them what they need to do, or how they need to feel, or how to make things better. Also, sharing anything they told you in private could be a significant violation of their trust. Explain that you will keep their story private, and then do so unless they are going to hurt themselves or someone else. In that case, it would be important to get them help (call their therapist, emergency medical personnel, or law enforcement in extreme circumstances).

- *Manage other students who may have noticed that the student is upset.* If you have set a tone for your class that authenticity and feelings are welcome, this can help students trust and follow the instructor's lead. The goal is to give a fellow student respect and space if they are triggered. Let other students know that hovering with attention over a student who is upset is generally unhelpful and can draw even more unwanted attention.

- *Listen actively.* How you actively hold space for a person to express and process their feelings can have a significant impact. Mirroring back what they have said can help them feel heard and understood. Survivors are often left feeling misunderstood and dismissed. You might simply state, "If I heard you correctly, it's like . . ." You could also validate their feelings and experiences. Depending on what they have said, you might state, "I could see why you feel that way." Normalize that all emotions and tears are okay in this space. Emotions are simply a normal healthy part of our human experience. People are generally only open for being challenged into action after they have been heard and validated.

- *Don't minimize, which includes telling someone what/how to feel.* People often attempt to comfort someone by telling them how to feel. Saying things to someone who is upset like, "You're safe, you're okay," "It could be worse," or "Don't cry'" minimizes the importance of what that person has experienced. Imagine that they have the original ball of pain in their hands and they are showing it to you and you tell them that they shouldn't feel that way. Your response doesn't take the original ball away; it simply adds a layer of "you should" on top, making the ball even bigger. In addition, we would add that this is not necessarily the time to share your story or another student's story. Again, your job in this moment is simply to hold space for their experience. There may indeed be wisdom from your story and/or others that directly applies and may be very helpful at some point, yet timing is everything. Honor their story first, and on another day, ask if you might share your story with them.

- *Do not give unsolicited advice.* You have probably gathered by now that it is not your job to know how to fix your student. Ask if they need suggestions before you provide any. Unsolicited advice suggests that you know better than they do. Even if they ask for help, suggestions can be phrased as questions: "Have you considered . . . ?" or "Would you consider/think about . . . ?" are how we start many difficult dialogues with our clients and students.

Checking In

If someone has shared their story and has put their trust in you, it can have a positive impact if you reach out later to check in. Be prepared for the fact that students can have a range of reactions to having been triggered or from sharing information with you. Shame and vulnerability specialist Brené Brown (also a clinical social worker) discussed a phenomenon that she calls *vulnerability hangover*.[3] Students and clients alike can feel a deep sense of regret or "Oh no, what did I just do!?" after potentially feeling that they shared too much or became emotional in front of others. Such responses are especially common if students grew up in invalidating environments in which showing emotion or asking for help was labeled as weakness.

A phone call or a simple text after class or the next day may be appropriate, depending on the student and the context. If the student is a minor, make sure that you involve their parents in the process of contacting them, at the very least getting permission from the parents or guardians. If the student sent an email, you may consider emailing them back. The goal of the contact is to show them you are continuing to support them and to connect them to resources if they ask you to. You can begin by normalizing their emotions and any trigger reactions. Asking if they have support will let you know if there is an opportunity to recommend a licensed clinician who specializes in trauma recovery. It is a privilege to be chosen as a trusted person to talk to about feelings, triggers, or trauma. Ending the call or email by expressing your gratitude for their trust in you lets them know you feel that way.

Vicarious Trauma and the Importance of Taking Care of Yourself

With the prevalence of trauma in our world, you or someone close to you has likely experienced it. *Vicarious trauma* is a reaction in someone who is a witness to someone else's trauma, whether they are actually there during the experience, or they hear about it later. *Secondary trauma*, while generally not viewed with the same degree of seriousness as vicarious trauma, typically refers to someone being impacted by the trauma in some way. Perhaps a traumatic event happened in your community; one way or another, you are bound to feel the effects somehow. Maybe there is a death or tragic loss in your school or training community. If you've experienced that before, think of how the whole school was affected. The impact may still be lingering.

You don't have to be at the scene of the trauma to be impacted by it. Many people will have reactions to simply hearing the details of someone else's trauma experience. If you are going to teach jiu-jitsu, you need to be prepared that you will likely hear trauma stories at some point. Mark Barentine, a brown belt with over twelve years of training, relates how this affected him. He was teaching a church camp self-defense workshop when he was first confronted with the realization that women in his inner circle had been assaulted. "I was surprised to find out that a person I knew very well, a colleague that I worked with daily, had been sexually assaulted." Shortly after she told him, several others started telling him about their assaults and traumas as well. Mark recalls a sixteen-year-old girl from the class telling him, "I'm glad you're teaching this class because it happened to me." He shared how it stunned him:

> It was one of those moments where everything just stopped. I knew the statistics. I knew that one in four women had been assaulted. I had heard these stats from Rener and Ryron. She said "it happened to me a couple years ago. I'm glad you're doing the class." She didn't give details and I didn't ask for them. I simply sat and listened.

It blew me away. Despite knowing the stats, I never considered that it would have happened to someone in my class. That thought feels naive as I looked back. Of course someone would be a trauma survivor, but it just didn't occur to me. It took the better part of the night to process what I had just experienced. I felt incredibly sad that she went through that and it opened my eyes. I knew it conceptually, but it wasn't real to me because I felt it had never happened in my life or to someone directly connected to me. On the last day of camp, one of the girls said, "Thanks for making sure this never happens to me again," and gave me a hug. I just broke. It was one of the most unexpected things I've ever heard. That first year teaching the camp shifted something in me. The stats were now connected to my inner world. It was unexpected, powerful, and it blew me away.

Although Mark was affected by the pain evident in their stories, he also clearly saw their resilience. Mark was reminded of lessons jiu-jitsu had taught him, "Sometimes the pressure sucks, but you handle it. The more experience you have, the more pressure you are able to handle."

Given these realities, and the fact that helping people who are survivors is not always easy, it is important that you have your own support system and plan for taking care of yourself in place. To quote a well-known folk saying, you cannot pour from an empty vessel. All of the toolbox strategies that we've covered throughout this book can be used by you, too! We also feel it's important that your life not become so dominated by teaching that you forget to also train yourself. Not only does it make you a better teacher to also remain a student, it can assist you in continuing to work through what may need release in your body. And there is never any shame in seeking out professional therapy or healing assistance of any kind from someone qualified. Perhaps seeing the healing miracles in your students has prompted you to want to go further with your own wellness journey. Being a jiu-jitsu player or other martial artist, you already have much of the healing foundation in place. A professional may help you take your goals for life to the next level, especially if unhealed trauma or stress in your life is keeping you stuck.

May we continue to be good examples and to practice what we share with our students!

Find Clinical Resources and Collaborative Opportunities

As a jiu-jitsu instructor, chances are high that you will be in contact with trauma survivors. Because unpredictability in healing is normal, it is best to do some homework and preparation in advance. Reading books like this one is a start. In addition, we highly recommend that you search your local community for therapists who specialize in trauma recovery. Aim to have three trusted people that you could refer students to if and when it is appropriate. It's also a good idea to have their information available in paper form (business cards or a flyer, for example) so that students can take them without a referral from you. Unfortunately, there is still much stigma around mental health and getting help. Many people will want to seek help in private, so having the options easily available to take in private is key. Hearing from you, an instructor or coach, that it's all right to seek out help might just be the motivation and subtle permission that your students need.

Like anyone else you would have connected to your business, you need to vet these therapists. Interview them. Ask questions. In particular, ask about their experience with trauma survivors and their approach. If they verbalize an understanding that working with trauma entails more than just talking about it, you are generally in good hands. In this day and age, trauma specialists have an understanding that we must work with the entire person, their body-mind complex, and their spirit, which can be as simple as honoring the client's search for meaning in life. You may hear them share that they are trained in specialty modalities like trauma-focused cognitive behavioral therapy (TF-CBT), cognitive processing therapy, eye movement desensitization and reprocessing (EMDR), brainspotting (BSP), Gestalt therapy, hypnotherapy, art therapy, expressive arts therapy, dance/movement therapy, the *Seeking Safety* method, trauma-informed or trauma-sensitive yoga, Somatic Experiencing (SE) or Sensorimotor Psychotherapy (SP). Typically having at least one modality that they've received extra training in for trauma work (above and beyond standard graduate school education) is optimal. In many states licensing boards are easily accessible online where you can type in a therapist's name and verify that their license is valid and see if any complaints have been made against them. Many therapists have their own websites with videos and blogs where you can learn more about their philosophy and specialties.

If their approach and level of experience sounds reasonable to you, and they are understanding and supportive of the philosophy of your facility, invite them to visit and train on the mats with you. Share this book with them and let them know what you are doing to support the trauma survivors on your mats. A clinician who has experienced and/or actively trains in jiu-jitsu or some other martial art in person will be much better equipped to be helpful to their clients. That said, just because they have a license in your state and they train jiu-jitsu does not mean they are right for your clients. Licensed clinicians and psychologists are flawed and often injured human beings like everyone else. So we cannot emphasize enough that you interview them and make sure that they seem ethical and honest in their approach. If, for example, you have referred people to them, you might check in once with that student to see if the therapist has been helpful. If you get a sense that they are not being helpful, be sure your student has other resources. This is why having three therapists (or more, if possible) to recommend is great.

When clinicians make referrals to other clinicians, we always try to provide the person with three options and recommend that they interview them over the phone. In that conversation over the phone, they can try to get a sense of whether that particular therapist will be a good fit for them. A well-trained, ethical clinician will not be negatively impacted by or punishing to a client who is not having a good experience. They will often attempt to adjust what is not working and make it clear that it is perfectly okay to switch to another therapist. As mental health clinicians, we often ask for feedback to see if what we are doing is working. We will emphasize that everyone is different, making it normal that some treatments work and some do not. We also normalize that we are surely not everyone's cup of tea and that we have absolutely no hard feelings if they need to switch for any reason. We emphasize that this is not about the therapist's ego and the goal is simply to make sure they get the best possible care.

You may be surprised by how such collaborations with local therapists will unfold in your community. Let's summarize the three purposes of collaborating with a therapist:

1. To make sure you have three good referrals to provide to your students if they are having mental wellness difficulties.

2. To have a therapist present during larger general public workshops to assist any students who might need emotional support.

3. To have therapists become familiar with jiu-jitsu so that they will be better informed in how to help when students experience mental health challenges on the mats.

We are not asking them to present anything, instruct, or even participate necessarily on the mats unless these opportunities organically emerge and work for all parties. Both of us have had the chance to work with our jiu-jitsu instructors at our schools, offering therapeutic support for workshops. One of Jamie's most special professional experiences was introducing members of her Dancing Mindfulness and expressive arts community, along with some female members of her recovery and blood family, to Micah via a special workshop on trauma-informed jiu-jitsu that they hosted in the community. As we've pointed out several times, creating collaborative opportunities for people in the community is a quality of trauma-informed care that can help to facilitate whole-brain and whole-body healing in the individual. If you've read the book this far, we can already tell that you are a part of this solution, and we thank you for your commitment.

TRY THIS Collaborative Conversations

The collaborative relationship between clinical mental health professionals and jiu-jitsu instructors holds great power and potential for transforming the healing shape of the world. As a jiu-jitsu instructor, this particular "Try This" exercise is meant for you!

- If you know a clinical mental health therapist, psychologist, or social worker, especially if one trains at your school, set up a time to meet with them. This can be outside of the academy, over coffee, or through videoconferencing. Ask them about their approach to mental health and healing and where jiu-jitsu can fit in. Inquire how what they learn on the mats, if they train, relates to what they do as a therapist.

- If you do not know a therapist personally, consider letting your fingers do the walking and look up some therapists, specifically those who specialize in trauma, in your area. Send out a few emails or perhaps make some calls to set up a time to talk, stressing that this is for community collaboration. You can mention that you are reading this book and are interested in building a wider base of referrals for your students. Generally, if a therapist knows that you will be a source for referrals, they will make time to speak with you.

- Whether you're speaking to a therapist you already know or one you've met through searching, consider sharing a bit of your jiu-jitsu story with them, specifically how jiu-jitsu has helped you to heal or just become a better human being. In the spirit of free flow, see where the conversation may lead!

Nine

Conclusions and Future Directions

Even if they don't know it, everyone has the instinct to survive.

—RONDA ROUSEY

In writing this book, we've listened to and read so many stories that testify to the healing power of jiu-jitsu. We've met people from around the United States and around the world who add their voices to the chorus of how meaningful this practice has been and can be as a healing art. Although every voice had an impact on us in some unique way, both of us especially marvel at the teaching philosophy of Alex Ueda. Alex is a young father of Chinese and Japanese descent, has a college degree in physics, and is a long-time jiu-jitsu practitioner who earned his black belt and teaches at Gracie University in Torrance, California. Alex epitomizes something special among those who share their practice of jiu-jitsu. He sees jiu-jitsu as more than just a sport or a physical activity—he sees it is as a practice in which you can learn to heal and grow into the best version of yourself. Not just that, if you are an open vessel, you learn tremendous lessons about life, how to treat your fellow humans, and indeed, how to transform the world.

Alex expresses that in the right environment, healthy self-worth will be fostered. But in the wrong hands, jiu-jitsu has the capacity for the opposite. He continues, "I will never in any teaching capacity divorce myself from humanist ideals. To teach one without the other is to miss the point of martial arts entirely."

Our sincerest hope is that this book has given you, in whatever role or roles you occupy in life, insight into how the fusion of humane ideals and jiu-jitsu training is possible. One truly does enhance the other if we foster a commitment to make it so. Every voice we consulted in this book, whether through interviews or through reading their insights on the page (many of which are passed down through oral tradition), offers perspective into *how* we can make this possible. In this final chapter, we review and further explore some issues that were perhaps left unresolved or incomplete in the chapters themselves. Part of our intention is to tease out or explore what feels incomplete to help shape future directions not just in the evolution of jiu-jitsu, but in the evolution of trauma healing as well.

An Unexpected Shift

Our plans for writing this book were unexpectedly altered due to the COVID-19 pandemic that began to change our personal worlds as well as the global landscape in the beginning of 2020. The original intention for the book was to include more of a physical focus; Anna was planning to visit as many of the gyms in other jiu-jitsu traditions as she had access to in Southern California. Yet COVID-19 restrictions forced so many gyms to stay closed long-term, especially in California. While we were still able to bring in the emphasis on important physical components in the book, our focus became increasingly more philosophical than we originally anticipated. We actually believe that this shift allowed for a better book. This shift blessedly invited us to look into more of the Asian roots of an activity we had been exposed to as Brazilian. And it challenged us to see, with greater clarity, how the lessons of our physical jiu-jitsu training transferred into our lives and into the lives of others, even when gym access wasn't available or optimal.

We are grateful that our physical training has not stopped altogether. As we explored in various chapters, the pandemic has forced practitioners to get creative with solo drilling and extending what it means to train. Jamie lives in a state (Ohio) that opened up sooner, so she was able to return to a gym for some in-person training with Micah Bender and Brian Needham. Indeed, one of our most special moments in writing this book together was, through an Internet meeting platform, having Anna and her husband be able to take a weapons defense seminar that Brian led Jamie through at his gym. While the possibilities of technology were expanding the reach of jiu-jitsu even before the pandemic, our COVID-19 reality is allowing us to consider how much more important technology and getting creative will become in widening jiu-jitsu's reach in the future.

In many of our interviews, issues around the professionalism and adaptive capacities of various schools were addressed. Keeping students safe both mentally and physically is the hallmark of a good school, and that physical safety is likely to be of great concern to trauma survivors as well when they are seeking out an ideal training environment. We were both moved by contributor Staci May's acknowledgment of her current school's ability to handle the transition back to in-person training. By its nature, partner training in jiu-jitsu is the opposite of physical distancing, which can naturally raise concerns for students, many of whom might not feel safe about returning to in-person training at the moment. As Staci noted, her gym owner's focus has been on making sure that students' questions are addressed and ensuring that class sizes are responsible with an even higher focus on hygiene. We were both concerned with many gyms' choice to operate with a business-as-usual mentality, including those that continued to host large seminars and training camps prior to widespread availability of vaccinations. While we want to be empathetic to the reality that physically run businesses have struggled during the pandemic and that students ought to have a right to choose what they are comfortable with in terms of risk, negligence concerns us.

If you are a trauma survivor thinking about beginning your jiu-jitsu journey now, we encourage you, in addition to everything else we've mentioned in this book, to investigate the school's health and safety protocols. We believe that the pandemic has changed the way we operate in life and may continue to leave an impact for some time after COVID-19 is no longer something we think about daily. Even if you are picking up this book years after it was published and you haven't thought about the pandemic for a while, we believe that the lessons learned during it can still resonate. If something doesn't feel right to you about a gym you are considering, honor that prompting and consider looking somewhere else. A careless attitude around physical health concerns around the pandemic can be a sign of deeper issues within the culture of the school.

Social Injustice and Healing

Over the year that this book was written, several incidents also amplified the deep social divides that remain in our world, especially in the United States, around race, injustice, and police violence. We've encountered people from all political backgrounds and philosophical ideologies on jiu-jitsu mats. There can be a tendency to make jiu-jitsu this great equalizer that helps us to meet each other where we are, regardless of what we believe or how we identify. Jamie recalls a previous experience at her old gym where she deliberately embraced the challenge of doing some training drills in class with a man whose truck was so decked out with all kinds of political stickers that it made her feel unsafe. He was nice enough and certainly very respectful on the mats, which helped her in meeting that challenge. Yet we have to be careful not to fall into these feel-good tales about jiu-jitsu's potential to help us meet each other as humans without also exploring the very real social injustices that still exist throughout our world.

Privilege is a word that can make some people squirm in discomfort, especially when they perceive it as an attack on them. Having privilege does not make you a bad person. Rather, the challenge is to recognize what your privileges are in this life and identify how you can use them to make the world a better place. A very real privilege that many jiu-jitsu players must confront is that they have the money—often a great deal of it—to join a gym. Jamie recognizes that her financial privilege has allowed her to train via private lessons almost exclusively. And while this can be ideal for trauma survivors (it certainly was for her), having this privilege is not most people's realities. As a jiu-jitsu community, we must continue to discuss and try out ideas on how to make jiu-jitsu more consistently available to people at a lower cost.

Staci May has been involved with taking jiu-jitsu-based self-defense to a club of local runners. Several of the contributors to this book, including

Micah Bender and Eve Gracie, have experimented with or are continuing to adapt jiu-jitsu content to places that they can share it outside of academies. For many women, for instance, jiu-jitsu may feel more accessible at places like yoga studios, general gyms, or even at domestic violence shelters and in social service programs designed to help them. Also, organizations like Girls with Gis have an active scholarship program to help those who are not able to access training or the costs associated with required gear (i.e., gi, rash guards). We encourage you to take notice of schools and organizations that offer such assistance and, if you are in a position to contribute as someone with a degree of privilege, consider doing so.

We've both been impressed by Rener Gracie's ability to use his privilege, not just as Helio Gracie's grandson, but also as a successful business person within jiu-jitsu, for the common good. First, he and his collaborators (including his wife Eve and his brother Ryron and Ryron's wife Victoria) make a great deal of content available at no cost via online platforms like YouTube and other social media. For us, this free content distribution is a mark of how someone can still be successful in a jiu-jitsu-based business while also contributing to the greater good. Many other teachers engage in this practice as well, and in our experience, this is typically a good sign of a teacher being committed to making a real difference in the world, not just running a business.

Ryron Gracie regularly shares his philosophy on de-escalation and how not to fight on various social media platforms and on the GracieBreakdown YouTube channel. In a podcast interview, he describes what he calls "verbal jiu-jitsu" as an ability to stay calm and offer empathy, compassion, and patience when someone is saying something that could otherwise instigate a fight.[1] Rener regularly does a "Gracie Breakdown" of fight videos and how they either did a great job staying safe or how they could have done better. In a video describing how a person interrupted a potential kidnapper, Rener highlights the use of jiu-jitsu as a way to not only stop or shut down violence but also have humanity for people going through difficult times. In this interview with a citizen named Brian, who happens to be a professional kickboxer with a black belt in Muay Thai, Rener asks Brian to share what his mindset was going in to a street fight. "So in that moment," he asks Brian, "why did you use jiu-jitsu instead of punching the guy's face in?"[2] Brian explains that this was a public safety issue, and he felt it should be about "de-escalation by approaching things as non-violently as possible." He shared how he wanted to keep everybody safe, and in the process of disabling the attacker, he discovered that the man was severely mentally ill and that he wanted to keep him safe from the crowd until police arrived.

Rener has very directly taken on the social stain of systemic police brutality through many of his online talks and workshops. While he clearly recognizes the unhealed threads underneath our current crisis, in a well-received online workshop he gave in the Fall of 2020, Rener contended that police officers are poorly trained at managing conflict and the dynamics of escalation. He makes a case that jiu-jitsu can provide much of what they are missing. The Gracie family has a long history of training military service personnel and public safety professionals, and Rener issued a call, even offering his services for free in some contexts, for a paradigm shift around the way that we handle conflict. You can access this talk (*Police Training Reimagined*) on YouTube or through Gracie University social media platforms.

Trauma-focused professionals are also working long and hard on the issues of how we can heal a broken world and the legacy of violence, discrimination, and brutality that exists at the root of it all. While it may seem counterintuitive to employ a marital art that many associate with the "violence" of sports like MMA and programs like the UFC in this process, we hope this book has taught you otherwise. Tapping into the age-old wisdom of Sun Tzu's *The Art of War*, a principle of conflict management is learning how to avoid conflict in the first place. Well-delivered jiu-jitsu training imparts many of these vital skills to people. Jiu-Jitsu training can also help people experience necessary completion tendencies in their body connected to past trauma in a safe and contained way that does not lead to explosive violence.

In his best-selling book *My Grandmother's Hands: Racialized Trauma and the Pathway to Mending Our Hearts and Bodies*, Somatic Experiencing practitioner Resmaa Menakem emphasizes the need for trauma survivors to experience at least twenty minutes of active movement each day; he claims that it helps them move energy through their body.[3] The entire thesis of his book is that the current state of affairs in which we find ourselves can be explained by people spewing their unhealed, *dirty* pain onto each other. We must encourage people of all races and in all professions to feel through their pain in what he calls a *clean* way so that it can be metabolized without causing violence to others. We highly recommend his book to anyone working with trauma survivors in a way that is responsive to the issues of racial and systemic injustice. Clinical professionals, jiu-jitsu instructors, educators, and anyone interested in really doing their own work can benefit.

Future Exploration of Therapeutic Benefits

As we continue to explore and investigate, via research and lived field experience, how the practices of jiu-jitsu can best be of service to trauma survivors, we must first recognize its potential in helping those of us who are offering the services. Here are a few questions to consider: If you already practice jiu-jitsu or share its practices with the people that you serve, how has jiu-jitsu helped you feel through your unhealed pain? Have these practices of jiu-jitsu allowed you to do this humanely and in a way that does not spew violence, either physical or emotional, onto others? How has jiu-jitsu helped you discover the totality of your body and renegotiate your relationship with it? If you have not yet practiced jiu-jitsu and are thinking about it, or if you are a professional of some kind who is feeling a call to share it as a referral option for those you serve, what is calling you about jiu-jitsu? Where do you see it as filling in a missing piece? Can you transform what you feel is missing into a clear intention for yourself going forward? How can engaging in all of this deep personal work help you transform yourself, healing your own traumas in the various ways that they show up, and ultimately make you a real force for change in a broken world?

Jiu-Jitsu and other martial arts have clearly been a part of culture, healing, and transformation since ancient times. Thus, what we are writing is not something new, and we must acknowledge that. However, in this Western world that can be very biased against ancient and indigenous systems of inquiry and that wants to see the hard data and numbers, we are only just beginning to codify and even quantify what jiu-jitsu can do for people and how it can enhance their journeys. We thank, from the bottom of our hearts, our interviewed contributors to this book who have contributed to this process by sharing their lived experiences. Moreover, we thank those who have offered to participate in research—both ours and projects conducted by other investigators—to continue enhancing jiu-jitsu's credibility in the arena of healing options.

If you are someone who is seeing the benefit of jiu-jitsu in your trauma healing process, consider writing up your experience, even if it's on a blog, or by reaching out to talk on a podcast. If you see the opportunity to take part in a research study, consider doing that. Because of the way that Western medicine operates, widespread acceptance within systems is not generally adopted unless there are hard numbers and research to support it. Sadly, this is the best way that we can convince the establishment about what we might already know to be true for ourselves. If you've benefitted from the healing power of jiu-jitsu, be an ambassador for it in whatever way that you can.

We, along with many of our contributors, are very keen on seeing what the research and practice knowledge will continue to reveal about how jiu-jitsu is helping lives transform and how it can be best implemented. In this book, we've given you the best possible presentation of where we see things standing at the moment of our writing. Yet there are still so many areas to be explored and other voices to listen to, especially those who have been traditionally marginalized. This includes those voices from Asian cultures that carry the origin story of jiu-jitsu and the martial arts. We would like to see more research in the clinical world on the specific best practices and treatment protocols for using jiu-jitsu as a healing tool for trauma survivors. Questions surrounding best practice protocols still remain: Which jiu-jitsu students need the support of a therapist, and which do not? Could a screener be developed to identify who this is appropriate for and what type of supports such students would need before, during, and after training to maximize the healing benefits of jiu-jitsu? Are there more environmental or character factors at schools that need to be considered?

How Can We Better Serve Trauma Survivors?

Like all martial arts, jiu-jitsu is a living, breathing practice that evolves over time. The history we've presented in this book shows how it can be adapted to both culture and context. From spending so many hours coding data, reflecting on parts of our own story, listening to others' stories, and investigating what exists in the written and oral tradition, we have several recommendations to make. Most of us who are socially conscious and working in mental health are constantly talking about how we can *do better*, and we've seen that same drive present in many educators and jiu-jitsu instructors as well. As we cover some of our recommendations, perhaps notice if you would like to add any others to the list.

Are the Statistic Accurate? Better Studying the Needs of Trauma Survivors

As we have shared already, weapons defense is an important topic. We would like to see more current research on the specifics of how attacks are committed. In order to create "self-defense" programs with adequate breadth and depth in their curriculum, we need more exact details, not just topline categories labeled "assault with a deadly weapon."

- What specific weapons (gun, knife, taser, bat, blunt object) were used?
- Were strikes used? Where did the strikes land (nose, chin, stomach, etc.)?
- Was someone dragged or controlled by their hair?
- Was their clothing grabbed? Were they tripped or thrown to the ground or backed into a wall?
- Were they forced into a vehicle (trunk, backseat, etc.)?
- Were they drugged?
- How many attackers were there?
- Were they brought to a secondary location?
- Were they tied down (with what to what)?

The last thing you want is for a student in your school to have a successful assault perpetrated on them due to common assault tactics of which you were unaware. We cannot expect schools to be responsible for every type of attack happening on the streets. However, we do believe it is fair to ask that the average attack specifics be understood and incorporated into your programs. We do not want survivors walking away with a false sense of safety. If you are a survivor and you feel that this is in danger of happening, know that you have options: to address it with your school, to bring it up with your clinician or other healing presence in your life, or perhaps to explore other pathways, especially different schools, where you can get your needs met.

The Future of Teaching Jiu-Jitsu to Trauma Survivors

We hope that this book showcases how much jiu-jitsu has evolved, clearly changing the lives of many practitioners throughout the centuries. Yet for jiu-jitsu to catch on as a more universally accepted modality for healing and attending to the impact of trauma, much more work needs to be done, or at least refined. In this section, we review some of our thoughts on what steps will need to be taken for jiu-jitsu communities to be the best possible ambassadors for healing.

BASIC CURRICULUM

Some schools are already providing classes on situational awareness and healthy vigilance, embodying a strong and aware presentation, break falling, breathing for jiu-jitsu, and base. That said, even some of the top schools in the US are missing these very basic and key elements. And jiu-jitsu schools that market themselves as self-defense focused may need to fortify what is offered at their schools with cross-training in some other practices. For instance, we've both found that the Israeli martial art Krav Maga may be able to fill in some of the missing pieces. Jamie benefited from doing some cross-training in Muay Thai kickboxing and traditional boxing (which her coach Micah also teaches). An openness to integration is vital in trauma therapy, and we feel it can be appropriate for jiu-jitsu-based self-defense programs as well.

Our first defense on the streets is our awareness. *Awareness* is our ability to sense danger in order to take preventative action. Where and when we can be distracted on our phone and not paying attention is an important discussion to have. Schools should share information on what predators are looking for in an "easy victim." Brian Needham includes *threat profiling* in his curriculum. He explains that there are *tells* or pre-incident indicators that someone is about to do something bad, from clenching fists and jaws to looking over their shoulders and pulling up their sleeves. Students can learn to send nonverbal messages that they won't make a good target to these potential attackers. Sometimes simply standing in awareness and confidence is all that is needed.

Other curriculum techniques we consider critical are standing in base and break falling. Standing in base is also often a first line of defense. Standing in a way that makes you hard to move helps you execute on most other standing techniques. Break falling, or learning how to fall without hurting yourself, is the next logical line of defense if your base is lost. It's critical for that reason, but also because many throws and takedowns require good break falling ability, without which there is a potential for physical injury. Anna and many of our contributors attest to the potential for concussions if you are not tucking your chin during a throw. For obvious reasons, we would have this technique taught and mastered before throws and takedowns are attempted.

Breathing when you are nervous, physically exerting yourself, or someone is putting pressure on either your chest or stomach is a skill that can be taught, enhanced, and mastered. Anna recalls being told for years that she needed to breathe by a variety of instructors across a variety of sports, but it wasn't until she started jiu-jitsu that she actually began to learn how. In Marty Josey's Breathing for BJJ training program, you learn more than fifty different techniques to expand and optimize your breathing capacity during physically and mental stressful situations. Anna completed Marty's breath training program and was impressed by the wide variety of ways to expand lung capacity. She shares that Breathing for BJJ not only showed her how to breathe better during jiu-jitsu and other sports, but had other unexpected benefits. "I explicitly remember feeling defeated and hopeless as a kid when my doctor told me that there was nothing I could do to expand my lung capacity. Thank goodness, the medical world has evolved since then and people like Marty are creating tools that help. I have a new awareness as a trauma survivor of how I am breathing and how to fix it, which has led to a direct decrease in anxiety in general but also when triggered." We agree that breath work would be a welcomed addition to programs that don't have it for both the physical and the mental health benefits it can provide. As mentioned in prior chapters, holding your breath is not uncommon as you exert yourself or when you are feeling nervous, yet holding it is exactly opposite of what we typically need in that moment.

If you are an instructor of jiu-jitsu, we hope you are covering the best techniques to keep students safe on the streets, as we discussed in Chapter 6. We suggest ongoing curriculum evaluations every six months to a year to make sure you stay current with trends in how violence is committed. Student surveys may be one way to check on whether you are addressing student curriculum needs. As our world evolves, curriculum will be expected to evolve as well.

ADVANCED STUDENT AND INSTRUCTOR CHARACTER

Anna and Jamie agree that schools have an ongoing and evolving opportunity to screen for and positively impact the character qualities of their students. Videos setting expectations for an inclusive, culturally responsive, trauma-sensitive, and compassionate approach are one way to set expectations. We invite schools to consider having instruction time, workshops, and/or videos on these topics. We also ask jiu-jitsu schools to consider taking it a step further by testing a student's understanding of these topics as part of the belt testing process. In truth, the higher belts are also instructors and leaders in your school. Another option could be a special stripe added to the belts of students who have passed the character test and who want to help newcomers. This protocol could help to ensure that your newcomers are having a positive experience.

Contributors Katie Gollan and Tony White's school has a leadership team. Whomever a school elects to promote to their leadership team definitely has the power to shape culture and instruction and explicitly model what leadership and character mean. At a bare minimum, Jamie and Anna would ask that jiu-jitsu schools prominently display a code of conduct board and have instructors refer to it often in class. Mark Barentine, brown belt and certified instructor, shared his disappointment in witnessing a pastor's interview process as just being an academic exercise to recall specific bible passages, "but no questions were asked on are you a good husband? How do you behave in the community? Character is important." There is more than technique being taught. "There is a quality of character that students and instructors need to possess." Mark recommends classes and/or seminars on how you treat others, how you approach students, and how you deal with certain situations, especially with students that you may not know. "Empathy is lacking in our world today, and that can get magnified on the mats."

We agree that class time spent on these topics has many potential benefits. Obviously there is the benefit of creating a trauma-sensitive environment for survivors. However, teaching such topics also potentially helps to provide healing to the bullies of the world who might have been raised in abusive households or who simply lacked communication and problem-solving skills to de-escalate issues in a kind, gentle, and respectful fashion. Ultimately, the question schools need to answer is: How do we treat people on the mat? Your students in general should know the answer, but especially the higher belts and instructors.

Protocols for Collaborative Services

As we shared in Chapters 6 and 7, if your jiu-jitsu school is open to the general public, trauma survivors will walk through your front door at some point. Even if you don't want to promote your school as trauma-informed, we still think it is in your best interests to prepare your staff and instructors to handle a variety of situations. We suggest that schools have protocols for how to respond, not only when someone is physically injured, but also when someone is needing mental support. Anna and Jamie have heard numerous stories of students leaving the mats triggered, tearful, frustrated, angry, and more. We would like to see more research and general investigation put toward establishing best practice protocols in schools and in clinical practice. These are some areas to consider:

- Protocols on how to check in with students, as it may not always be visually evident that someone is unwell.

- Protocols on when and how to provide referrals for support.

- Protocols on the depth and breadth of support that should be readily available (clinicians, support groups, etc.)

- Protocols on how to partner in the healing process (students, clinicians, instructors).

- Protocols on inclusive and trauma-sensitive messaging communicating codes of conduct and ways to elevate concerns and solve problems.

- Exploration of best practices around language in school and gym settings to create as inclusive of an environment as possible, while also honoring the Japanese and Brazilian roots of how the practice of jiu-jitsu has contextually evolved.

Some jiu-jitsu schools have made significant efforts in providing trauma-informed instruction. For others, trauma-informed approaches will be a new concept. We hope that the experiences and ideas in these chapters will inspire growth no matter where your school falls in the spectrum. We urge continued, on-going investigation, as it is the only way we will all get to the most-relevant and best solutions.

We also wish there was a unifying association with which most jiu-jitsu schools were united to set policy and to police themselves with rating systems to identify who is qualified to teach in what domains (e.g., sport jiu-jitsu, self-defense jiu-jitsu, healing- and trauma-informed jiu-jitsu). Guido Jenniges, third-degree black belt instructor for Gracie University, shares that the jiu-jitsu community can be very political and competitive. This results in a variety of organizations competing for legitimacy (American Ju-Jitsu Association, United States Ju-Jitsu Federation, International Brazilian Jiu-Jitsu Association, and more). Guido explains that the International Brazilian Jiu-Jitsu Federation (IBJJF) is currently the biggest, but their focus is on sport jiu-jitsu. Guido shares that you need to be a member to enter their jiu-jitsu tournaments. "Schools focused on competitions measure their success by how many medals are coming in. Their focus is not on self-defense or trauma healing per se."

Conflict over allegiance, business, and other matters has also affected the Gracie family, as documented in the 2010 Viktor Cesar Bota documentary *The Gracies and the Birth of Vale Tudo*.[4] It's truly hard to watch this piece and read some other perspectives on the history of jiu-jitsu and not feel sad that a practice so meaningful can still be the subject of great division, even within its most famous family. We feel that it's important to see the Gracies as human and thus vulnerable to the same kind of worldly squabbles all of us face in daily life. They are not to be placed on a pedestal, and we are grateful that we had a chance to look at some of the problems with modern jiu-jitsu as we created this book. Even through this process, we remain in love with the practice of jiu-jitsu and hope for a future where a greater sense of unity on the mats and in life exists.

Until the jiu-jitsu community is more united, it will be up to the students to decide where they feel safest and are getting what they need out of their training experience. We wonder what it would be like if there were medals awarded for healing hearts and minds, and saving lives too . . .

The focus would inevitably shift.

Final Thoughts

As with anything good, with growth and diffusion can come headaches and growing pains. This phenomenon can happen on top of societal dynamics—not just in the United States but around the world as well—that make for an already complicated background. We certainly hope that the ideas promoted in this book can help the practice of jiu-jitsu, and the various ways that it shows up in the world today, preserve itself as a healing art and grow in this spirit. We also hope that survivors of trauma can make their way to this healing practice in a way that serves and benefits their overall journey—and in a way that can teach them to further respect themselves and their process.

Jiu-Jitsu taught us both a great deal about respect. There is an ethic of respect toward elders fostered in many martial arts schools in keeping with the precepts of Japanese cultural norms. Yet we are most delighted to see when that respect is not solely linear or based by rank. When respect can be practiced toward every member in the school, a truly productive space for healing and transformation is being created. And when a trauma survivor, who may be low on showing respect for themselves, can see this in action, they will hopefully be inspired to turn the respect inward. From this place of respecting oneself the deepest transformations possible can occur. And when we change ourselves, we are truly empowered to change the shape of the world.

TRY THIS The Triangle

The move called the "triangle choke" made jiu-jitsu famous. In an interview for this book, third-degree black belt Guido Jenniges shared how "Royce Gracie choked out a much bigger opponent from the inferior position using triangle choke on the bottom in one of the first Ultimate Fighting Championships (UFC). It was something no one had ever seen or thought possible. It was a miracle move back in the days for most martial artists."

You might notice that the logos of many schools have a triangle in them. The surprising power of this technique has inspired students the world over. Being on your back on the ground with a person in your guard may look like a vulnerable position. For those of us trained in jiu-jitsu and who know the power of the triangle, though, this is a position of fierce and potentially lethal power. For trauma survivors, this reality can teach us that even in positions of great vulnerability we can muster great strength.

Triangle is a relatively complicated technique, and we do not recommend that you try it from reading this book alone. In teaching this technique, an instructor would spend time describing the numerous ways in which one might even arrive at being in a position to execute it. They would also spend time discussing its lethality on the streets and when and where one would consider using something so dangerous. Sharing that depth of information is beyond the scope of this book. Instead, we would like to share a prep drill exercise that can be used to begin preparing your body to learn the technique. In many ways, this may feel similar to a yoga stretch.

- Lying on the ground, bend your left knee so that you are able to grab your shin on that leg with your right hand.

- Then take your right leg and hook it over your left ankle. Release both legs back to the ground and try again.

- If you are feeling comfortable, switch sides.

- Lying on the ground, bend your right knee so that you are able to grab your shin on that leg with your left hand (see Figure 9.1). Then take your left leg and hook it over your right ankle (see Figure 9.2). Release both legs back to the ground and try again.

- Do eight to ten reps on each side.

Figures 9.1 and 9.2 show how such a prep drill would prepare you for the full technique.

Figure 9.1: Preparing for triangle.

Figure 9.2: Triangle.

As a final reflection on this journey we've taken together, perhaps you should take some time to contemplate what it means to muster some of your greatest strength from a place of vulnerability. How have you managed to do this in your life, on the jiu-jitsu mat, or in both arenas? You can meditate on this, write in your journal, create other art, or share in conversation with a trusted friend, coach, confidant, or even your therapist. Notice how the insights derived from this process can serve you going forward as you step onto the mat at the academy, or on to the mat that is life.

Appendix

CHECKLIST: WHAT DO I SPECIFICALLY LOOK FOR IN A SCHOOL?

✓ Is friendly and approachable.

✓ Puts safety first.

✓ Curriculum is structured so I know what to expect.

✓ Curriculum separates sport from street self-defense.

✓ Curriculum is designed especially for a particular demographic: (beginners, women, children).

✓ Curriculum includes weapons defense.

✓ Curriculum includes striking.

✓ Curriculum includes a mix of standing and ground.

✓ Curriculum includes reflex development.

✓ Delays sparring.

✓ Keeps facility clean: mats are cleaned regularly.

✓ Emphasizes proper attire and hygiene.

✓ Provides individualized pacing.

✓ Offers private lessons.

✓ Has flexible policies on stopping or leaving.

✓ Has successful female students.

✓ Has a high rate of student retention.

✓ Pairs advanced students with the new students.

✓ Encourages questions.

✓ Takes part in *joy-jitsu* fun.

✓ Provides a sense of community.

✓ Shows concern for partner's progress.

✓ Demonstrates techniques that are applicable.

✓ Provides realistic explanations of attacker's goal.

✓ Teaches to avoid the fight.

✓ Explains the multiple attackers fiction.

✓ Has certified instructors, not just another black belt.

✓ Keeps facility and lessons up to date.

✓ Specifically teaches break falling as a technique.

✓ Provides student references.

✓ Uses training agendas and collaborative language.

Resources and Further Study

Books

There are many great jiu-jitsu and marital arts titles available, including many of the sources that we cite for this book. We decided to not overwhelm you and keep this list specifically limited to the books that will most likely supplement ideas for trauma-focused jiu-jitsu covered in this book.

Anna Pirkl, *12 Creative Experiences for Personal Growth in Recovery* [eBook] (One Heart Counseling Center), https://www.oneheartcounselingcenter.com/personal-growth-in-recovery/.

Christine Caldwell, *Bodyfulness: Somatic Practices for Presence, Empowerment, and Waking Up in This Life* (Boulder, CO: Shambhala Boulder, 2018).

Dan Siegel and Tina Payne Bryson, *No Drama Discipline: The Whole-Brain Way to Calm the Chaos and Nurture Your Child's Developing Mind* (New York: Bantam Books, 2016).

Jamie Marich, *Process Not Perfection: Expressive Arts Solutions for Trauma Recovery* (Warren, OH: Creative Mindfulness Media, 2019).

Katie Maloney, *Cake Pops and Coffee: A New Conversation About Trauma—How to Laugh, Cry, and Love Your Whole Story* (Pittsburgh, PA: Katie Maloney Coaching, 2019).

Resmaa Menakem, *My Grandmother's Hands: Racialized Trauma and the Pathway to Mending Our Hearts and Bodies* (Las Vegas: Central Recovery Press, 2017).

Websites & Podcasts

Ayesha Kamal Blog: Plum Petals
https://sheisfierce.co.uk/

Breathing for BJJ (Marty Josey)
www.breathingforbjj.com

Chewjitsu Podcast (Nick "Chewy" Albin)
https://chewjitsu.libsyn.com/

Girls in Gis
www.girlsingis.com

Gracie University
www.gracieuniversity.com

Tada Hozumi (The Selfish Activist)
https://tadahozumi.com/

Team BJJ Hashashin
https://medium.com/@harrysuke

Trauma Made Simple (Dr. Jamie Marich)
www.traumamadesimple.com

Valente Brothers Jiu-Jitsu
www.valentebrothers.com

Notes

Chapter 1

1 Robert Scaer, *The Body Bears the Burden: Trauma, Dissociation, and Disease*, 3rd ed. (New York: Routledge, 2014), 95.

2 *Oxford English Dictionary* online, s.v. "martial arts," accessed July 21, 2021, https://www.oxfordify.com/meaning/martial_arts.

3 Jamie Marich, *Trauma Made Simple: Competencies in Assessment, Treatment, and Working with Survivors* (Eau Claire, WI: PESI Publications & Media, 2014), 6.

4 Gino L. Collura, "Brazilian Jiu Jitsu: A Tool for Veteran Reassimilation" (unpublished doctoral dissertation, University of South Florida, 2018).

5 Alison Willing, Sue Ann Girling, Ryan Deichert, and Rebecca Wood-Deichert, "Brazilian Jiu Jitsu Training for US Service Members and Veterans with Symptoms of PTSD," *Military Medicine* 184, no. 6 (2019): 1–6.

6 Aleksander E. Chinkov and Nicholas L. Holt, "Implicit Transfer of Life Skills through Participation in Brazilian Jiu-Jitsu," *Journal of Applied Sport Psychology* 28, no. 2 (2016): 139–153.

7 M. Ann Phillips, "Classical Martial Arts Training: A Zen Approach to Health, Wellness and Empowerment for Women," *Canadian Woman Studies* 29, no. 1/2 (2011): 67–71; Phillipa Velija, Mark Mierzwinski, and Laura Fortune, "'It Made Me Feel Powerful': Women's Gendered Embodiment and Physical Empowerment in the Martial Arts," *Leisure Studies* 32, no. 5 (2013): 524–541; Julie C. Weitlauf, Daniel Cervone, Ronald E. Smith, and Paul M. Wright, "Assessing Generalization in Perceived Self-Efficacy: Multidomain and Global Assessments of the

Effects of Self-Defense Training for Women," *Personality and Social Psychology Bulletin* 27 no. 12 (2001): 1683–1691; Darah Westrup, Julie Weitlauf, and Jennifer Keller, "I Got My Life Back! Making a Case for Self-Defense Training for Older Women with PTSD," *Clinical Gerontologist* 28, no. 3 (April 2005): 113–118.

8 Stuart W. Twemlow, Frank C. Sacco, and Peter Fonagy, "Embodying the Mind: Movement as a Container for Destructive Aggression," *American Journal of Psychotherapy* 62, no. 1 (2008): 1–33.

9 Niamh Bird, G. McCarthy, and Kevin O'Sullivan, "Exploring the Effectiveness of Integrated Mixed Martial Arts and Psychotherapy Intervention for Young Men's Mental Health," *American Journal of Men's Health* 13, no. 1 (2019), https://doi.org/10.1177/1557988319832121.

10 M. Weiser, I. Kutz, S. J. Kutz, and D. Weiser, "Psychotherapeutic Aspects of the Martial Arts," *American Journal of Psychotherapy* 49, no. 1 (1995): 118–127.

11 Christine Caldwell, *Bodyfulness: Somatic Practices for Presence, Empowerment, and Waking Up in This Life* (Boulder, CO: Shambhala Boulder, 2018), 155.

12 G. Zivin, N. R. Hassan, G. F. DePaula, D. A. Monti, C. Harlan, K. D. Hossain, and K. Patterson, "An Effective Approach to Violence Prevention: Traditional Martial Arts in Middle School" *Adolescence* 36, no. 143 (Fall 2001): 443–460.

13 Adam Croom, "Embodying Martial Arts for Mental Health: Cultivating Psychological Well-Being with Martial Arts Practice," *Archives of Budo Science of Martial Arts and Extreme Sports* 10 (2014): 59–70.

Chapter 2

1 Bessel van der Kolk, *The Body Keeps the Score: Brain, Mind, and Body in the Healing of Trauma* (New York: Viking, 2014), 21.

2 Earl Grey, *Unify Your Mind: Connecting the Feelers, Thinkers, and Doers of Your Brain* (Pittsburgh, PA: CMH&W, Inc., 2011), 68.

3 American Psychiatric Association. *Diagnostic and Statistical Manual of Mental Disorders: DSM-5* (Arlington, VA: American Psychiatric Association, 2013).

4 Christine Courtois and Julian Ford, *Treating Complex Traumatic Stress Disorders: An Evidence-Based Guide*, 2nd Ed. (New York: The Guilford Press, 2020), 1.

5 Adam O'Brien and Jamie Marich, "Addiction as Dissociation Model," Institute for Creative Mindfulness: *Redefine Therapy* (blog), October 15, 2019, https://www.instituteforcreativemindfulness.com/icm-blog -redefine-therapy/addiction-as-dissociation-model-by-adam-obrien -dr-jamie-marich.

6 Christine Forner, "What Mindfulness Can Learn about Dissociation and What Dissociation Can Learn from Mindfulness," *Journal of Trauma and Dissociation* 20, no. 1 (2019): 1–15.

7 Stephen Porges, foreword to *The Polyvagal Theory in Therapy*, by Deb Dana (New York, Norton Professional Books, 2020): xiii–xvii.

8 Deb Dana, *Polyvagal Exercises for Safety and Connection: 50 Client-Centered Practices* (New York: W.W. Norton & Company, 2020), 10–14.

9 Arielle Schwartz, "Polyvagal Theory in Psychotherapy: Practical Applications for PTSD Treatment," *Arielle Schwartz, Ph.D.* (blog), March 2, 2020, https://drarielleschwartz.com/polyvagal-theory-in-psychotherapy -dr-arielle-schwartz/#.YEo15eZOnAa.

10 M. Pagani, G. Hogberg, I. Fernandez, and A. Siracusano. "Corrélats de la Thérapie EMDR en Neuroimagerie Fonctionnelle et Structurelle: Un Résumé Critique des Résultats Récents" [Correlates of EMDR Therapy in Functional and Structural Neuroimaging: A Critical Summary of Recent Findings], *Journal of EMDR Practice and Research* 8, no. 2 (2014): 29E–40E.

Chapter 3

1 Darrell M. Craig, *Japanese Jiu-Jitsu: Secret Techniques of Self-Defense* (North Claredon, VT: Tuttle Publishing, 2015), 7.

2 Craig, *Japanese Jiu-Jitsu*, 8.

3 The Valente Brothers, "The Origin of Jit-Jitsu," accessed May 26, 2021, https://valentebrothers.com/jiujitsu-history/.

4 3Sixty Jiu-Jitsu. "History of Brazilian Jiu-Jitsu," accessed June 24, 2021, https://www.360-bjj.com/jiu-jitsu-history/.

5 Thomas Hyunh and Sun Tzu, *The Art of War: Spirituality for Conflict* (Woodstock, VT: Skylight Paths Publishing, 2008), 114.

6 Nihongo Master, "Chikarakurabke," accessed June 24, 2021, https://www.nihongomaster.com/dictionary/entry/57495/chikarakurabe.

7 Judo Info, "Origins of Kodokan Judo," August 19, 2003, https://judoinfo.com/jhist3/.

8 Evolve MMA, "The History and Origins of Brazilian Jiu-Jitsu," *Evolve Daily*, accessed July 21, 2021, https://evolve-mma.com/blog/the-history-and-origins-of-brazilian-jiu-jitsu/.

9 Evolve MMA, "History and Origins."

10 Donn F. Draeger and Robert W. Smith, *Asian Fighting Arts: Techniques History Philosophy* (New York: Kodansha International, 1969), 132.

11 Draeger and Smith, *Asian Fighting Arts*, 132.

12 BJJ Hashashin, "Differences between Jujutsu and Judo," *Medium*, August 19, 2015, https://medium.com/@harrysuke/difference-between-jujutsu-and-judo-2fcfe0fe5951.

13 Kenei Mabuni, *Empty Hand: The Essence of Budo Karate* (Chemnitz, Germany: Palisander-Verlag, 2009), 26.

14 Valente Brothers, "The Origin of Jiu-Jitsu."

15 Lao Tzu, *Tao Te Ching*, trans. Charles Muller (New York: Barnes & Noble Classics, 2005), 78.

16 Andy Pruin, "Karate Compendium: Karate Histories from Te to Z," *Black Belt Magazine* (June 1990), 18.

17 Helio Gracie, *Gracie Jiu-Jitsu* (Torrance, CA: Gracie Publications, Inc., 2005), 1.

18 Martial Arts Federation (MAIF), "The Art of Kodokan Judo," accessed May 26, 2021, https://www.maifhq.org/the-art-of-kodokan-judo.html.

19 United States Ju-Jitsu Federation, "Tenjin Shinyo-ryu," accessed May 26, 2021, https://www.usjjf.org/usjjf_book_-_tenjin_shinyo_ryu_jujutsu.html.

20 John Stevens, *The Way of Judo: A Portrait of Jigoro Kano and His Students* (Boston: Shambhala International, 2013), 19, 48.

21 Raul Sanchez Garcia, *The Historical Sociology of Japanese Martial Arts* (New York: Routledge, 2019), 159.

22 MAIF. "Art of Kodokan Judo."

23 Stevens, *Way of Judo*, 19, 48.

24 Valente Brothers, "The Origin of Jiu-Jitsu."

25 Combat Otaku, "Fusen Ryu Jujutsu," accessed July 1, 2020, http://combatotaku.blogspot.com/2019/10/fusen-ryu-jujutsu.html; Martial Arts Tube, "Fusen Ryu jujutsu video," accessed June 24, 2021, https://www.martialartstube.net/fusen-ryu-jujutsu/.

26 Stevens, *The Way of Judo*, 99.

27 Shane McFarland, "Mitsuyo 'Count Koma' Maeda, The Man Who Taught the Gracies," World Mixed Martial Arts Rankings, accessed May 26, 2021, https://sites.google.com/site/mixedmartialartsrankings/home/mixed-martial-arts-hall-of-fame/mitsuyo-count-koma-maeda--the-man-who-taught-the-gracies; Joseph Svinth, *Martial Arts in the Modern World* (Santa Barbara, CA: Prager-Greenwood Publishing Group, 2003), 69.

28 Thomas Green and Joseph Svinth (Eds.), *Martial Arts of the World: An Encyclopedia of History and Innovation* (Santa Barbara, CA: ABC-CLIO, 2010), 1.

29 Nori Bunasawa and John Murray, *The Toughest Man Who Ever Lived* (Costa Mesa, CA: Judo Journal, 2007), 38.

30 Gracie, *Gracie Jiu-Jitsu*, 1.

31 Evan Meehan, "The True History of Brazilian Jiu-Jitsu" (blog), BJJ Success, April 9, 2020, https://www.bjjsuccess.com/history-of-brazilian-jiu-jitsu/.

32 Valente Brothers, "Origin of Jit-Jitsu."

33 3Sixty Jiu-Jitsu, "History: History of Brazilian Jiu-Jitsu," accessed May 26, 2021, https://www.360-bjj.com/jiu-jitsu-history/.

34 Roberto Pedreira, "Top 30 Myths and Misconceptions about Brazilian Jiu-Jitsu" (blog), Global Training Report Archive, March 16, 2016, http://global-training-report.com/myths.htm.

35 Gracie, *Gracie Jiu-Jitsu*, 11.

36 Jeff Reese, "Survival Mindset" (blog), Gracie Nepa Grappling Club, December 26, 2013, https://www.gracienepa.com/blog/survival-mindset/.

37 Christopher David Thrasher, *Fight Sports and American Masculinity* (Jefferson, NC: McFarland and Company Publishers, 2007), 206–207.

38 *The Gracies and the Birth of Vale Tudo*, directed and written by Viktor Cesar Bota (Vale Tudo LLC, 2010).

39 Valente Brothers, "The Origin of Jit-Jitsu."

40 Valente Brothers, "The Origin of Jit-Jitsu."

41 Pedreira, "Top 30 Myths and Misconceptions."

42 Valente Brothers, "The Origin of Jit-Jitsu."

43 Valente Brothers, "The Origin of Jit-Jitsu."

44 Pedreira, "Top 30 Myths and Misconceptions."

45 Valente Brothers, "The Origin of Jit-Jitsu."

46 Pedreira, "Top 30 Myths and Misconceptions."

47 Louis Martin, "How Long Do Street Fights Actually Last? We Watched 200 of Them to Find Out" (blog), *High Percentage Martial Arts*, March 10, 2020, https://www.highpercentagemartialarts.com /blog/2019/3/6/how-long-do-street-fights-actually-last-and-what -can-we-learn-from-that.

48 Gracie, *Gracie Jiu-Jitsu*, 9.

49 Pedro Valente, Guilherme Valente, and Joaquim Valente, *The 753 Code: Introduction to Jujutsu Philosophy* (Miami, Florida: Valente Brothers Jujutsu, 2020).

Chapter 4

1 Shira Hantman and Zahava Z. Solomon, "Recurrent Trauma: Holocaust Survivors Cope with Aging and Cancer," *Social Psychiatry and Psychiatric Epidemiology* 42, 5 (2007): 396–402; Jamie Marich, *Trauma Made Simple: Competencies in Assessment, Treatment and Working with Survivors* (Eau Claire, WI: PESI Publishing, 2014).

2 Jamie Marich and Stephen Dansiger. *EMDR Therapy and Mindfulness for Trauma-Focused Care* (New York: Springer Publishing Company, 2018), 45, 87.

Chapter 5

1 Helio Gracie, *Gracie Jiu-Jitsu* (Torrance, CA: Gracie Publications, Inc., 2005), 14.

2 Rener Gracie and Ryron Gracie, "Surviving the First 6 Months of Sparring," *Gracie University*, accessed July 21, 2021, https://www.gracieuniversity .com/pages/public/lesson?enc=3Y0W2PnMaIBLFuTvLK4jLqV5Y Sr8kF7Z8RiO13Oiwlc%3D.

3 Helio Gracie. *Gracie Jiu-Jitsu* 11.

4 Helio Gracie, 13.

Chapter 6

1 U.S. Department of Justice, "Full Report of the Prevalence, Incidence, and Consequences of Violence Against Women," National Institute of Justice, accessed June 9, 2021, https://www.ncjrs.gov/pdffiles1/nij/183781.pdf.

2 U.S. Department of Justice, "Full Report."

3 US Department of Justice, "Criminal Victimization, 2018 Bureau of Justice Statistics, accessed June 9, 2021, https://www.bjs.gov/content /pub/pdf/cv18_sum.pdf.

4 U.S. Transgender Survey, "The Report of the 2015 Transgender Survey, accessed June 23, 2021, https://www.ustranssurvey.org/reports.

5 Centers for Disease Control, "NISVS: An Overview of 2010 Findings on Victimization by Sexual Orientation," National Intimate Partner Violence and Sexual Violence Survey (2010), accessed June 9, 2021, https://www.cdc.gov/violenceprevention/pdf/cdc_nisvs_victimization _final-a.pdf.

6 Helio Gracie, *Gracie Jiu-Jitsu* (Torrance, CA: Gracie Publications, Inc., 2005), 14.

Chapter 7

1 Tada Hozumi, "On Somatics Being an Asian Practice," September 9, 2020, https://tadahozumi.com/on-cultural-somatics-being-an-asian-practice/.

Chapter 8

1 Robert Drysdale, "*Do Vale Tudo Brasileiro ao 'Mixed Martial Arts,'*" by João Alberto Barreto, Reviewed by Robert Drysdale," Global Training

Report, May 2, 2018, http://global-training-report.com/DrysdaleJABrev 2018.htm.

2 "Before You Get Angry, Watch This Terry Crews Video" Motivational Speech/Goalcast, May 8, 2020, https://www.youtube.com/watch?v =F1v4o646SsA.

3 Roman Krznaric, "Ready for a Vulnerability Hangover? Five Ideas from Bréne Brown," October 16, 2012, https://www.romankrznaric.com /outrospection/2012/10/16/1729.

Chapter 9

1 "Jiu-Jitsu Secrets and Principles featuring Ryron Gracie," Brute Strength, April 29, 2019, https://www.youtube.com/watch?v=SofEPmvbUIA.

2 "BJJ vs. Kidnapper (What REALLY Happened in This Viral Video?) Gracie Breakdown, November 25, 2020, https://www.youtube.com /watch?v=vMXAkV1JUo0&list=UUNMZWa1QP42jHrmmzayFEeg.

3 Resmaa Menakem, *My Grandmother's Hands: Racialized Trauma and the Pathway to Mending Our Hearts and Bodies* (Las Vegas: Central Recovery Press, 2017).

4 *The Gracies and the Birth of Vale Tudo*, directed and written by Viktor Cesar Bota (Vale Tudo LLC, 2010).

Index

About the Authors

JAMIE MARICH, PhD, (she/they), speaks internationally on topics related to EMDR therapy, trauma, addiction, dissociation, expressive arts, yoga, and mindfulness, and maintains a private practice in her home base of Warren, Ohio. She founded and directs The Institute for Creative Mindfulness and developed the Dancing Mindfulness approach to expressive arts therapy as well as Yoga for Clinicians. Marich has written numerous books, notably *Trauma and the 12 Steps: An Inclusive Guide to Recovery*. She has won numerous awards for LGBT+ and mental health advocacy. In 2017, she earned her *Women Empowered* pink belt through Gracie University of Jiu-Jitsu. Learn more about Marich's work at www.jamiemarich.com.

ANNA PIRKL, LMFT, specializes in recovery from complex trauma, addiction, and anxiety disorders. She has worked with a wide range of clients from adolescents at Los Angeles Central Juvenile Hall to men in recovery at sober livings to pregnant and parenting teens. She is the author of *12 Creative Experiences for Personal Growth in Recovery* and is a seasoned presenter, booking speaking engagements at community and high school mental health events, mental health conferences, and for corporate wellness events. Pirkl earned her *Women Empowered* pink belt, combatives belt, and blue belt at Gracie University Jiu-Jitsu. Learn more about Pirkl's work at www.one heartcounselingcenter.com.

ALSO BY JAMIE MARICH

available from North Atlantic Books

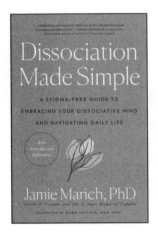

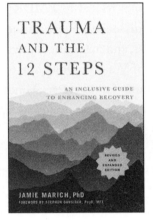

Dissociation Made Simple
978-1-62317-721-8 (print)
978-1-62317-722-5 (ebook)

Trauma and the 12 Steps,
Revised and Expanded
978-1-62317-468-2 (print)
978-1-62317-469-9 (ebook)

Trauma and the 12 Steps:
The Workbook
978-1-62317-932-8 (print)
978-1-62317-933-5 (ebook)

North Atlantic Books
www.northatlanticbooks.com

North Atlantic Books is an independent, nonprofit publisher committed to a bold exploration of the relationships between mind, body, spirit, and nature.

About North Atlantic Books

North Atlantic Books (NAB) is a 501(c)(3) nonprofit publisher committed to a bold exploration of the relationships between mind, body, spirit, culture, and nature. Founded in 1974, NAB aims to nurture a holistic view of the arts, sciences, humanities, and healing. To make a donation or to learn more about our books, authors, events, and newsletter, please visit www.northatlanticbooks.com.